When the Garden Was Eden

When the Garden Was Eden

*Clyde, the Captain, Dollar Bill,
and the Glory Days of the New York Knicks*

Harvey Araton

With Photographs by George Kalinsky

An Imprint of HarperCollinsPublishers

HarperCollins books may be purchased for educational, business, or sales promotional use. For information please write: Special Markets Department, HarperCollins Publishers, 10 East 53rd Street, New York, NY 10022.

Photographs by George Kalinsky

FIRST HARPERLUXE EDITION

HarperLuxe™ is a trademark of HarperCollins Publishers

Library of Congress Cataloging-in-Publication Data is available upon request.

ISBN: 978-0-06-208878-9

11 12 13 14 ID/OPM 10 9 8 7 6 5 4 3 2

To Zelda Spoelstra, the Angel of the NBA,
and to the nurturing women in my life:
Marilyn Araton, Sharon Kushner, Randi Waldman,
Ruth Albert, Michelle Musler, Sophia Richman,
and my special love, Beth Albert

Contents

Part III: Fallout

Part IV: Paradise Regained

PROLOGUE:
IN A PARADISE LOST

Last man out of the tunnel was Willis Reed. The Captain emerged to a rousing ovation at Madison Square Garden and made his stiff-legged way toward his teammates waiting at center court. It was Wednesday night, February 23, 2010, halftime of a thoroughly ordinary Knicks-Bucks game except for the presence of the assembled legends. Bill Bradley and Walt Frazier, Reed's fellow Knicks in the Hall of Fame, stepped out of the spotlight fringe on either side of the Walter A. Brown world championship trophy—a silver cup that takes more than one man to lift—while Dick Barnett and the beloved "Minutemen" Cazzie Russell and Mike Riordan applauded Reed as if he were coming to their rescue all over again.

This was, in fact, the 40th anniversary of the Knicks' rise to the summit of pro basketball, and all the men at center court wore varsity jackets custom-made for the occasion: blue-and-white sleeves and 1970 stitched to the left shoulder. Four decades had passed since *"Here comes Willis!"*—since Reed, with a numbed and practically immobilized right leg, hit the Knicks' first two shots before Frazier and the others followed his lead and buried the Lakers in Game 7 of the NBA Finals.

And yet the celebration seemed tinged with sadness. Teri McGuire appeared for her husband, Dick, the venerable organizational lifer—player, coach, and scout—who had suffered an aortic aneurysm and died earlier that month. Eddie Donovan, the architect of the team fondly known in city basketball circles as the Old Knicks, had suffered a fatal stroke and was represented by his son Sean. Gail Holzman Papelian stood in memory of her father, Red, the wily and streetwise coach of both championship teams. The DeBusschere boys, Peter and Dennis, came for their father, Dave, dead seven years from a sudden heart attack in 2003.

But the legacy lives on. When Frazier stepped to the microphone, the fans in the lower bowl rose, shouting their approval, aiming their cell phones. The man they called Clyde conjured the memories that still, despite the years, *abound and astound*: "I see the Captain coming through the tunnel, I see three of the greatest players ever to play the game—Baylor, West, and Chamberlain—mesmerized by his presence."

He paused for effect, letting the few fans old and lucky enough to have seen the looks on the faces of the Lakers for themselves linger for just a second longer in the reverie. "I say to myself, 'We got these guys.'"

The disconnect of eras was starkly apparent, 37 years and counting since the Old Knicks had claimed the franchise's second and last crown, in 1973. A new generation of fans, long suffering and paying staggering prices for an inferior product, constituted that night's crowd.

In the second half, a team of young players and short-term rentals—filling roster space as the front office readied itself for the unprecedented 2010 free-agent sweepstakes, the Summer of LeBron—played miserably, falling far behind Milwaukee. There would be no glorious comeback, nothing even close to that storied game of November 11, 1972, when Reed, Frazier, and friends ran off the final 19 points to nip the Bucks right here at the Garden. But tonight, as the stands emptied before the end of the fourth quarter, so, too, did the guests of honor retreat from celebrity row, opposite the Knicks' bench, with only Barnett resisting the urge to bail. Or, as he might have put it: *fall back, baby*. The man who had TRICKY DICK stitched into the right sleeve of his commemorative jacket remained in his seat until the final buzzer of the home team's brutal showing. Sitting alone, Barnett watched through sleepy, expressionless eyes the young men coming off the court, players whose collective achievements pale in comparison with his own but whose individual salaries amount to more than Barnett had earned over his entire career.

"It is what it is," he said philosophically, staring out at the deserted court as if it were a vandalized cathedral. "And it's still just a game."

But when the Captain and Clyde and the rest of the Old Knicks played, when the city and the country convulsed with fury and pain: oh, what a beautiful game it was.

PART I

Roots

1

DOWN HOME

It was a hot summer night in Ruston, Louisiana. The air inside Chili's, a bustling outlet just off I-20, was almost heavy enough to make breathing not worth the effort. The A/C system appeared to be waging the same losing battle as the makeup on the faces of several waitresses. But Willis Reed paid the wet heat no mind. He was much too tickled at tonight's role reversal. Here, a few thousand miles south of Manhattan, Reed's best buddy and oldest friend—Howard Brown—was the name brand, the guy with fans clamoring for his attention, the celebrity.

"That's what happens when you're a teacher and you have a long career in the same area," said Reed, former NBA champion and national sports hero. "You know everyone."

Reed and Brown, both age 67, live not far from here on adjacent properties near the Grambling State University campus where they once shared a dorm room.

"Howard helped me get the land," Reed said.

"Whenever Willis would come back to visit, he'd stay with me," Brown said from the seat across from mine. "And about the time he was moving back, he said, 'If you want to build a house, why not right here?'"

The two might as well be brothers, and Reed calls them that. They met in the late 1950s at the all-black Westside High School, a few miles away from Bernice, a 30-minute drive north from Ruston. Willis and Howard both played on Westside High's basketball team, Reed the star big man and Brown a 6'0" guard who, according to Reed, never met a shot he didn't like.

Well, only "until it came down to the wire," said Brown. "Then Coach would say, 'Get it inside'—which meant 'Give it to Willis.'"

Give it to Willis. A smirk grew across Brown's face, and he looked across the table at Reed: "Remember how Coach Stone would hold the bus for you?"

Reed cackled at the memory, while Brown narrated: "We'd all be there, ready to go, except Willis. There was a guy named Duke who drove the bus, and he'd be looking at Coach, waiting for him to say, 'Let's go.' But then Coach would stand up, put his hands in his pocket, and say, 'I've got to go get my keys.' He'd go back in the building and wait until he saw Willis walking up to the bus. Then he'd come back on and say, 'Crank it up, Duke.'"

And so the bus would roll with Reed on board, on the way to another all-black school, another audition for a young man destined for stardom in the heart of New York. But all of that had happened decades ago. It was ancient and unknown history to the Chili's crowd, sweating over their fajitas.

The night manager stopped by our table while making her rounds to comment on my accent, which doesn't sound too Louisianan.

"He's here to work on a book," Brown informed the perky young woman.

"Really," she said. "What's it about?"

"This man right here and the basketball team he used to play for," Brown said. "This is Willis Reed of the New York Knicks; his photo is on your wall."

He pointed to the entryway of the restaurant and there it was, along with other greats from this area, one uncommonly rich in basketball lore: Bill Russell, a native of Monroe, due east on I-20; Robert Parish, another Celtics Hall of Fame center, out of Shreveport, an hour away on the interstate in the other direction; Karl Malone, who put Ruston's Louisiana

Tech on the college basketball map; Orlando Wool-ridge, a cousin of Reed's and a gifted kid who played for Digger Phelps at Notre Dame—on Reed's recommendation—and later in the NBA; and, of course, Reed himself, who hilariously wasn't good enough for most of the major universities up north that deigned at the beginning of the sixties to recruit a player or two from the growing pool of African Americans.

In the end, after a brief and uninspired flirtation with the University of Wisconsin and Loyola University of Chicago, Reed was more comfortable moving on down the road to Grambling, where he could play for Fred Hobdy, a protégé of the coaching legend Eddie Robinson, and stay connected with his best friend. Howard Brown might not have been cut out for college basketball, but Reed was more concerned about having a freshman roommate.

"I bet my husband knows who you are," the night manager assured Reed. Then she asked for an autograph, which seemed like the polite thing to do.

If Willis Reed had instead retired to a high-rise perch in Manhattan, maybe his fame would still precede him every time he stepped out the door. Whenever he got a hankering to aim his gun or cast his rod, he might have simply trekked upstate (just as he used to blow off practice—with Red Holzman's permission—on opening day of hunting season).

In some ways, remaining in New York would have been the easier life. He would have spared himself the discomfort of climbing aboard prop jets designed for Lilliputians when flying out of small airports in Shreveport or Monroe, on his way to Montana to hunt or to New York City whenever the Knicks or the NBA called. But the perks of celebrity were never his guiding aim. What mattered to him was this: "I just wanted some quiet, to be able to get in my car without worrying about traffic and being able to walk outside on my property and take a piss without worrying about my neighbors."

He knew himself well enough to know that he didn't need strangers to remind him of who he'd once been. For Reed, basketball was about the competition, the wins, and, because he's a practical man, the financial windfalls. Basketball was a life primarily defined by lessons gleaned from his parents and coaches—even from a few people he was once forbidden to so much as sit next to on the local bus.

"If you're going up to Bernice," Reed told me, "then you've got to go see Harry Cook." We were sitting in the den of the modern home he had built in 1989, on the property scouted for him by Howard Brown. Here, in an otherwise bland rural expanse off the Grambling I-20 exit, the roadside dotted with tired wooden houses and a low-slung Baptist church, was where Reed envisioned and developed his gated dream palace on a rolling landscape with three specially designed ponds he stocked himself with fish.

Three Ponds Road: the retirement address of Willis Reed and his second wife, Gail.

Mounted on the walls of the den were his beloved hunting prizes—the stuffed heads of a bison and a mountain lion killed in Montana, a moose bagged in the Yukon, and an elk felled with his arrow, among other stuffed heads and . . . a basketball trophy, an MVP award.

Nodding, Reed added: "Harry is a character, a great talker, and he can tell you everything about Bernice."

Harry Cook is a retired biologist who used to work for the Louisiana Department of Wildlife and Fisheries. For years, Inell Reed, Willis's mother, worked as a domestic for Cook's family, among others. When Reed called Cook to tell him of my visit, Cook's wife answered. Reed addressed her as Miss Alice, and, in keeping with the theme of country quaint, he told her he'd been meaning to drop by anyway because he and

Gail were all out of Miss Alice's delicious mayhaw jelly and they were craving a fresh jar. (Eventually, Cook would send me off with two—one for the Reeds, one for myself.)

"Willis was a big boy, but Inell, she called the shots," Cook was quick to say as we settled down in his living room with glasses of fresh lemonade. "She kept him on the straight and narrow. I've pretty much known Willis all his life. Yes, we were segregated in those days, but we all came up together, black and white. It was without conflict. When you're living in a town with 1,500 people, everybody's on a first-name basis."

Later, I asked Reed if he'd sent me to Cook, a white man, in part to dispel whatever preconceived notions that I, a lifelong New Yorker, might have had about the rural South—and by extension his childhood. The question made him chuckle. "I always said that about Bernice—people did get along," he said. "I mean, I knew there were things I didn't have. Didn't have the kind of houses the white folks had; didn't have a car. The situation was what it was. But you know what? We all made the best of it in Bernice until it changed."

Founded in 1899 as a stop on Captain C. C. Henderson's Arkansas Southern Railroad, Bernice was created to give Henderson an industrial foothold in an area known as the Big Woods, due to its huge virgin pines.

In the days of Cook's and Reed's youth, the town, all of three square miles, was a thriving lumber-and-agricultural center, its two-light downtown a vibrant shopping district with a movie theater. Strategically placed were the warehouses—more than you would expect in a town that size, and owned by the man who employed most of Bernice's working-class members, including Willis Reed Sr. and, for one unforgettable summer, his strapping teenage son.

"Mr. Donald Lindsay," Reed said. "My dad worked for him, building the warehouses to store cotton for the government. I had a chance one summer to work at my dad's job, the summer before my senior year in high school. So I was at these warehouses, with the scaffolding and all. Worked all summer in the heat for 75 cents an hour. Had these big old calluses on my hands and, man, that whole experience was life-changing for me.

"After the summer, my dad said, 'Well, you don't have to go to college; you can stay here and work for Mr. Lindsay.' Now, it wasn't like today, where a kid who's a basketball star is thinking he is going to play in the NBA someday. When I was in Bernice and even at Grambling, there were only maybe eight NBA teams. So what did I want to do? Well, after that summer working for Mr. Lindsay, I would see my dad coming home with sweat down to his knees, and, having been there with him, I knew why. And then I went back to school and there was Coach Stone, wearing a jacket and tie to school, nice car, much nicer house. So my real dream was about being a high school coach and a teacher like Coach Stone. I said, Boy, I want to be like him—I'm going to college."

He majored in physical education and minored in biology at historically black Grambling State. Beyond rooming with his friend, Reed had been drawn to a place where there were many role models like Coach Stone, and where his new mentor, Hobdy, would teach him not just the fundamentals of the game but how to cope with the degradations of the day.

"He used to say to us, 'Listen, you guys are athletes, and you don't need to be out there demonstrating and all that,'" Reed said. "The best thing you can do is do what you do best. Become as good a player and as good a team, and all of that is going to be a good example."

This was hardly black militancy, or even the kind of nonviolent protest that Martin Luther King was championing then, at the start of the civil rights movement. By nature, Reed was no iconoclast. At least not like his idol, Bill Russell, whose family fled Louisiana for the California Bay Area, settling in Oakland when he was 12. Reed wasn't blind to the fact that there had been only one car, in the rear, in which he was allowed to ride on the train from Bernice to Ruston, and he knew why the white kids like Harry Cook could enjoy their burgers and fries in "the real nice part" of the café on Fourth Street while he and his black friends were relegated to the counter in the back. All these years later, a smirk creased his face when he said, "Separate but equal," recounting the segregationist mantra that had prevented him from formally competing against white players until 1961, his freshman season at Grambling, in the NAIA basketball tournament.

What, then, could he—or any athlete—do for the Cause without involving himself directly in the struggle? He could win. He could show what black ballplayers brought to the court in direct competition with whites. Decades after the NAIA semifinals in Kansas City, where he had done exactly that, Reed could still summon the satisfaction of the tight game, his jumper on the baseline that gave Grambling a late 45–44 lead, and then the horror of watching a Westminster, Pennsylvania, shooter—the same one who had nipped Winston-Salem State in the Elite Eight—coming off a screen, wide-open for another buzzer beater.

"I jumped out at him and he missed the shot, ball hit the front of the rim," Reed said. He himself had missed only one shot the entire game, free throws included. Grambling won the title by blowing out

Georgetown of Kentucky in the final. For Reed, the execution of Hobdy's strategy—social change via on-court performance—was another example of what had made Grambling the right choice for him. "For me, as a kid growing up in the segregated South, certain things were probably not as tough as for other people in areas where they were integrated but more exposed to those hard feelings," he said.

He believed this based not only on his own experiences but on what he had observed in some black teammates and opponents from the northern states: a lingering bitterness that at times prevented them from putting aside the past and focusing on the tasks at hand. He had come to believe there were some unintended advantages to having grown up in a malevolent system set up by whites. As one historian, Jennifer Ritterhouse, author of a book about the social implications of Jim Crow, told me, "Many people have argued that growing up black in the South was less segregated than your urban housing project in the North, which was so isolating, not only from the white world but from the middle-class black community that could separate itself from that environment."

Reed came to believe that *separate but equal* gave him one benefit that a young African American male living in an urban northern ghetto was not guaranteed:

the proximity of the upwardly mobile black role model, the man in a suit with a college degree. With regard to race and class in 1960s America, perhaps that was the starkest antidote to a hard day's work—*sweat down to his knees*—that represented the status quo.

"I always said that Mr. Lindsay was very inspirational to me and he didn't even know it," Reed said. When he referred to his father's employer as "Mister," he was not as much making a point about southern manners as showing respect to a man who had helped make Bernice a working town and something of a destination within Union Parish. However abhorrent the domestic hierarchies may have seemed to outsiders— especially northerners who never lived through Jim Crow—there was a personal history in these relationships that was complicated, lasting, and real.

To elaborate on this point, Reed told me about an invitation he'd received to speak at a Kiwanis Club luncheon from an insurance guy on June 25, 2009, a few weeks before my visit. As that happened to be his 67th birthday, he'd hedged, asking the guy to call him back at a later date, but he finally decided, What the heck? It was for a good civic cause. He put some notes together for a speech about his life as a young man and included his summer of hard labor working with his father for Lindsay.

"I give the speech, and afterward this guy comes up, looks a little younger than me, had glasses on, a little pot belly, and says, 'Do you know who I am?' Reed recalled. "I look at him, and I look closer at him, and I say, 'Yeah, I do. You're Robert Albritton. Donald Lindsay's your uncle.' He was amazed that I recognized him. He told me that he always remembered the time we went bullfrog hunting and I was paddling the boat on Mr. Lindsay's pond and a big moccasin snake was laying up there by the side. I pulled over too close, almost got my head bit off. We laughed about that. He invited me over to see his mounts, said he's got four alone of African game."

As a proud hunter himself, Reed said he might have to go have himself a look, if only because it would be the neighborly thing to do. And here was the essence of Willis Reed, a man who had long ago discovered that there was currency in overcoming differences, building bridges, and cultivating relationships.

That I—the writer of a story that had contributed to his being fired by the only organization he ever wanted to work for—was sitting in his den, still apparently welcome in his life, was a testament to that very fact.

In April 2007, Reed retired from basketball, concluding a four-year stay in the front office of the New Orleans

Hornets. He had taken the job in part because he was bored with the ceremonial position he had with his bedraggled Knicks, but even more so to be closer to his ailing mother. Dutifully, Reed went home to his native state in July 2003. Mother and son, long the essence of mutual devotion, had those summer weeks in closer proximity before Inell Reed, almost 80, died that October. To Reed, it seemed that God's plan had brought him home to see her to the end and finish his working days; but two years later, with a biblical vengeance, there came a hurricane named Katrina that—perhaps least among its consequences—forced a relocation of the Hornets to Oklahoma City.

Nearing 65 years in a life that conditioned him to believe that fate is more than a four-letter word, Reed decided to quit just as the Hornets were returning to New Orleans. I called him to do a tribute column in the *New York Times*, and of course it couldn't be done without reminiscing about a certain May 1970 night, the most memorable of his long and hardworking life.

As for the most forgettable?

"Well," he said, "you can guess that one."

There was no retreating from the unsavory subject and from my role in what was another infamous walk by Reed, this time out of Madison Square Garden and into the chilly New York City night: when he was fired as coach of the Knicks only 14 games into his second season.

November 1978. I was 26 years old, the new beat reporter for the *New York Post,* not so far removed from a Staten Island housing project and from hero worship of the man and his team.

The *Post* at that time was an afternoon newspaper with a long tradition of cagey sportswriting, but was being remade by Rupert Murdoch into the country's most sensational daily. Reed was beginning his second season as the Knicks' head coach after replacing Red Holzman, maestro of the franchise's only championships. He was learning on the job, mainly how to deal with players whose work ethic fell far short of his own. Reed made the playoffs as a rookie coach but the team began the 1978–79 season slowly; as they pulled into Seattle, the word was that David "Sonny" Werblin, the new Garden president, was eager to make a move.

More impresario than sports executive, best known for landing Joe Willie Namath and putting the Jets and the old American Football League into the ring with the establishment NFL, the nearly 70-year-old Sonny didn't know a pick-and-roll from the first pick of the college draft. Neither did his friend Howard Cosell, but it was Cosell who apparently made perfect sense to Werblin when he whispered in his ear that Reed was no worthy coach and that Holzman, who had been relegated to a nominal position in the organization, never should have been replaced.

In Seattle, following an afternoon workout, I asked Reed if the rumors were hurting the young team. He nodded, wearily. "It hurts our gate and it kills team spirit," he said. "Either I'm in or out."

The last quote was incendiary, fast-tracked for the *Post*'s back page. But while I accepted my no-holds-barred Murdochian mission to search and disrupt, if not actually distort, I also had to consider Reed's facial expression, his reasoned tone of voice. He seemed more bewildered—hurt, actually—by Werblin's refusal to acknowledge what he had meant to the organization.

When I called Werblin the next day for a comment, I told him that Reed's words amounted to more of a plea than an ultimatum, although the *Post* headline sitting on his desk had certainly read like the latter. Werblin said he understood the nature of the tabloid newspaper. Days later, when he fired Reed and replaced him with Holzman, Werblin confided to a member of the organization, "Nobody gives me an ultimatum."

That story was my first big splash as the Knicks beat reporter, but it came fraught with conflicting emotions. No matter how much I reminded myself that I was just doing my job, the advancement of my young sportswriting career at the expense of the most essential Knick in the history of the franchise did not feel much like a triumph.

Through the years, Reed and I never talked about the story or its consequences. After he went across the Hudson River to work for the New Jersey Nets in 1988, he always returned my calls, greeting me at the arena with an outstretched hand. But I nevertheless wondered if there was resentment on some level, subliminal or not. Professionalism aside, it mattered to me on a deeper and more personal level. The space in my memory reserved for Willis Reed was more vast than what an occasional quote might fill.

"You know what? Sonny had come in wanting to make changes," he said when I finished a rambling but sincere recounting of the *in-or-out* story, the call to Werblin included. "He came in and fired other people, and he wanted to fire me. So if it didn't happen that day, it would've happened the next week or the next month. So . . . ."

So the case was closed, finally and forever? Yes, he said, I shouldn't give it another thought. I thanked him for his graciousness, for everything he'd given to New York. And when I asked what he was most looking forward to in retirement, he laughed and said, "That's easy. If you happen to call, my wife will tell you that I've gone fishing."

I hung up the phone and wondered why a man who had been the biggest fish and most important catch the Knicks had ever made would want to return to a pond in north-central Louisiana.

Sure enough, when I went to visit, Harry Cook volunteered to show me around Bernice. We rode in his truck and made a quick stop at the Depot Museum, a two-room boxcar with artifacts from the town's bustling sawmill era, a time when, as Cook noted, there were as many as 75 warehouses in operation. Inside, under glass, was a frayed copy of the book *Willis Reed: The Knicks' Take-Charge Man*, by Larry Fox, who happened to have been the sports editor of the New York *Daily News* for a spell when I covered basketball there in the eighties. (You could damn near fill a library with Old Knicks tomes produced in the first half of the 1970s.) Folded neatly beneath the book was one of the seven Eastern Conference All-Star jerseys Reed wore during his ten-year career with the Knicks.

Cook drove to the end of Third Street, stopping in front of the gleaming one-story house Reed built for his mother, just a few hundred feet from the remains of the more ramshackle home he had inhabited as a child and where he had, on his own, built a backboard and rim. "That was a proud day for Willis when his mother moved into that place," Cook said.

The next stop was the mayor's office in the town hall on Fourth Street, in the heart of what was once a busy town center. "On Saturdays, the streets were crowded with folks from here and the towns from all around us," Cook said. "This street here, it had everything. You didn't have to leave Bernice to get anything."

Now, with the sawmill industry long gone, with the remaining warehouses abandoned, Bernice was just another sleepy, depressed town. At one corner of Fourth Street were the remnants of a gas station. Several storefronts were shuttered; what remained open was hardly uplifting: Union Paper & Chemical, Professional Home Health Services, Rexall pharmacy. Across Highway 167 was the town's lone fast-food emporium, a Sonic Drive-In.

Without the industry, Cook said, a slow, steady exodus of townsfolk had occurred in recent years. Bernice High—once the white school—was targeted for closure, with local students soon to be bused to a regional school in Farmerville, 17 miles away. Westside, the school Reed and Brown attended, sat empty and unkempt several miles north on 167. Even the two stoplights in town were gone, along with the welcome sign that once informed visitors that Bernice was THE HOME OF WILLIS REED.

Inside the town hall, Mayor Joe Hicks promised that the sign would soon be replaced by a new one, with a second one to be posted at the north end of town. Bernice was also planning a day in Reed's honor, because, as Hicks said, "Willis is still giving back to the community and to the church here, even though most people don't know about it because he does it so quietly. All people here have to do is ask."

Hicks had left Bernice as a young man for work in Detroit, returning much later in life, presumably to retire. He wound up being elected Bernice's first black mayor. Granted, it had taken a while for the historic event, about 35 years after the desegregation of the town's schools. But Hicks said he was proud to have received biracial support. "It couldn't have just been the black vote, because in general, black folks don't vote," he said.

Hicks and Cook said that any of the town's old-timers, black or white, would tell you that all folks in Bernice could always agree on one thing, and that was their affection for Reed. Nothing united the town more back in the day than a Knicks playoff game against the Bullets, Celtics, or Lakers. "I can tell you that my father didn't care a thing about basketball, but if there was a

Knicks playoff game on, he was in front of that TV and he didn't move until the end of the game," Cook said. "The whole town came to a standstill when Willis was playing. It wasn't a black thing or a white thing . . . "

"It was a Bernice thing," Hicks added.

"That's right," Cook said. "Everybody here felt good about Willis. You'd see him on TV, a star in New York, and then he'd be back in town and it was the same Willis we'd all known growing up."

The same Willis Reed who appeared during my last stop in Bernice—the Third Street home of his aunt Grace and her husband, the Reverend Clyde Oliver. Aunt Grace, his father's sister, had been a teacher in the town's black school system. The Reverend Oliver was the principal at Westside High School for part of Reed's time there.

"I remember when Junior—we all called him that—was playing in high school, everyone came out to see him, white folks, too," Aunt Grace said. "As a boy, he was always all-out, never a problem for anybody. He always wanted to work, just like his mother and father, and he always loved money. He'd do anything to get that money: mow lawns, whatever."

When Reed arrived, in his fishing uniform, after a morning out on a lake in Farmerville with a friend, he asked me: "Did the Reverend tell you that he coached basketball?" No, I said, he hadn't. But it turned out that Oliver had coached scholastically in the area, against Reed. Apparently, Reed never suffered for role models.

When he was a senior at Grambling, Reed was offered an invitation to try out for a 1964 Olympic team for which he had surprisingly little interest in playing.

It was nothing political—or personal. He was just fatigued after a long senior season that was preceded by the Pan American Games the previous summer in São Paulo, Brazil. His body was still expanding, putting on natural weight. His knees were hurting. And with the '64 Summer Games scheduled for October in Tokyo, any NBA draftee on that team would miss not only his first NBA days of training but also the opening game of his rookie season. Reed decided he wasn't up for the sacrifice. More than a gold medal, he wanted the hardware that came with being named NBA Rookie of the Year.

With his attention focused on his future, he settled on the belief that he was going to be drafted by Detroit, which had sent Earl Lloyd, one of the league's first African American players, to scout him in a game against Southern University and the future Chicago Bulls star Bob Love. "I had about 40 that night," Reed said.

The Knicks looked at him, too, and a smile spread across Reed's face when he recalled Red Holzman standing in the corner of the Grambling gym, raincoat draped over his arm, watching him arc soft southpaw jumpers and dominate the boards against an opponent long faded from memory. They shook hands afterward, but Holzman didn't say much.

When word spread within Grambling that he wasn't planning to try out for the Olympic team, Reed was called to the athletic office. Hobdy was waiting, along with Eddie Robinson, who was the athletic director as well as the football coach. The school president also weighed in. Their judgment was unanimous and firm: he had to go to the Olympic trials at St. John's University in New York.

"But I'm kind of banged up," Reed argued. "I'm tired. I want to be ready for my rookie season."

He was told to put his school first, to recognize how rare it was for a player from a historically black school to even be invited. Months before President Lyndon Johnson would sign the landmark Civil Rights Act of 1964, Reed was reminded of the greater struggle, the team that needed him most. He packed his bag and flew to New York for the first time.

As it turned out, he failed to impress, and didn't make a squad that would include a Texas Western

forward, Jim "Bad News" Barnes, along with a heralded Princeton man named Bill Bradley. Reed didn't
worry about it. He had done what his Grambling men-
tors had asked. He had tried. He accepted the result.
In Brazil the previous summer, he had competed with
the best American collegians for playing time on the
way to a gold medal and had been convinced that he
was NBA material—to the point that he was furious
to learn that spring that he had not been a first-round
pick in the 1964 college draft.

"Matter of fact, I was finishing up my student teaching when Eddie Donovan called to tell me I was the
first pick of the second round," Reed said. "Boy, was I
pissed."

With the number-one pick, the woebegone Knicks
had selected Bad News Barnes, whose Olympic trials
performance had convinced the Knicks that he was the
quicker, better athlete. Reed wound up as the first pick
of the second round, the eighth overall, not counting
two territorial selections. Upon arrival in New York, he
bumped into Holzman at the Knicks' Madison Square
Garden office.

"I guess you liked what you saw," he said.

"A little," Holzman said.

Looking back now, Reed could laugh about the quip
as "typical Red." But that day, he vowed (to himself, at
least) to prove that the Knicks had made a mistake.

Whether it was a consensus decision—from Ned Irish, the Knicks' president, at the top to Fred Podesta in the general manager's seat to Donovan as the coach and Holzman the scout—to spend the first pick on Barnes, an African American who had played at Texas Western before that school's five black history makers humbled Adolph Rupp's all-white Kentucky team in the 1966 NCAA title game, or whether doing so came on Holzman's recommendation alone, the rationale is of little relevance now. But it must be acknowledged: the organization got away with a blunder that could have spelled disaster.

What if the teams drafting behind them hadn't been so enamored of players from the predominantly white or all-white universities and generally dismissive of those from all-black schools? What if Baltimore had taken Reed with the third pick, instead of the immortal Gary Bradds of Ohio State? What if San Francisco had resisted the charms of NYU's Barry Kramer with the sixth pick? What if Red Auerbach, the NBA's reigning Nostradamus, hadn't gone for Mel Counts, a spindly seven-footer from Oregon State, with the final selection of the first round?

Granted, the system and standards of scouting amateur talent had been primitive before cable television turned the college basketball season into a blizzard of nightly matchups and the Internet connected the world and ushered in the age of national power rankings for pre-adolescents. Films were grainy black and white and not always easy to come by. Even the most itinerant scout could see only so much. Far from the year-round science it is today, the selection process was based on word-of-mouth sleuthing—on hunches, if not actual guesswork.

Maybe it was fate all along that nurtured and developed the concept of the Old Knicks. But from Reed's point of view, the draft-day slight was just another slice of reality that, however objectionable, he could do nothing about other than prove it wrong.

Reed was so sure of himself that he made the Knicks an offer they couldn't refuse when he sat down with Podesta and Donovan to negotiate his first contract (for $11,000, with a $3,000 signing bonus). "I was trying to bargain for an extra $2,500 as part of a bonus, but I told them I knew I would have a good year and would deserve it, so they could pay me after the season," he said.

Stunned by the self-assuredness of this country kid, Podesta made eye contact with Donovan, a look that said, Can you believe this guy? He turned back to Reed and said, "I like that." They shook hands, and Willis Reed was officially part of the worst team in the NBA.

Growing up in his small-town culture of once punitive inequity had prepared him for that challenge. His days in Bernice had taught him to look past limitations, to imagine what was possible if people could just band together. The man who would soon be captain of the Knicks would make the best of the situation in the big city until he had the right firepower—the right teammates—to change their losing ways.

2

RED AND FUZZY

R ed Holzman died on Friday the 13th, of leukemia and maybe of heartbreak, too. It was November 1998. Months earlier, Red had lost his wife and beloved sidekick, Selma. The last time he appeared in public had been soon after she died, at the second wedding of George Kalinsky, the longtime Madison Square Garden photographer. Holzman kept worrying aloud about whether his monetary gift was sufficient. Selma had always known about such things. He seemed, to the Knicks extended family around him, unmoored and defeated. He was 78.

Two days after Holzman's death, on a brisk Sunday morning, a funeral service was held in his honor at the Parkside Memorial Chapels on Queens Boulevard in Forest Hills.

Not surprisingly, the chapel overflowed with a who's who of New York basketball. I chose a pew in the back, having arrived early enough to watch the procession of the Madison Square Garden executives, along with the most celebrated and famous players in the history of the franchise, take their seats.

Reed . . . Frazier . . . DeBusschere . . . Bradley . . . Barnett . . . Monroe: a lineup that needed no introduction, even after three decades. It was a strange, poignant scene: seeing in mourning players who had collectively caused so much joy—for each other, for New York, for Red Holzman himself. They were solemn in their realization that their basketball family would never again be whole, but Holzman would have been the first to tell any weepers in the congregation to knock it off already. He'd lived the life he wanted to live, and it had turned out a hell of a lot better than he could ever have envisioned. His own idea for a memorial would probably have meant cracking open a bottle of his beloved scotch and raising a glass to the players who had won him those two cherished titles.

But I also wondered what Holzman—not a man disposed to being publicly fussed over—would have said to the tall white-haired gentleman who stiffly entered the chapel, accompanied by his wife and looking as if he hadn't slept in the days since he'd heard the news.

Noticing the man's unmistakable grief, a reporter from another newspaper, younger and apparently unfamiliar with the old Garden crowd, leaned into me and asked, "Who's that?"

"That," I said, "is Fuzzy." And even in the saddest of moments, I found myself smiling at the sight of one of pro basketball's most likable lifers, one of the sport's true characters: Andrew "Fuzzy" Levane. Seeing him had instantly triggered a long-dormant memory. Years before, with Fuzzy himself at death's door, lingering in a coma, I had called Holzman to ask about his old teammate, someone Holzman had known longer than anyone else in the game.

Holzman told me: "You never heard anyone say, 'Here comes that asshole Fuzzy.'"

Though he had a reputation for being perhaps the lousiest quote in the long, loquacious history of the coaching profession, it was classic Holzman: witty and wise and—due to the profanity—unprintable without alteration.

The chain of events ultimately leading to the creation of the most democratic team in professional basketball history began with a steamy shower scene in postwar Rochester, New York. Les Harrison, the owner and coach of the National Basketball League's Royals, loitering in the locker room after a game, couldn't help but take a peek as one of his new players lathered up. Harrison gave the unmistakably uncircumcised Fuzzy Levane a look as if to say: What the hell?

"I thought you were Jewish," he said. "That's why I signed you."

"What are you talking about?" Levane said. "I'm Italian."

"Christ," Harrison swore, exasperated by his erroneous presumption and still anxious to have a player who would appeal to his team's Semitic fans. "Get me a goddamn Jew."

In 1945, this wasn't such a tall order, by any means. Eager to please the boss, and knowing exactly where to look, Levane got Harrison two of Brooklyn's finest Yids. From his home borough, Levane summoned Jack Garfinkel and William Holzman, who, not unlike Fuzzy Levane, were known to their friends as Dutch and Red, respectively. Both were guards, though Garfinkel was considered one of the more creative passers of the day, while Holzman was fancied a gritty and overachieving defender.

Harrison signed the two of them in 1945, and the assist by Levane wouldn't be the last in a long symbiotic relationship between him and Holzman. "If it wasn't for me," Levane said with the sardonic license he and Holzman had granted each other for decades, "Red would've been selling insurance, or peanuts."

Levane and Holzman became friends during their college careers, Levane playing for St. John's and Holzman for City College of New York, where he was an All-American in 1942. They worked together at a resort in upstate New York for a couple of summers before the war, when Levane joined the Coast Guard and Holzman the Navy. Home again, Levane had an easier time launching his pro career as a Frank J. Haggerty Award winner, given annually by the New York writers to the college player voted best in the metropolitan area. Holzman was eager to play, too, despite his wife's fears that basketball would lead to a financial dead end. But he needed his friend's intervention. He sat on the bench as Levane badgered Harrison to let Holzman be more than a marketing ploy. Given a chance, Holzman became an eight-year backcourt fixture, winning two NBL championships and another in 1951 after the league merged with the Basketball Association of America to form the NBA.

For their NBA championship, the Royals had to defeat Joe Lapchick's New York Knicks. The series was the first league final to go the distance: seven games, ending with Holzman dribbling out the dying seconds of a four-point win. Clever man: by helping to beat the

Knicks, he kept the New York franchise and fans waiting for a title that wouldn't come until 19 years later—when Holzman himself would deliver it, as coach.

That 1950–51 season is often regarded as the season that broke the pro basketball color line in Boston, Syracuse, and New York. But Holzman and Levane always scoffed at the imprecise historical reporting. Long before that, in 1946, they had welcomed William "Dolly" King to Rochester. King was a 6'4" swingman, a three-sport star out of Brooklyn's Alexander Hamilton High School and Long Island University—and a black man. Levane insisted that it was Harrison, "that old son of a gun," who deserved to be recognized as the Branch Rickey of professional basketball.

Given the meagerness of their paychecks, the three Brooklynites banded together, renting a small space at the downtown Seneca Hotel on Clinton Avenue. "Room 308," said Levane, his memory astonishingly sharp. "Imagine that, in 1946: a Jewish guy, a black guy, and a *paisano*."

On the road, the story did not always inspire, and the treatment of the team by locals was often far from royal. The three New Yorkers would walk into a restaurant, hoping for a late-night bite. "We had an agreement that if they wouldn't serve all of us, then none of us would eat there," Levane said. "We'd say screw you and walk out." Most of the time, they wound up eating in their room.

In the early years of pro basketball, destinies and dynasties depended upon the enlightenment of a single individual, the willingness of an owner to risk a backlash of ignorance. In a world that refused to pander to hate and fear (or plain stupidity), a world that didn't yet exist, Holzman's coaching career might have been very different. Perhaps he would have been the long-reigning standard for NBA coaching greatness, rather than that other Brooklyn Red, the cigar-smoking pit bull named Auerbach.

Holzman got a call from Levane upon his release by Rochester in 1953. Levane had by then worked his way into the coaching ranks with the Milwaukee Hawks. "Come up here and be my tenth man," Levane said. It wasn't long before the rescue mission took a fateful turn: Levane was fired and was succeeded on the bench by his buddy.

Under Holzman, the Hawks' losing continued, all the way to St. Louis, where the team moved in 1955. One year later, his 33-win team had the second pick in the college draft, behind the Rochester Royals. The most accomplished collegian, far and away, was an elusive, dominating big man named Bill Russell. "I had seen Russell," Levane said, "and I thought he couldn't shoot, but he would revolutionize the game with his defense and intimidation."

To his everlasting credit, Auerbach also believed Russell was a game changer, the perfect player to ignite his fast-breaking offense, which already starred the ball-handling and passing magician Bob Cousy. According to Auerbachian legend, he conspired to have the Celtics' owner, Walter Brown, send his popular Ice Capades show to Rochester if Harrison would conveniently draft someone else. Brown agreed and, hungry for the revenue on ice, so did Harrison, who took a forgettable guard named Sihugo Green.

That left St. Louis with the next pick, and the chance to grab the man who would become the winningest player in NBA history. But it was also common knowledge around the league that the Hawks' owner, Ben Kerner, did not want to pay Russell the $25,000 in bonus money that he had demanded upon signing. Nor was Kerner eager to risk a convulsive reaction in St. Louis by making an African American (one whom he perceived as having a combative personality) the centerpiece of his team.

Auerbach made it easy for Kerner with a trade offer for Russell that he couldn't refuse: St. Louis native and six-time All-Star Ed Macauley—who had requested a move to his hometown to be with his ailing young son—and giving in to Kerner's demand for another touted player, Cliff Hagan, who was returning to basketball after military service. The deal didn't immediately look as lopsided as it would in the ensuing decade: the Hawks made the Finals in four of the next five seasons, losing to the Celtics in 1957 and reversing the result a year later when Russell was injured. Unfortunately for Holzman, the Hawks' success came too late. Before the team could mesh, he was fired after a 14–19 start.

"Imagine if Red had gotten Russell and not that asshole Auerbach," Levane said. Unlike Holzman—who privately referred to Auerbach as Oyerbach but was a model of circumspection publicly—Levane was never too reticent with his feelings about the other Red and his trademark victory cigar. Every time he saw Auerbach chomping on one, Fuzzy was overcome with the desire to "shove it up his ass."

Levane offered another intriguing hypothetical: Imagine if the Knicks had gotten Russell! By 1956, after being dismissed in Milwaukee, Levane had drifted home to New York and joined the Knicks as a scout. That spring, he went to his boss, Ned Irish, and told him that Kerner didn't want Russell in the upcoming draft—the very thing Auerbach had done in Boston.

"He asked me what it would take to get him," Levane said. "I told him it would take a player, draft picks, and cash. He said, 'How much?' I said $15,000. He said, 'I'm not paying that.' That schmuck—we had a chance to bring Bill Russell to New York, and didn't even try because of $15,000."

Edward S. "Ned" Irish was one of the 11 founders of the Basketball Association of America in 1946 and was instrumental in its merger with the National Basketball League three years later. He had founded the Knickerbockers (named for a pseudonym of Washington Irving) simultaneously, after quitting his job as a sportswriter for the *New York World-Telegram*. Under his stewardship, Madison Square Garden transformed into the so-called Mecca of Basketball (a name derived from the Shriners' Mecca Temple, a depression-era boxing venue) as Irish promoted college basketball games at the event-starved arena, where previously the largest crowds had assembled to watch hockey.

Though the Garden technically owned the Knicks, Irish was virtually a one-man executive office, using the leverage of New York and the Garden, along with his blustery personality, to create a bully pulpit. In the early days of pro basketball, Irish was arguably more powerful than the league commissioner, whose office was in the Garden. When difficult decisions had to be made—should big markets share home gate receipts with teams less financially endowed?—Irish typically got his way.

"He was a dour man, never seemed happy," said David Stern, who would replace Larry O'Brien as commissioner in 1984 but who knew Irish from his time as a league counsel dating back to the seventies. Stern theorized that Irish had never recovered from the death of one of his two sons. Others said he always came across as arrogant, aloof, and humorless. The journalist and author Roger Kahn interviewed Irish for a 1967 profile in *Sports Illustrated* and found it difficult to believe that Irish had been a newspaper reporter. His answers were mostly gibberish, although Kahn took special note when Irish let slip, "I don't care what they say about me as long as they buy tickets." Kahn described Irish as so obsessed with the Garden's business that he would occasionally lurk in the shadows and pounce when he spotted an usher moving a patron into a better seat in exchange for a fifty-cent tip.

As with James Dolan years later—the current owner of the Knicks and scourge of their twenty-first-century fans—the front office and coaches had to put up with his moods and his meddling. After early success under Joe Lapchick, when they reached the Finals three straight years, the Knicks became one of the worst teams in the NBA, a franchise with a knack for picking losers in the draft and firing coaches. Fuzzy Levane got his chance in 1958 and actually led the team into the playoffs, something that wouldn't be repeated for nearly a decade. But Irish could never leave alone the people he hired long enough for them to do their job. Nor was he above forcing his own discriminatory and ultimately self-defeating practices upon his team.

In the fall of 1959, Levane's early-season roster included a rugged 6'4" forward out of New York University named Cal Ramsey, who began his rookie season in St. Louis but quickly became an ex-Hawk after appearing in only four games. In New York, he lasted just seven, despite averaging an eye-opening 22.9 minutes, 11.4 points, and 6.7 rebounds as Levane's first man off the bench. Levane liked Ramsey; he believed the Knicks had found themselves a solid rotation player, and a homegrown one at that.

"Cal and I had something pretty good going," Levane said. "But we already had three other black guys on the roster: Willie Naulls, Johnny Green, and Ray Felix. So I get a call from Irish, who says that's too many, I have to get rid of one." Levane complied, reluctantly. Ramsey went to Syracuse, where he roomed briefly with a young, flamboyant shooting guard named Dick Barnett. Then he injured his knee and drifted, like many a deserving black player, into the Eastern League, more or less playing for carfare.

Levane wasn't on the Knicks' bench much longer, either. After an 8–19 start, he was replaced by Carl Braun. By then he had made his most significant contribution, throwing yet another career lifeline to Holzman, convincing Irish to bring him on as a scout in 1959.

Fate would much later allow Holzman to repay Levane, or at least lend him a hand when the Garden's corporate bean counters cut Fuzzy loose as a scout in the 1980s, forcing him to live on Social Security benefits. As company legend has it, Holzman successfully lobbied the new regime of Al Bianchi and Rick Pitino to return Levane to the payroll, where he remained long after his scouting days were over. Always mindful of how Levane never did make any real money in the game, Holzman also left his friend a nice piece of change in his will.

Strange how these things work out.

In 1959, upon buying a sturdy suitcase and a couple of suits to dress the part of the distinguished scout, Holzman would tell anyone within earshot that he had no desire to return to the bench. He was content to hit the road and scour remote college towns across the country.

"When I was coaching with Frank McGuire at South Carolina in the sixties, I remember Red coming down and actually getting on the court and doing some workouts with us," said Donnie Walsh, the longtime NBA executive who returned to his native New York to run the Knicks in 2008. "Frank knew him from New York and really liked him. He was this tough little guy, spinning these two-hand set shots off the backboard from all over."

All over. That was the story of Holzman's itinerant life for almost a decade. During the college season, he packed a suitcase and hit the road, a man in his forties logging too many miles for not enough money.

Jerry Krause—a young scout for the Baltimore Bullets, who much later would fit all the right pieces around Michael Jordan for the Bulls' six-title dynasty—remembered meeting Holzman for the first time. Krause had just disembarked from a flight on a Saturday morning in St. Louis—like Red, a travel-weary soul in need of a week's worth of sleep.

"You're Krause, aren't you?" Holzman said. "I hear you work hard. Where you been?"

Krause was flattered that someone as experienced in the business as Holzman knew who he was, but he wasn't keen on sharing trade secrets.

"Oh, up the road," Krause said. Holzman shot him a don't-shit-a-shitter look.

"Now listen, Krause," he said. "I know for certain you were in Oklahoma City last night, because there were only two games worth seeing, and I was at the one in Wichita. Secondly, I know you're going to scout the Van Arsdale boys tonight, because that plane over there is to Indianapolis and I know they're the only ones worth seeing up there. So don't try to lie to old Red again and maybe I'll let you drive with me."

Holzman even imparted some road wisdom, telling Krause how to maximize his time in a town by spending the afternoon before a night game at the school, watching tapes of earlier games, instead of wasting time watching television in a cheap hotel room.

Beyond the car and the counsel, Holzman didn't reveal much, saving whatever he knew about the players for the detailed scouting reports he prepared for the Knicks' front office. On those pages was evidence that he had even more of an impact on those two Knicks championships than is commonly known.

Not all the reports were saved. Some have inevitably been lost in the shuffle of lives lived. But a couple of bound volumes went into the back of Holzman's closet with the rest of the keepsakes he never displayed at his modest Cedarhurst home in the Five Towns area of Long Island (where the Holzmans resided with a listed telephone number). His daughter and son-in-law would have other ideas. After Holzman's death, in the finished basement of their Westchester townhome, Gail and Charles Papelian created a display of photos and memorabilia. There was the framed, player-autographed photo of the Rochester Royals' 1951 NBA championship team, the net Holzman had worn around his neck after Game 7 of the 1970 Finals; even one of Selma's old scorecards was framed and mounted on the wall. But the scouting reports were kept out of sight, delicate and protected like expensive family heirlooms.

When I spent time with Gail and Charles in their basement, talking about the qualities that can lead one to success, she posed a question that sounded right from the Holzman lexicon: "Doesn't it always come down to character?" She seemed to have inherited her father's personality, private and modest and unwilling under any conditions to publicly share anything that might be construed as negative. I could peruse the reports as long as I didn't share some of what I saw—the various critical appraisals of players long retired and, in some cases, dead. Her father would not have approved.

She explained to me that it wasn't as if she and her husband had created a shrine for mass consumption. It was their way of paying private tribute to a man who loved the game, and who proved it with a decade's worth of oppressive travel and toil for $5,000 a year well into the sixties.

Born to Eastern European immigrants on Manhattan's Lower East Side, Red moved to a tenement in the Brownsville section of Brooklyn when he was four. His early life was focused resolutely on the school yard and its games—basketball and handball—and his daughter figures he would have been a basketball lifer, one way or another. Just like his lifelong friend Fuzzy.

"Red didn't mind scouting; he just wanted a job," Levane said. "Me, I always wanted to coach. So what happens? I end up as a scout and he winds up coaching the perfect basketball team." Not the best team, Levane would have to admit, in deference to Russell, Sam and K. C. Jones, and, yes, even that other, less likable Red. But take it from a guy who had been around long enough to have seen every NBA season from day one: "As far as five men working together, the Knicks were the perfect team."

A decade after Red was buried, I called Fuzzy at his daughter's home in South Carolina during the summer of 2009, unaware that his wife, Kay, had recently passed away. Quick to offer condolences, I said I would call back another time, but, no, the 89-year-old Levane insisted he didn't want to hang up. He wanted to talk about basketball, the other great love of his life—a welcome distraction from yet another season of grief.

Death had been too much a mainstay since he'd lost his sister, Marie, in the late nineties, followed by a couple of close friends and finally his best friends, Selma and Red. The sadness sent him into an emotional tailspin, in part because he just couldn't figure out how he had outlasted all of them after his own near-death experience in 1991. Driving home with his wife after his induction into the New York City Basketball Hall of Fame, Levane suffered a ruptured aortic aneurysm. Had it occurred an hour later, he would have died of internal bleeding in his sleep, doctors later told him. Instead he was rushed to St. Francis Hospital in Roslyn, Long Island, where he needed a minor miracle to survive the next 72 hours in a coma. Holzman visited him every day for two weeks, until he was out of danger.

Beyond all the ribbing, Holzman and Levane had deep and abiding respect for each other. However famous or successful Holzman would become, he never forgot to credit Levane. "He always said that Fuzzy paved the way for him, every step of the way," Gail told me.

When Holzman died, in 1998, Levane felt as if doctors had excavated a chunk of his heart. He especially missed him when the Knicks made a shocking run to the NBA Finals the following spring with a socially dysfunctional team that had finished eighth in the Eastern Conference during a season shortened by a lockout.

After they eliminated the Larry Bird–coached Indiana Pacers in the Eastern Conference finals, I was working my way through the crowd in the lower stands of the Garden when I bumped into Levane near his seat behind the Knicks' bench, tears streaming down his face. I asked him about that. The emotional unburdening was part joy, he said, but also the result of all the funerals and wakes, the post-traumatic stress his doctor had explained to him. Despite the Knicks' success, he was still hurting, most of all when he looked across the court to where Red once sat, Selma faithfully keeping score by his side, as she had ever since Holzman was on the bench, leaning forward, immersed in his work.

If only Red could have lived to see the Knicks back in the NBA Finals—Levane couldn't let go of the thought. Maybe it would have given him more incentive to fight, kept him going after Selma was gone. Basketball had always meant that much to both of them. He admitted to compulsively dialing Holzman's number throughout the stunning playoff run before hanging up, embarrassed and heartbroken all over again. He would think to himself: What the hell am I doing?

3

AN IRISH CARNIVAL

ifteen years before Magic and Larry, there were
Cazzie and Bill. Like Magic Johnson and Larry
Bird, who all but created March Madness with their
epic 1979 final, Cazzie Russell (Chicago) and Bill Bradley (Crystal City, Missouri) were native sons of the
Midwest. Like Magic, Russell played for a traditional
sports power, the Michigan Wolverines. And Bradley, for his part, was largely responsible for lifting Ivy
League Princeton into the national championship discussion, just as Bird would later do with a motley collection of Indiana State Sycamores. And then there was
the unmistakable color of their skin: Russell was black,
Bradley was white.

But unlike Bird and Magic, their teams met twice
during the 1964–65 season, including a semifinal

Michigan blowout of Princeton in the Final Four. It's difficult to imagine, in an age of "one-and-done" college prospects, that a matchup akin to Bradley versus Russell (or, for that matter, Lew Alcindor versus Elvin Hayes, which played out on January 20, 1968, in front of 52,693 fans at the Houston Astrodome and has been billed ever since as the Game of the Century) will ever happen again.

The use of the college game as a one-year springboard to the NBA, the lusting after network television money, and the obsession with postseason tournaments have long reduced the college regular season to a drone of revenue-generating exhibitions, nightly cable filler. But on December 30, 1964, at Madison Square Garden, Michigan-Princeton not only captivated the city; it helped restore college basketball's reputation after the 1951 point-shaving scandals had implicated four New York schools and brought disrepute to the basketball world in general.

The game was especially gratifying for Ned Irish, who had watched the Garden's reputation crumble along with the sport it showcased. The first college basketball game he promoted—a doubleheader in which NYU defeated Notre Dame and Westminster beat St. John's—had drawn 16,180 fans on December 29, 1934. He bragged that he didn't have to put up a cent, the

Garden demanding only that its percentage of the gate offset the $4,000 cost of renting the building. "Don't forget, it was the Depression, and the Garden was dark a lot of nights," Irish said. Under Irish, attendance for college basketball peaked at an average of 18,196 in 1946, when the pro leagues were in diapers. Five years later came the scandals; Irish watched helplessly as his gold mine collapsed, as the NCAA tournament made sure to steer clear of bookie-infested New York, and as the renowned CCNY program downscaled its involvement in the sport.

With the Michigan-Princeton matchup, the wounds seemed finally to heal. Michigan was ranked number one, with Russell leading its freewheeling offense. Playing for the first time in the Garden, Bradley was up from New Jersey, having months earlier captained the gold-medal-winning Olympic team in Rome, one of three Americans to average double figures in points. But he was still carrying the predictable Ivy stigma. Was he a dominant force because he had primarily been measured against scholarly white boys with secure futures in banking or law? "That was the number-one question: Is he playing against the kind of competition we were?" said Gail Goodrich, an All-American guard that season at UCLA. "I remember we played Yale and beat them by 40, so my first take was, well, probably not."

More than 40 years after being shuttered and de-
molished, the old Garden survives only in New York's
collective memory, romanticized in photographs of
an era gone by: outside, the landmark Nedick's sign,
where they served up hot dogs and drinks, the ritual
snack on the way in or at halftime; inside, the sorely
missed voice of the public address announcer, John F.
X. Condon, launching the night with his elegant opening: "Good evening, everybody. Welcome to Madison
Square Garden." The court itself was buried beneath a
gray, smoky haze that grew thicker and thicker among
the arena's steel girders as the night progressed. Bal-
conies hovered over the court as if the Garden were
an opera house, one filled with vociferous fans whose
rooting interests often had more to do with the point
spread than with home-team fidelity.

When I try to recall the old Garden's interior, I
only seem to summon Boston Garden (a building I
frequented as a reporter in the 1980s, when Bird and
company reigned). "It was actually a lot like Boston,"
said Marv Albert, who broke into the business at the
old Garden as a ball boy, on his way to replacing Marty
Glickman as the radio voice of the Knicks. "And if you
were able to go back to it now and saw everything that
was wrong with it, the tiny locker rooms and all, you'd
say, 'How did professional athletes ever play here?' Of

course, that was all they knew, and if you were around back then, you have a great nostalgia for the place, the same way people feel about Ebbets Field. There were some great games there."

That Garden incarnation was actually the second of three locations in the long history of the arena, dating back to 1879. The first two were located at East 26th Street and Madison Avenue. By 1925 the brand had moved to Eighth Avenue between 49th and 50th streets, where it remained until 1968. For the Michigan-Princeton game, the building was sold out, with scalpers outside demanding a princely sum of $35 for choice seats. Two NBA games on the same night in New York could be seen for a fraction of the cost.

But no Knicks game to that point was anywhere near as compelling an attraction as Michigan-Princeton, which was anticipated with a raw tension beyond any normal athletic competition. "I was at that game, and I can tell you that everybody was rooting for Bill," said Cal Ramsey, the would-be Knick who had gone into teaching but never strayed far from the Garden. By "everybody" he meant everybody who was white. "It was 1964."

In a positive light, it was also the year the Civil Rights Act was signed into law by President Lyndon

Johnson—a blow against racial discrimination and segregation. A couple of weeks before the Michigan-Princeton game, Martin Luther King Jr. had traveled to Norway to receive the Nobel Peace Prize. But 1964 was as much about violence and unrest as it was about peace. In June, three young civil rights workers were murdered in Mississippi. Race riots shook Harlem during a six-day period in July and then spread to Rochester and Philadelphia. At the end of the year, here came an event in the heart of New York that had all the trappings of social conflict: the white star from an elite private school versus the black star from a public powerhouse—Old World privilege versus the New World knocks of a Chicago housing project.

Even for basketball fans, the game took on a rare significance. Everyone was eager to see how Bradley and the Ivy Leaguers would meet the challenge of the Wolverines—though they should already have known that Bradley, at least, was not likely to be intimidated. When Princeton played Syracuse in its opening game of the Holiday Festival, the Orange immediately set up a box-and-one defense, assigning a tough kid from Brooklyn, Sam Penceal, to chase Bradley. Reporting for *Sports Illustrated*, Frank Deford wrote: "Penceal literally clung to him, clutching, grabbing, clawing. Suddenly, obviously furious, Bradley lashed back with an elbow that rocked the husky Penceal . . . the crowd gasped."

The scouts drooled. This particular Ivy Leaguer, no white wallflower, was not about to be bullied. Bradley, the only child of Warren (a banker) and Susan (a teacher), had been a natural at the game from the time he began playing in fourth grade. He was blessed with wide peripheral vision that made him an expert passer and a desire to work on the staples of his game, which depended more on repetition than physiological gifts. On school days, he would practice for three and a half hours after class. On Saturdays, from nine to five. On Sundays, he went from one thirty in the afternoon until five. He scored 3,068 points at Crystal City High School and could have gone to any basketball power he wanted.

Russell had no reason to question Bradley's qualifications and recalled having no interest in the social context of their confrontation. Growing up in a Chicago housing project, he had strong Baptist roots and blue-collar parents who told him that he was no victim as long as he had the ability and a job to showcase it. "We didn't have much, but enough to do what we needed to do," Russell said. "I had two or three pair of pants, but they were always clean. I always had to go to class, account for my grades. I came home late from high school one night and my father said, 'Where you been?' I said, 'I was at basketball tryouts.' He wasn't sure that's what I should be doing. He came to the school one day, the same day the coach made final cuts. He looked in the gym and saw I was still there. He turned around, never saw that I saw him, and never said a word. That was his way of saying 'Okay.' "

Russell said the prospect of playing a widely anticipated game in New York obscured everything else. "Madison Square Garden, a buzz in the city, everyone carrying their newspapers around, all hyped up," he said. "That's what I remember. Bradley didn't have anything to prove to us. We already knew he was good."

How good? That was what they had yet to find out. Not only did Bradley riddle the Wolverines for 41 points, but he brought the ball up against the press, controlled the offense, defended tenaciously, and went to the boards for 9 rebounds. Until he fouled out with 4:37 left in the game, it appeared that Princeton was going to win handily, the score 75–63 in the Tigers' favor. Bradley's commanding performance essentially overshadowed the 27 points scored by Russell, who at the time was reported to have struggled because he was playing with a damaged sneaker. Unless memory failed, that was news to him. "I honestly don't remember anything wrong with my sneaker," he said. "I know I didn't shoot well. I know Bradley did."

After Bradley left the court, Princeton extended the lead to 77–63 before its historic collapse. Without Bradley to steady them against the relentless pressure, Princeton might as well have sent its debate team to try to break the half-court line. Michigan closed the game with a 16–1 run that included wiping out a 78–68 lead in 65 seconds, beginning with a rebound by Russell and run-out for a fast-break layup. So toothless were the Tigers without Bradley that on three of their next four possessions, they failed to reach midcourt before turning the ball over. With the fans in pandemonium, Michigan had the ball with 36 seconds left for the last shot, and put it where it belonged: in Russell's hands.

He remembered the clock ticking down, the Princeton defender Ed Hummer trying to force him left so he couldn't use his explosive quickness to get to the rim. Russell thought: Fine, have it your way. He dribbled left, stopped, and launched a 15-footer that won the game by the time it hit the ground. The celebration began. But in a more general accounting, and one that would preview the Bradley-Russell chronicles to come, the shot came too late to steal the night.

This proved Bradley's show from start to finish. As he sat on the bench with a towel over his head, fouled out and helpless, the totality of Bradley's performance took on a whole new dimension.

In an era of reigning big men, it seemed all the more amazing that one player who was no goliath in the paint, no Chamberlain or Russell, could have such an impact on a game. In his *Sports Illustrated* dispatch, Deford called Bradley's effort "as fine an individual performance as has ever been given on a basketball court." Deford, of course, was also a Princeton man. But Joe Lapchick, the former Knicks coach whose St. John's team would upset Michigan in the festival final, was equally awestruck: "I always thought Oscar [Robertson] was the greatest, but Bradley is only a half step behind him," he told Deford.

This was heady stuff for a young man with the vertical range of a YMCA warrior and one who didn't appear quick enough to play in an NBA backcourt (or big and brawny enough, at 6'5", to survive as a forward). Bradley suspected that he received the zealous praise precisely because he was no exceptional specimen. Many coaches and sportswriters relished the opportunity to champion a so-called thinking man's player, and were inclined to celebrate him for that reason—if not strictly for the color of his skin.

Given the mounting evidence that the sport was well on its way to becoming a national stage for talented black men, and in the face of fomenting social issues, Bradley believed he may have been the first of the great white hopes. In hindsight, he admitted that it was not a role he was comfortable with; white and black players alike saw through the thinly disguised media stereotyping, he said. From Bradley to Bird and beyond, black stars would chafe at the blue-collar, hardworking characterizations that accompanied the shrinking number of their white counterparts, while they themselves were lauded for their God-given talent.

In 1987, the issue would for the first time become a public discussion when Dennis Rodman and Isiah Thomas suggested that Bird was the beneficiary of white hype. The timing was bad: Bird's Celtics had just eliminated the Pistons from the playoffs, and only two games separated the miracle (in Boston, at least) of Bird stealing Thomas's inbounds pass, which resulted in one of the all-time end-of-game heists in NBA history. The execution was clumsy. But given time to explain himself in a calmer setting, in an interview with Ira Berkow of the *New York Times*, Thomas captured the sentiments of many black players:

When Bird makes a great play, it's due to his thinking, and his work habits. It's all planned out by him. It's not the case for blacks. All we do is run and jump. We never practice or give a thought to how we play. It's like I came dribbling out of my mother's womb.

No one was quite ready to speak that way in 1964. By season's end, Bill Bradley had accepted a Rhodes scholarship and was on his way to England. If he was going to effect social change, he believed he'd do it as a Washington power broker, not as a basketball player.

He didn't mind telling people about his ambitions for the political arena. In Minneapolis for the announcement of the *Sporting News* All America Team, he befriended Gail Goodrich. They played a lot of Ping-Pong, Bradley determined to beat the quick-handed Goodrich before they left town. At one point they discussed their plans. Goodrich said he expected to play in the NBA. He asked Bradley what the future might bring. "He said, 'Oh, I'm going to Oxford. And then I'd really like to start working toward being president of the United States,'" Goodrich recalled. "Just like that—no big deal."

Ned Irish couldn't forget the furor Bradley and Russell had created in New York that late December night. He couldn't ignore the potential gate appeal Bradley in particular would have if he ever returned to basketball. Irish leaned on his people to secure Bradley with a territorial draft pick, in which a team could lay claim to a player based on his school's location in the same region.

Without question, Eddie Donovan and Red Holzman did not need to be convinced that the risk was an acceptable one. Fuzzy Levane and Dick McGuire, who'd succeeded Donovan as coach when Donovan was moved into the general manager's seat during the 1965–66 season, both said they believed the Knicks would have taken Bradley with or without the owner's approval. "Bill was too good not to play anymore—that's what everyone thought, anyway," Levane said. Once they had reached that conclusion, it made perfect sense for the Knicks to lock Bradley up with a territorial pick, even if he wouldn't play for two years while studying at Oxford, if at all.

As for Russell, he would deposit his game-winning shot into the bank of special memories. Sportswriters might never let him forget Bradley's transcendent effort, but his peers would remember who came through at the finish. Years later, when Russell attended a Lakers game, Kareem Abdul-Jabbar told him he had been at the Garden that night and that it was one of the best games he'd ever seen. He said he'd always admired how Russell had shaken off the subpar shooting night and risen to the moment.

Compared with Bradley, Russell may not have looked like the best player in the country, but there was at least one Garden witness on December 30, 1964, who believed Russell's performance was worth savoring, too.

"Guts to take the last shot," Red Holzman wrote in his scouting report, making special note after detailing Russell's offensive strengths, his impressive athletic gifts.

Though hardly irrelevant, the fact that Russell had made the shot to beat Princeton was not the main point. The way Holzman saw it, any team with serious NBA championship aspirations did not have room in its end-of-game lineup for conscientious objectors. The main point was that Russell had taken the shot. The team needed to be a complete coalition of the willing. Let the shots fall as they may.

One year later, when the Knicks won a coin flip with Detroit to determine who would get the first pick of the 1966 draft, they used it to bring Cazzie Russell to New York. The Pistons, desperate for Russell as an in-state draw, were crushed—especially the man who had called tails. Dave DeBusschere, their player-coach, was, after all, a lifelong resident of Detroit.

By the time Bradley and Russell squared off in New York, the Knicks were well on their way to another forgettable season, running a distant fourth in the NBA's Eastern Division (which at the time had only four teams). But there was hope. Three of the four rookies on the team—the front-liners Willis Reed, Bad News Barnes, and a guard, Howard "Butch" Komives—were all under 24 and already averaging double figures. Reed was in the process of winning the league Rookie of the Year award, posting at year's end 19.5 points and 14.7 rebounds, while taking over at center.

One night against the Warriors in San Francisco, Reed scored 32 against Wilt Chamberlain, using a variety of jumpers and agile post moves to keep the Stilt on his heels. The game went to overtime, where the Warriors pulled it out, but Reed was quite pleased with himself . . . until he picked up a box score. "I held him to 56," he recalled. "He killed me, man. One big step and jump, dunk it, or the finger roll."

It could have been much worse. The Knicks were already familiar with Chamberlain's otherworldliness. On March 2, 1962, when the Warriors were still based in Philadelphia, he'd scored a record 100 points in Hershey, Pennsylvania, while the team on the other side barely did more than watch. The young Knicks were eager to move past that and other franchise humiliations.

"The expectations were very low at the time, but even though we weren't a playoff-caliber team, the fans began to enjoy us because we played hard, we ran, it was more fun than the old style," said Emmette Bryant, the fourth rookie on the team, a 6'1" guard out of Chicago and DePaul who became Reed's first roommate and friend in New York.

They visited the World's Fair together at Corona Park in Queens. They went out for dinner, learned to navigate the subways, found their way uptown over the summer to play in the famed Rucker League. "We liked the idea that we were the guys making the transition from the old era—Richie Guerin and those guys—to the new," Bryant said.

Last place, though, was still last place. After averaging almost 12,000 fans per game at home in the late fifties, attendance had slipped under 10,000 by 1964–65. The front office was restless, ready to retool, sending the veteran forward Bob Boozer to the Lakers for the shooting guard Dick Barnett, who was moving to his fourth pro team at the age of 29, including a brief jump to the short-lived American Basketball League with George Steinbrenner's Cleveland Pipers to reunite with

John McLendon, his college coach at Tennessee A&I (now Tennessee State).

On the East Coast, Reed was ecstatic. At Grambling, he had heard all about Barnett, who had put on a few shows when visiting in the late 1950s. The black college legend of Skull Barnett—so nicknamed because he shaved off his hair—was such that Reed wondered if the stories were apocryphal. "Everyone said he was a character," Reed recalls. "When we got him, I thought, I'm going to enjoy playing with this guy."

He would be less sanguine about the next Knicks trade, early in his second season: Bad News Barnes, Johnny Green, Johnny Egan, and cash to Baltimore for a high-scoring center, Walt Bellamy. As much as Barnes's departure validated Reed's belief that he should have been the number-one pick, the acquisition of the 6'11" Bellamy meant that Reed would have to change positions.

"I think they thought because Bellamy was bigger that I would be better as a forward," Reed said. Throughout his career, he was alternately listed at 6'10" and 6'9", but Holzman had measured him at Grambling in his socks at a shade under 6'9". The conventional wisdom was that if they were to contend for a title, the Knicks would need more size at the position to confront the likes of Bill Russell and Wilt Chamberlain.

Already convinced that he could compete in the paint, Reed wasn't happy. The deal didn't make sense to him. Bellamy was already in his late twenties, and his reputation as a talented and statistically prodigious but enigmatic and occasionally unmotivated player preceded him. Eddie Donovan had told Reed upon his arrival in New York that the Knicks intended to build a championship team, largely through the draft. Now Reed wondered: was the blueprint already being abandoned?

For the moment, perhaps it was; while the additions of Barnett and Bellamy didn't get the Knicks into the playoffs, the team did achieve a winning record at home for the first time in four years, typically a sign of better things to come. The following season, 1966–67, they would creep within nine games of .500. They were no longer league doormats, and their draft status reflected that. With the fifth pick, their choice wasn't as obvious as it had been with their selections of the previous two years.

At a crucial time in the team's development, the front office was about to be tested. Luckily for the Knicks, as had been the case with Bradley and Russell, the best place to study again turned out to be Madison Square Garden.

. . .

Red Holzman never said a word to Walt Frazier. He scouted him assiduously throughout the 1966–67 season and watched Frazier drive Division II Southern Illinois to a series of stunning upsets: over the largely intact defending champions from Texas Western; against second-ranked Louisville, with the All-Americans Wes Unseld and Butch Beard; and opposite another top-ten team, Wichita State. Holzman would later surprise Frazier by telling him that he'd had the privilege of seeing him torch the likes of Kentucky Wesleyan. Wherever Frazier went, Holzman was sure to follow. He hopped flights and rented rooms a step behind Frazier, all the way to Madison Square Garden for the National Invitation Tournament.

But it never made any sense to Frazier that right up to the 1967 draft, Holzman and the Knicks never said so much as . . . *one . . . freaking . . . word.* Maybe they didn't want to tip their hand, or preferred to remain noncommittal until they saw as much of Frazier as possible after he'd missed his junior season because he had been ruled academically ineligible.

"My sophomore year, I was so upset with my coach, Jack Hartman, I actually thought he was discriminating against me," he said. "I was already a Division II

All-American, playing great, but there were times I just couldn't get the ball. There were three white guys and two black guys starting, and it was always, 'Swing the ball, Walt. Swing the ball.' I started thinking maybe it was a black-white thing. I was unhappy. I stopped going to class. I was planning on leaving, and Hartman, he didn't even call me. If it wasn't for the athletic director, I would have been gone."

Frazier hailed from Atlanta, the eldest of nine children, seven of them sisters—an urban version of Willis Reed's lower-middle-class family. His grandparents on his mother's side had been farmhands on the very land where their own parents were enslaved. Early in Frazier's life, he spent summers with his siblings in the Georgia countryside, as comfortable around pigs and cows as he would later be at the wheel of his Rolls.

In Atlanta, his family lived in Summerhill, a neighborhood just south of downtown that was established after the Civil War as a home for freed slaves and Jewish immigrants. His father's parents lived next door, his grandfather working on the assembly line at the Atlanta Paper Company. Frazier recalls a strong male presence in his life, though his father, also Walt, was an irascible sort, drifting between running a cafeteria with his wife, Eula, and gambling on the neighborhood's "numbers." Still, the family was stable. Frazier's uncle Eddie

Lee Wynn was in the dry-cleaning business and took a special interest in the family's star athlete. "We had a house, a lot of love," he said. "I actually cried when I left for college."

Echoing Reed, Frazier said he believed there was an unintended but palpable benefit to growing up black in the South of the 1950s. "I don't care how much money you made; in the South, you were still black," he said. "And when you are openly denied something and discriminated against, it brings people together. Unlike the North, in a way, we were raised by a village. If you were doing something wrong, everybody in the neighborhood had carte blanche to make it their business. We were always taught to have a tenacious work ethic, to get an education. Because no matter what names they called you, once you had that, no one could take that away."

At the all-black Howard High School, Frazier was the catcher on the baseball team and a good enough quarterback to draw scholarship offers from historically black colleges. But why play football? he thought. Beyond college, there was no professional future for a black QB. He had neither the desire nor the speed to change positions. He saw himself as a quarterback, a leader. But the most important reason for choosing basketball was a simple realization:

more than the other sports, he enjoyed practice, even on ramshackle neighborhood courts. He was a fan, watching games on television with his father and uncle. He had a favorite player, Skull Barnett. "My idol," Frazier said.

He had never heard of Southern Illinois University before being steered there by a local college scout for a tryout that brought him, in turn, a scholarship. Carbondale, Illinois, was a largely white environment in which Frazier felt immediately overwhelmed. "I was so far behind academically, because our schools were inferior," he said. Befriended by a white teammate, Ed Zastrow, they enrolled in the same classes, studied together. Frazier's confidence began to grow. Until his frustration with Hartman boiled over and his class attendance suffered late in his sophomore year, he pulled decent grades.

But it was during his season of ineligibility that Frazier moved off campus and became more personally accountable. With the help of the team's trainer, he went on a strict workout regimen and adopted a healthier diet. He grew stronger and quicker, and when he scrimmaged with the freshmen against the varsity, he dedicated himself to defense, roaming passing lanes, stripping the guards, talking trash—all of this newfound aggression really directed at his coach.

"It got to the point where Hartman would have to say, 'Walt, sit down,'" said Dick Garrett, a talented freshman guard that season, a young man who would later learn, in a more public setting, what it was like to deal with a supermotivated Walt Frazier. "He just didn't want the varsity guys getting too discouraged."

The following year, Frazier was back in the lineup and Hartman was happy to ride him all the way to the NIT. "At that point, playing with Walt, we felt we could run with anyone," Garrett said. "We weren't all that big, but we were really athletic. We also knew we could beat a lot of the teams in the NCAA tournament, but at the time they could only take 32. So going to New York for the NIT was a big thing for us, for any Division II team."

Frazier remembered being wide-eyed on the bus ride from Kennedy Airport, and the mob scene of players from the 14 NIT teams housed in one Midtown hotel, along with one very special guest who every day that week held court in the lobby, mobbed by fans. Muhammad Ali, training nearby for his heavyweight title bout with Zora Folley, needed no introduction to a young black basketball player.

"It felt like the center of the sports world," said Clarence Smith, another college teammate of Frazier's. "We went to the Garden to see Ali train. Howard Cosell came to one of our practices." Smith, a 6'4" defensive stopper who allowed Frazier the luxury of gambling for steals, offered a convincing imitation of the famed broadcaster: "Just who are these Salukis from Southern Illinois?"

And what the hell was a Saluki in the first place? Over the course of the tournament, as no one got within nine points of them, with Al McGuire's touted Marquette team falling in the final by 15, New York discovered why the team's nickname derived from a breed of dog known for its beauty, endurance, and speed.

Most of all, the city was introduced to the ball hound named Frazier, the tourney MVP and now certain to be a first-round draft pick. He had no great reason to stay for his final year of eligibility, and two good reasons to leave: a wife and young son, living with him in a trailer home. "I just wanted to make sure I would be going to the right team for the right price," he said. "Otherwise, we did have our whole team coming back."

Detroit had the first pick and zeroed in on Providence guard Jimmy Walker. Next up was Baltimore, whose college scout, Jerry Krause, had had his eye on a black college sensation, Earl Monroe, from the time Monroe was an unknown sophomore at Winston-Salem State in North Carolina. By his senior year he was averaging 41.5 points and was such a sensation that Winston-Salem games had to be moved off campus to the downtown coliseum, where there were almost as many white faces in the crowd as black. But there were others in the Baltimore organization, including the coach, Gene Shue, who didn't think Monroe was worthy of that high a pick. They had their eye on the Saluki.

"My coach had gotten a lawyer to advise me," Frazier said. "Baltimore called. They offered me $15,000 for my rookie season. The lawyer said, 'What about the bonus?' They said, 'It's in there.' The lawyer said, 'Don't waste your draft pick—Frazier's going back to school.'" Spurned, the Bullets turned their attention back to Monroe, for whom Krause was vehemently lobbying and who had also been scouted by Holzman.

"Cool and good poise with the ball . . . shooting and range . . . should be a No. 1 this year," Holzman wrote in his book under a box score pasted onto the page. "Hits the free man good when double-teamed. Knows the game."

When I mentioned to Monroe what Holzman had written about him—proof that Holzman knew exactly what he would be trading for years later—the man they called Black Magic (or Black Jesus in college) recognized how different his pro basketball life could have been from the start.

"I guess if the Bullets hadn't drafted me, I could have wound up a lot sooner in New York," he said. And had Frazier not had the attorney's advice and accepted the Bullets' lowball offer, it could have been him having to strong-arm his way out of Baltimore to join Monroe in New York, instead of the other way around. Instead, Monroe signed with the Bullets, who paid him $20,000 a year—more than they'd offered Frazier but still the lowest salary among the top rookies.

Life is laden with serendipity, to borrow one of Frazier's pet broadcasting words. The Seattle SuperSonics, an expansion team, informed his lawyer that they were prepared to take him with the sixth pick. Clem Haskins went third to Chicago. Detroit, with another pick, chose Sonny Dove of St. John's. Until the moment when the Knicks selected Frazier with the fifth pick, they still hadn't made contact. "When the lawyer called, I was like, 'The Knicks?'" Frazier said. "I thought he was kidding."

Now the Knicks, for $100,000 over three years, had Walt Frazier. How did they reach their decision? Jimmy Wergeles, a longtime Knicks public relations man, told me it was another case of Ned Irish bigfooting his front office, as he had with Bradley. "After the NIT, Irish said, 'Take Frazier,'" Wergeles said. But there also was evidence that Holzman, at least, agreed with Irish. His scouting archive suggested he knew from the beginning that Frazier was the real deal. In fact, it read like a dead-on preview of a Hall of Fame career.

> Very few weaknesses . . . Good size, strength and weight for guard position . . . good jumper and rebounder for his position . . . Hands and ball-handling steady . . . Gets the big basket and steal . . . Good leader . . . Team goes to him in the clutch . . . Seems to have good knowledge of the game . . . Might even be tougher in the freelance game . . . Could be great defensive man in NBA.

Thanks largely to Frazier, the 1967 draft would turn out to be Donovan and Holzman's most propitious, the growth spurt the Knicks desperately needed. In the second round, they took a gangly big man, Phil Jackson, out of North Dakota. Holzman had watched Jackson stumble around in a tournament game, only to miss his 50-point explosion the next night in a consolation effort. But he liked Jackson's length and unorthodoxy, which seemed to speak well of his defensive potential.

Now the Knicks had Reed, Barnett, Frazier, Russell, and Jackson, with Bradley in their purview and prayers. From the '67 draft, they also gained the rights to a guard from Great Neck, Long Island, named Mike

Riordan, chosen in the 12th round (or, as Riordan liked to say, "the 127th pick of the first round")—a position typically reserved for selecting somebody's nephew.

No one had paid Riordan any mind at Providence College, where he partnered in the backcourt with Jimmy Walker. But there was something about Riordan's classic Irish mug and southpaw, working-class game that resonated within Holzman, reminded him a little bit of himself. His report on Riordan labeled him a sleeper, a guy you would want on your NBA bench.

Riordan at the very least would fit right in with the team's developing mix of eclectic upstarts and outsiders from schools historically black, bookishly white, or categorically remote. Only Cazzie Russell, the Michigan Wolverine, was from what could be considered a traditional college sports power. With representation from Grambling to Southern Illinois to North Dakota, the roster was shaping up as a cross-section of Americana. On Broadway, in the midst of America's most violent political and social storms, which were threatening to tear the country apart, the Old Knicks were gradually coming together.

4

THE REAL WORLD

Straight between the eyes. Young Bill Hosket, just 21 and spending his first day in New York, sat down for an introductory interview as a member of the New York Knicks, and Howard Cosell fired him a question as if by slingshot:

"Your thoughts . . . in a nutshell . . . on the black boycott . . . of the '68 Games."

Hours off a plane from Mexico City after the Summer Games ended that September, his Olympic gold medal in hand for what he believed would be a pleasant exchange of show-and-tell, Hosket felt his cheeks, already of rosy Midwestern vintage, begin to blush.

Hosket had arrived late at the ABC radio studio, rushed from his contract signing at Madison Square

Garden (a team ritual) and into a taxi by the Knicks' public relations man, Frankie Blauschild. When the two of them arrived, Cosell was irate, screaming at Blauschild for the delay and turning all of a sudden to Hosket: "Hey, kid, you got the medal? Gimme the medal."

Just like that, the interview began:

"This is Howard Cosell, speaking of sports. In my hand, a gold medal from the Summer Olympics . . . And to my right, the young man who was the recipient of that medal . . . Bill Hosket."

Then the question dropped.

What did Hosket have to say about the African American 200-meter medalists, Tommie Smith (gold) and John Carlos (bronze), raising a Black Power salute from the podium? Not much. Something quickly manufactured about how Hosket and his teammates were focused on what they had to do, nothing more or less.

When the interview concluded, Hosket stared at Cosell in total disbelief. Cosell ignored him, exulting in his ability to make another member of the jockocracy—an institution he both promoted and railed against—squirm. He looked over at Blauschild and chuckled in that macabre Cosellian way.

"Threw the farmer a hanging curve and he singled up the middle," he said.

Hosket wasn't too insulted. At least he had mustered some response. He recounted the story to me as he no doubt had to friends and associates in the years since he had returned to Ohio and gone into the insurance business—with an enduring appreciation for what he called "the fun part of being in New York." But there had been a larger lesson in Cosell's presumptuous query, a new paradigm for reporter-athlete protocol, based on the politics and social upheaval that were crashing through the once heavily fortified boundaries of sport.

"It was a tumultuous time and the first time that it seemed the outside world had invaded ballparks and arenas," said Larry Merchant, who at the time wrote a critically acclaimed sports column for the *New York Post*, a destination read during my teenage years the minute my father walked through the door before dinner, the afternoon paper rolled up in his back pants pocket. With a literate, acerbic touch and an eye for the offbeat, the column was called Fun 'n Games. But now, all of a sudden, the questions being asked and the answers given were not always fun and were about much more than games.

"It wasn't just the [Vietnam] war; it was the social upheaval, the civil rights, women's rights, who stood up and who didn't," Merchant said. "So many issues that were controversial, to the extent where a number of the athletes decided they could not avoid it. What had always been a sanctuary began to reflect the outside world."

Wilmer (Bill) Hosket Jr. was the Knicks' first-round draft pick in 1968, a 6'8" forward/center out of Ohio State, the tenth player chosen overall. In Mexico City, his Olympic teammates had included some famous names (Jo Jo White, Charlie Scott, Spencer Heywood) and others (Calvin Fowler, Don Dee, John Clawson) already retreating into obscurity. Hosket would fall somewhere in between as he embarked on a short four-year NBA career, two with a rising Knicks team.

That first visit of his to New York, though, came four years after the Civil Rights Act of 1964, after Martin Luther King Jr. had electrified the nation with his "I Have a Dream" speech in Washington, D.C., and three years after black players in the upstart American Football League's All-Star game were turned away by New Orleans hotels and businesses, leading to a boycott that forced the game to be moved elsewhere. Sixteen months had lapsed since Muhammad Ali refused to join the Army, famously explaining, "I ain't got no quarrel with them Viet Cong." The unsavory tensions of the real world had intruded resolutely upon athletics. Smith and Carlos had used the international Olympic stage to condemn the ongoing oppression of their people, Carlos unzipping his track jacket in a show of solidarity with American blue-collar workers because, he said, it wasn't just African Americans who were being held down by the rich American establishment.

The country was choosing sides, and many sportswriters were beginning to ask the players they covered, "For or against?" In the Knicks' locker room, many of the players with serious points of view were initially reticent to answer. "The players were very outspoken about their sentiments among each other but were private in public," Phil Jackson said. "We did have a few guys serving their country." The counterculture maverick in Jackson, camped somewhere within the graying boomer who in 2010 would opine that the controversial Arizona immigration policies were not the NBA's business, couldn't resist accentuating the word *serving*.

Measuring in under the 80-inch disqualification height, Cazzie Russell was one of them. For the first three years of his career, Russell was on a plane many weekends, heading back and forth to the Illinois National Guard. "I would fly to Chicago on a Friday afternoon, attend a Saturday meeting, fly back to New York for a Saturday-night game," he said. "Then back to Chicago for Sunday duty and rejoin the team for the week." He cackled at the thought of LeBron James, Nike's current major general, having to do his duty as a weekend warrior, tweeting his displeasure while his private jet was de-iced for takeoff.

Russell, an infantryman, saw live action during the summer of 1968 when he was assigned to scan and patrol Chicago rooftops for snipers during the infamous Democratic National Convention that embroiled student demonstrators, protesters, and a massive police presence fortified by the National Guard. The explosion of violence was a reflection of the tensions and frustrations in a country that was reeling from unspeakable tragedy and festering wounds: the assassinations that spring, two and a half months apart, of King and Robert F. Kennedy.

"They mobilized us because they knew there was going to be trouble," Russell said. "I saw it all—the protests, the police brutality, the craziness in the streets. It made you sad. It made you think about a lot of things that were a lot more important than basketball."

That year, 1968, New York had its own reverberating conflict. In the Brownsville section of Brooklyn—a neighborhood that was of particular interest to me, since I had lived there between the ages of five and ten before moving with my family to Staten Island in

1962—the community was given control of its schools in a decentralization test case. It responded by attempting to rid itself of white teachers. New York's teachers' union moved swiftly to defend its members and authorized a citywide strike. The strife between the black community and the union was a window into a city teeming with racial tensions. But it was merely one of many fiscal and social issues that plagued John V. Lindsay from the very first day of his mayoralty, which included a strike by the Transport Workers Union of America that shut down mass transit for twelve crippling days and a nine-day sanitation walkout in 1968 that turned the city into a mountain of reeking, burning garbage.

That same year, a young Queens attorney who would later become a political force in his own right was amazed by what he saw in his beloved native New York. "It was a crazy, crazy time, but very different from what would come later, the hangover from the seventies, the crack epidemic and HIV and on into the twenty-first century, when the problems would become much, much greater because the world has gotten so much smaller and what happens in Iran is as important as what happens in Chicago," said Mario Cuomo, the future governor of New York and father of Andrew, who in 2010 would ascend to the same Albany office that Mario had occupied from 1983 through 1994. "In the sixties, Vietnam was driving people crazy and brought all the drugs, and then the political violence and assassinations. But because we were fighting for all kinds of freedoms, it was also a time that you could shape an ideology, an identity."

When Cuomo was growing up in the South Jamaica section of Queens in the 1940s, playing baseball (seriously enough to land a minor league deal with Pittsburgh) and throwing elbows in schoolyard pickup and church league hoop games, pro basketball had no real identity to speak of. It was an inelegant game, the domain of whites and fittingly confined mostly to small, industrial cities. The Knicks might as well have been in one, too. They played many home games at the 69th Regiment Armory, where Jimmy Wergeles, the public relations man, would steer people in from outside for free. "To fill it up a little bit upstairs," he said.

But by the summer of '68, the infusion of black talent was lifting the pro game to higher athletic and cultural levels. It could be argued that the metaphorical curtain was raised on this sport—destined to soar in the American social arena—by one little-known or long- forgotten exhibition on August 16, 1968. The site was the 15,000-seat outdoor Singer Bowl on the site of the 1964 World's Fair in Flushing Meadows, Queens. Underwriting the event was the F. & M. Schaefer Brewing Company. Televising it in the New York area was WPIX (Channel 11). Tickets were scaled at $5, $3, and $2, with 350 VIP seats selling at $25.

The goal, said the game's celebrity organizer, Oscar Robertson, was to memorialize Dr. King and raise money for his Southern Christian Leadership Conference. "A quarter million dollars would be a nice round figure for us to raise," Robertson, the president of the National Basketball Players Association, was quoted as saying in the *New York Times* on the morning of the game.

At a time when pro basketball was no main attraction, only 7,500 people cheered the talents of Robertson, Wilt Chamberlain, Willis Reed, Walt Bellamy, Dave DeBusschere, and Earl Monroe. Hindsight tells us that the size of the crowd or the proceeds from the gate weren't really the point. When asked about the game, Robertson had scant memory of where it was played and who had shown up to participate, or that he had appeared the following morning in a *Times* photograph, shaking hands with the dapper Mayor Lindsay, who had to be thrilled to be attending an event that united people instead of inciting them to general mayhem.

Time has a way of blurring the details of even the most worthy endeavors, but what Robertson would never forget was the profound grief he felt that summer, the consuming need for him and his colleagues to collectively cry out. "It was a depressing time for blacks in America," he said. "If you grew up as an African American, with the poverty and despair, I always said it was almost like being a nurse in a hospital, where you see blood and suffering all the time but eventually you get used to it. But when Dr. King was killed, a man who was showing us a way out, it was almost too much to bear. It was a terrible time, but I wanted us to stand up and say something, even though you had to be careful what you said if you were black, because you could lose what you had."

The man who never once slammed a ball through the hoop in an NBA game because he believed it was an inelegant act seldom had to be prodded to belittle the diminished state of fundamentals in the modern game. To the chagrin of David Stern and other league officials, Robertson rightly linked the lack of movement and teamwork to the dunk-and-pony shows that were seemingly designed to suit the pyrotechnic NBA arena experience. In other words, Robertson had made it his life's calling to speak his piece, whether people wanted to hear it or not, on subjects related to what happened inside the lines or out.

To some, he came off as bitter: born too early to be justly appreciated or compensated for the magnificent player he was. In an age before free agency, Robertson had to take what his owners gave him, but was typically front and center when the players began to collectively fight back, beginning with a movement to procure a pension plan. Robertson and the Celtics' Tommy Heinsohn, mentored by union general counsel Larry Fleisher, were enraged when the owners didn't take them seriously. They made plans for the players to boycott the 1964 All-Star Game.

Scheduled to be televised nationally by ABC, the game represented a major marketing leap forward for the NBA. Unaccustomed to such player effrontery, the league was in a foul, combative mood. On a snowy day in Boston, the Lakers' owner, Bob Short, sent a Boston Garden security officer whom Heinsohn knew as "Chris the cop" to inform the players that they would be fired if the game was canceled. Robertson told his colleagues that the owners had to be bluffing. Burying the biggest names in their marginal business would amount to professional suicide.

"I remember we were in the locker room and some of the guys didn't want to go through with it," Robertson told me. "I said, 'If you don't, I suggest you leave.'"

If there is a moment to which the modern-day millionaire ballplayer—from Jordan to James—might trace the genesis of his staggering wealth, it would be when Elgin Baylor took his cue from the Big O and sent back the message: "Go tell Bob Short to fuck himself." The owners bent on the pension plan. Robertson then went out and demonstrated what they would be getting in return for their money, staging a basketball clinic with 26 points, 14 rebounds, and 8 assists. His MVP award might have stood for Most Valuable Proletariat. And if his All-Star leadership wasn't enough to sufficiently pry open the owners' wallets, it was Robertson, again, who risked their wrath by attaching his name to an antitrust suit against the NBA in 1970. Six contentious years later, the era of free agency dawned.

Robertson was born in a small Tennessee town but grew up in one of those more northern inner cities that lent credence to Reed's and Frazier's contention that the segregated South had its advantages. Robertson starred on an Indianapolis high school that fielded the city's first all-black squad to win state championships in Indiana, but was ordered to celebrate out of town by local leaders who were afraid that they, as Robertson said, "would go on some kind of rampage and burn the city down."

As much as any triple double (he remains the only player to average one for an entire season, 1961–62), he could still summon the ignominy and outrage of being in a restaurant in the uniform of the United States Army and being made to feel like the invisible black man. "I couldn't even get a sandwich," he said.

In the entirety of his career, Robertson made a fraction of what Jordan and later James could claim in salary and endorsements from a single season. But he was, indisputably, a man of and for the sixties, hotwired for a decade that was dedicated to challenge and change. The rewards that he carried across the years could be stored only in his mind and heart, never the bank. Nonetheless, Robertson was eager to disclose all that he'd earned.

"A lot of guys will say now they were involved in the movement, but what did you do at that time?" he said. "What did you say?"

As a matter of personal policy, the most political of all basketball players chose to say nothing, skirting inquisitions with a skilled evasiveness that occasionally struck interviewers as churlishness.

"I was extremely suspicious of being asked about the war," Bill Bradley said. Nor did he care to expound on the country's issues related to race, religion, or poverty, he added. "Why were they asking me? They were asking me because I was a well-known basketball player and therefore I was a celebrity. I would basically say, Look, I'm no different than any other 24-year-old. There are a lot of other people whose answer to that question is going to have a lot more import."

Bradley was seated across a conference room table at the Fifth Avenue offices of Allen & Company, a boutique investment firm serving media and entertainment moguls, where he worked as a managing director. Far from my working relationships with Reed, Frazier, Monroe, and others, this was the first time I had sat down with the former senator from New Jersey for a formal interview. He had departed the New York basketball scene before I arrived on the beat, though I had been around him when he returned for special events—Old Knicks jersey-retirement ceremonies and the like. For a few years, we actually lived in the same town, Montclair, New Jersey, and occasionally I would see him at the local YMCA, usually on the treadmill.

"You know, I've read your column for years," he said upon sitting down. "I would have sworn you were black." Startled, I took the mistake as a compliment, an acknowledgment that without a face to identify me by (the *Times* does not run columnist photos), he had made a judgment based on what he had read and that I had come across as an empathetic analyst of the NBA's majority African American player base.

But I wondered: Was Bradley's unwillingness as a player to share his political and social thoughts also a result of his own sensitivity to the commotion he had caused just by deciding to play in the NBA? Did he intuitively understand that to become part of a truly committed team meant that his personal ambitions beyond basketball could not become part of any public locker-room discussion?

As it was, Bradley thought he was already attracting too much undeserved attention. After two years at Oxford, in April 1967, Bradley signed a record four-year, $500,000 rookie contract, $25,000 a year more than Cazzie Russell was being paid. The Knicks called a major press conference at Leone's and bought the Oxford man of honor a new suit.

So eager were they to show off their prize that they arranged a scrimmage with some of their players and draft picks—including Walt Frazier—at the old Garden. They invited the press to watch, and that was just the beginning of the hype. By the time Bradley finished a stint with the Air Force Reserve and joined the Knicks in mid-December, it was out of control. The Garden attracted a sellout, 18,499, for his debut game, against a team, the Pistons, who would have normally drawn 10,000, tops. Fans roared at the sight of Bradley on the layup line. Photographers were shooting his every move. In the radio booth, the levelheaded Marv Albert was caught up in the frenzy, too. "I was literally calling his pregame shots," Albert said.

Two minutes after Bradley sat down on the bench between Butch Komives and Dick Van Arsdale for the start of the game, the fans were chanting his name, screaming for the coach, Dick McGuire, to put him in. McGuire didn't relent until the second quarter. Bradley played seven minutes, hitting one of his patently coiled jumpers on a fast break, the ball delivered by Cazzie Russell. The building erupted.

The general reception to Bradley was so overwhelming that it was bound to provoke the opposition. He remembered Bill Russell having the Celtics run him into bone-crunching picks in the backcourt that season, most of them set by a brick wall named Wayne Embry. When he played for the first time against the Lakers, coached by his college mentor Butch van Breda Kolff, the Lakers were forced to sit through a long-winded pregame discourse on Bradley's prowess. At the end of it, Elgin Baylor piped up from the back, "Uh, Bill, is it okay if we try to guard him?"

Bradley understood the capricious nature of both fan and reporter. He knew how long he had been away from regular and high-level competition and what he was being set up for. "I came in, I'm the Great White Hope, I've got a big contract, I'm supposed to save the team," he said. "But I'm playing guard, and after ten games it's pretty clear that I'm not cast properly. I'm failing and then the public turns, people spit at me, throw coins at me, it goes from great adulation to hostility and anger. Then I go out on Eighth Avenue one day, get hit by a car, and that was kind of a symbol."

He was only shaken up in the accident, but the Oxford man wasn't enjoying the school of hard knocks when all he had wanted to do, at least for a season or two, was break in slowly, on and off the court. "I felt that I had been dropped into a black world and therefore I had a lot to learn," he said. "I knew that I was going to learn a lot more from the black players than they were going to learn from me."

While Bradley has often said that he had "unlocked the part of me that I'd closed off" while shooting around in an Oxford gymnasium, there was more to the story of his decision to play in the NBA. In trying to settle the inner conflict, the competing callings to public service and the pro game, he sought out Mo Udall, the Arizona congressman, who had briefly played pro basketball in the old NBL. Udall, in turn, sent Bradley to see

Byron "Whizzer" White, who had shoehorned in a few years of pro football in the early NFL before going on to become a JFK-appointed Supreme Court justice.

Udall told him, "If you like playing, you ought to play. The key is what you do with your free time." What Bradley quickly discovered—beyond the social education of traveling with men whose life experiences were for the most part nothing like growing up as the only child in a Republican home in Crystal City—was that basketball was an itinerant, high-pressure life, but one also filled with an extraordinary amount of down-time along with a lengthy off-season.

Outside the arena, Bradley happily slipped the dreaded White Hope syndrome. Without fanfare, he found his way uptown to Harlem, to work with kids who were trying to manage their own escape—from the cycle of poverty and drugs—and salvage an education in Urban League street academies, which were considered early versions of charter schools. Its employees and volunteers were called street workers.

Dr. Eugene Callender, who was executive director of the Urban League's Greater New York chapter, didn't need to be told who Bradley was. Callender had been a pretty fair ballplayer himself, a 5'10" guard who was one of two black players on the Boston University team in the mid- to late forties. "Basketball was huge in

Harlem, but so was heroin," he said. "I remember the sound of the ball—*bomp, bomp, bomp*—all day and night, or whenever they weren't shooting up." There were other players who were civic and socially minded, native New Yorkers like Kareem Abdul-Jabbar. But Callender especially appreciated Bradley's involvement. "I always gave him a lot of credit," he said. "Especially in those days; it couldn't have been easy for him to come uptown."

It wasn't long before Bradley was traveling much greater distances, to more forbidding places, shaping a more global perspective. He read Kipling's "The Man Who Would Be King," a short story about two adventurers from British India who travel to a remote part of Afghanistan. Wanderlust grabbed him.

"One off-season, for two months, I was in India, Iran, Afghanistan, all over, and this was a trip that was very formative for me," he said. "I mean, here we are with Afghanistan in the center of the news for how long now? Well, I've been to the northwest provinces, went with a Pashtun guide, into villages that were 15,000 to 18,000 feet high. In one we met the village elder, and I'm sitting on his rug, shoes off, legs crossed, having tea, and what did he want to talk about? The Israeli-Palestinian issue, 40 years ago. So when people say now, 'Oh, that's not important to people in Pakistan and Afghanistan,' well, that wasn't my experience. So my point is that basketball allowed me to grow in ways that were unforeseen when I began, in terms of my personal and social experiences. If I had left Oxford, gone to law school, and never played pro ball, I would never have done that."

Traveling the country with the Knicks provided an abundance of downtime built into the itinerant madness. "Bradley never wasted a minute on the road, at the airport," Marv Albert said. "He always had a book, a newspaper, a discussion with someone he met. There was never any idle time, goofing around."

But Bradley also relished sharing a locker room with Reed and Frazier, a room on the road with Dave DeBusschere, and the street-honed wit and wisdom of Dick Barnett. What other profession would have provided such diversity of people and places?

None would have provided weeks off to explore, maybe even get a feel for what it was like to work inside the political arena of Washington, D.C. "One off-season, I worked in a congressman's office," Bradley said. "He had graduated from Princeton, and I had handled the tenth reunion of his class when I was a sophomore. I took care of all the people coming back. I got to know him, and then when I was at Oxford he asked me to write a paper on NATO for him in, like, 48 hours. I couldn't do that, but then he asked me to come out to a place close to Oxford, and I did and he introduced me to Mo Udall. And then he asked me to come down and work for him in the summer of '69."

That congressman was Donald Rumsfeld. Bradley recalled:

So I was there for about three weeks, and then Nixon appointed him the head of the Office of Economic Opportunity, the OEO, which is the poverty program. Well, Sargent Shriver and the whole Kennedy thing was a big deal to me, so when he said, "Do you want to come with me on the poverty program?" I said, "I only have about another seven weeks and I've got to go to training camp. But sure."

So I remember we walked into the seventh floor of the office building, his office—big office—and there was a rectangular table and a big stack of papers on it. And those were résumés. And Rumsfeld says to me, "Would you look through those résumés and make a recommendation as to who you think might be good on staff? And if you want to interview them, interview them." And so I interviewed several people.

Let the record show that Dick Cheney—whose political career officially began in 1969 as an intern for Congressman William A. Steiger—began his climb through the Republican ranks as one of Rumsfeld's OEO staff members in 1969. "You could say," Bradley sighed, "that I'm responsible for some of what's happened."

The moral from the left would have to be that the political world's learning curve was as challenging for Bradley as the NBA's. But as difficult as his rookie season was, 1967–68 wasn't a total write-off, collectively speaking. It ended in a new Madison Square Garden, with a new coach, Red Holzman, and the Knicks finishing strong with 43 wins, over .500 for the first time in nine years. After losing a six-game series to the Philadelphia 76ers in the first round of the playoffs, the team nevertheless brimmed with optimism.

A sobering context would come three days after the series ended, when Dr. King was assassinated on the second-floor balcony of the Lorraine Motel in Memphis, where he had gone in support of striking black public-works employees. Riots broke out in several cities, including the nation's capital. As spring turned to summer, and the presidential campaign of Bobby Kennedy was also struck down by an assassin's bullet in a Los Angeles hotel kitchen, the temperature and tolerance in the country would rise to near boiling point.

There were plenty of places to howl in pain or protest, or just quietly try to help with the healing. Most days, Bradley went to Harlem to volunteer in the street academy. But as much as he felt committed to a country in chaos, so, too, was there a fire burning within him to be a better basketball player. It was the part of him he could no longer deny. Disappointed by his rookie year, he knew he needed to remake and relaunch himself. On many summer afternoons, he got in the car and headed down to Philadelphia and to another prestigious educational institution: the reputable basketball hot spot known as the Baker League.

PART II

When the
Garden
Was Eden

When the
Garden
Was Eden

5

SCOUT'S HONOR

D ick McGuire made it to Christmas. On December 27, 1967, after a year in which the Knicks struggled and stratified under lax leadership, Red Holzman was abruptly named the team's head coach. He had, supposedly, been threatened with losing his job as a scout if he didn't accept the offer. According to legend, and the *New York Post*'s Leonard Lewin (a close friend of Holzman's and co-author of his autobiographical books), Holzman had wanted nothing to do with coaching ever since he'd been fired in St. Louis. He was said to be a man without grand ambitions, one who coveted attention and responsibility for wins and losses the way other men desired a root canal.

"He wanted to be left alone, and he wanted to leave you alone," said Larry Pearlstein, another Holzman pal.

Pearlstein made a living in the business world but loved the game and had cultivated enough friendships in and around the sport that he answered to a nickname befitting an entrenched insider: the Scout. He met Holzman in the early fifties on a handball court in Long Beach, Long Island, where Holzman was a regular. "He was with the Rochester Royals at the time, but I had been a big fan of his when he was at CCNY," Pearlstein said. "We all considered him a tough guy, an overachiever. But he was almost embarrassed when I told him that. He was friendly, but he wanted to talk about handball and other things, not basketball. That was Red. He was just very uncomfortable when you praised him. He had no ego, none whatsoever."

Rule number one for Holzman was to never glorify himself, especially at the expense of a colleague. "Red would come into your building, kick your ass, and tell the local media what a great job you were doing," Jack Ramsay, who coached against Holzman in Philadelphia and later Portland, said. "He was always aware of the position of the other guy. He thought the scoreboard was enough; he didn't have to gloat."

That said, ego and pride are qualities that share an unguarded border, and Holzman, in his own quiet way, was as stubbornly proud as he was pragmatic. Pearlstein saw that side of him firsthand when the coach was inducted into the New York City Basketball Hall of Fame.

According to Pearlstein, Holzman—who had several years earlier, in 1986, been inducted into the Naismith Hall of Fame in Springfield, also as a coach—bristled that the New York voters had overlooked him as a player. Hadn't he been a college star—a 1942 All-American at City College—in his own right? Didn't he have an NBA championship ring, something that McGuire—inducted as a player into the Naismith Hall—did not? Characteristically, Holzman would only reveal such feelings to those in his inner circle, and even then with a temperament to suggest that the oversight was no big deal, even if his friends suspected otherwise. That was Holzman: never revealing too much, never wanting his emotions to betray his intentions or ambitions. It was a coaching strategy as much as a personality tic.

In the case of McGuire, Holzman realized that the Irishman was beloved in the New York basketball community. The pride of Rockaway's 108th Street courts and St. John's University, McGuire had landed in the Knicks' backcourt in 1949, a born playmaker (or point guard, though there was no such designation yet). Before Bill Russell came along to make a champion of everyone in green, Boston had Bob Cousy—and the Knicks had McGuire, their own backcourt wizard. McGuire was such a passing genius that, deep into middle age, he could, with one adept look away, still bloody the ample nose (mine) of a sportswriter who dared put his head down in a pickup game when he should have honored the man's peripheral vision.

During my interview with Mario Cuomo, the former governor of New York went off on an impassioned tangent raving about McGuire, his Queens homey and favorite player of all time—and a onetime opponent in a church league game. Larry Pearlstein felt the same way about McGuire, as did scores of others, no doubt. But while no one ever had a bad word to say about McGuire, neither would anyone take to the street to defend him as a coach, least of all him.

McGuire was the first to admit that his younger brother Al—the college coach and NCAA television analyst, who died in 2001—was the family orator. Known around the game as Mumbles, Dick was a man of many words—only, like an AM radio station on the fritz, you couldn't understand any of them. He was no more a disciplinarian than he was a communicator. Improved personnel notwithstanding, his two-plus seasons coaching the Knicks produced a record of 75–102 and a me-first environment that shocked the rookie Walt Frazier.

"There was no camaraderie, a lot of selfishness, one or two guys getting back on defense," Frazier said. "I remember at first thinking that I wished I had gone someplace else, because I had never played on a team where guys wouldn't pass each other the ball."

He was talking, primarily, about Cazzie Russell and Butch Komives, whose dislike for each other was widely known. But there were other distractions and dysfunctions. Bellamy and Reed, who had made the move to forward, couldn't get out of each other's way in the lane. Phil Jackson, a rookie when McGuire coached the first 37 games of the 1967–68 season before switching roles with Holzman, recalled ball boys being sent out to the Garden lobby at halftime for hot dog runs to Nedick's. Others slumped in front of their lockers and fired up cigarettes. For road games—to Boston or Philadelphia, say—the players often traveled on their own. Even as a rookie, practically a deer from North Dakota caught in the bright lights of the big city, Jackson realized that any coach without leverage over his players could not last very long.

"The players were making tens of thousands, and you're paying the coach a few thousand dollars," Jackson said, looking back from the perch of 11 championships, the most by any coach in NBA history. The pre-Holzman days, he recalled, were chaotic and fraught with the vagaries of how money paid translates to respect earned, and McGuire didn't help himself by avoiding confrontation. He would even apologize to the forward Dick Van Arsdale when he would sub him out of a game, because Van Arsdale was the one player he knew wouldn't bitch.

("I should never have been coaching, because I didn't want to yell at anybody," he told me in his Long Island home during the summer of 2009, with his wife, Teri, nodding nearby.)

When Holzman took over, "he changed all that loose stuff," Jackson said. "We traveled as a team whenever possible." He told Frazier he'd be getting more time, because he wanted "guys playing both ends," but that he should also sit next to him whenever he was on the bench, absorb all that he could. He put an end to Bellamy's sweetheart arrangement of having his own room on the road, telling the veteran he wasn't earning the privilege. He implemented a fine system for rule breakers, nailing Bill Bradley for being a few minutes late to one of Holzman's first meetings.

But while establishing order, Holzman operated without autocratic zeal and with a wry sense of humor. When Russell broke the travel edict to test-drive a new Cadillac to Philadelphia, Holzman fined him $100 but wondered how much he'd spent on tolls. Russell figured about $8. Holzman said, "Okay, I'll only charge you $92." Russell went away thinking he'd made out.

"That was Red: always thinking of ways he could turn a situation, good or bad, into something better," said Jackson, who was watching closely, storing away little trade secrets he would draw on years later in Chicago and Los Angeles.

Holzman also had an indisputable and immediate impact between the lines, stylistically and statistically. "When he took over, we had like 25 practices—it felt like training camp except it was midseason—and it was always defense, defense, defense," Bradley said. Holzman believed that effective defense—much like great offense—was a collective act, five players coordinating as one. His emphasis was on extending it full-court, forcing dribblers into vulnerable positions, rotating to areas where they would most likely be forced to pass. Stressed most of all was the concept of covering for one another, of becoming a team whose proverbial calling card would one day read, simply: Defense.

The Knicks went from 15–22 to start the season under McGuire to 28–17 under Holzman, and steamed into the 1968 playoffs against Philadelphia. It's an established truism of sportswriting that coaches, in all sports and on every level, get too much credit and too much blame upon season's end, but what other explanation could there be for the Knicks' turnaround except that the right man had come at the right time? "Red was obviously the guy to coach us, because he was the one who scouted us, who knew us better than anyone," Reed said. "He knew that. People always said he had to be ordered to do it, but I think, deep down, he knew we had a chance to be really good."

In other words, he wanted the job. What man with Holzman's competitive instincts (to go along with the relationships he had with the players) wouldn't have? Of course, to admit that he desired another crack at coaching—and in his native New York—might have left the impression that he had undermined McGuire, a good man and a trusted friend. Holzman would have none of that. Hence, my theory: that he was all too willing to propagate the notion of his being forced to give up his comfy—and low-paying—scouting gig to assume the reins. Better for everyone's sake to have people believe he was just taking orders from Irish.

He was wily in other ways, too. On his office door at the Knicks' administrative digs, Red had scratched out measurement markers for various heights—6'2", 6'5", and so on. Wary of players who lied about their height, Holzman instructed his secretary, Gwynne Bloomfield, to usher incoming prospects by the door. This way, when Holzman got up to greet him, his head would align with the corresponding marker. The player never knew he was literally being sized up.

But Holzman never took his due credit. He would forever deny having anything to do with the immediate turnaround. That was a blessing bestowed by his players—at that point two in particular: Reed, who may still be the greatest second-round draft pick ever, albeit in a league with fewer teams (and thus shorter rounds), and Dick Barnett, a man who arrived from the Lakers in exchange for Bob Boozer and who fit in so well, it was almost as if he had been born to be an Old Knick.

Barnett was born and raised in Gary, Indiana, the youngest of three children in a close-knit family that lived in a poor neighborhood in the shadow of smoke-belching factories. His father at one time worked in a nearby steel mill but quit when he was ordered to do menial jobs that were below his skill level, and wound up being employed by the city's parks department.

Barnett was a reticent child, never looking for acceptance in gangs or places where trouble lurked. His refuge from the darker aspects of his adolescence was always the basketball court at the local Roosevelt High School. He played half-court games but spent more hours alone, sometimes well into the night, crafting an unconventional southpaw jump shot—the ball almost shot-putted from his left shoulder, legs bent behind him, practically parallel to the ground, as he elevated for his release.

Asked about his strange form, which defined the unorthodoxy of the man and his game, the original Tricky Dick said: "It was the unintended consequences of just being on the court, without rhyme or reason, something that came naturally and worked for me. It was in the playground before I even got to high school that I learned how to execute that shot without really knowing what I was doing."

Coaches shook their heads at Barnett's shot, tried to get him to change, but ultimately couldn't argue with the results: he became the best player in the city of Gary. As a high school senior, his school, Roosevelt, lost the Indiana state championship game to Oscar Robertson and Crispus Attucks High of Indianapolis. Barnett went off to college in Nashville, eager to play for John McLendon, if not as enthusiastic about going to class. McLendon took a look at his freshman grades and wanted to send him home, but school officials persuaded the coach to give Barnett time. A scholar he was not, but he did enough to "get by."

In Nashville, during his college years in the late fifties, he experienced lawful segregation for the first time. He unknowingly sat in the front of a bus and was ordered to move, in the stark language of the times. He tried to eat at a lunch counter in a whites-only restaurant and was spat on by the attendant. But if Nashville was jarring and occasionally humiliating, Syracuse, his first NBA stop, was downright depressing. Drafted in the first round in 1959, Barnett was paid $7,500 to play behind two established guards, Hal Greer and Larry Costello. After two years, he hated the snowy upstate New York outpost so much that he jumped at the opportunity to join McLendon, who had by then become the first black pro coach, with the ABL's Cleveland Pipers.

The Pipers were owned by the son of a rich shipbuilder, a guy named George Steinbrenner, who was every bit the madman you might imagine the young Boss would be. He threw tantrums. He drove McLendon crazy, then out of town. Worse, his checks bounced like basketballs pumped with helium. But before the ABL folded, Barnett and the Pipers won a championship under McLendon's successor, Bill Sharman.

After the Lakers purchased his NBA rights from Syracuse, Barnett went to Los Angeles, where he became the sixth man and third-leading scorer behind Jerry West and Elgin Baylor. Barnett's new mates appreciated his game and loved his idiosyncratic ways. He had a unique personality that brought people together. On the road, he appointed himself commissioner of late-night wagering. He summoned teammates with a typically colorful telephone greeting: "Darlin', they are playing the national anthem." The poker game was about to begin.

There was little that Barnett said or did that sounded or looked conventional. He brought a school yard swagger to the court, a knack for dropping back on defense after releasing his jumper and advising teammates out loud that there was no point in them waiting around for an offensive rebound, either.

The Lakers' famed announcer Chick Hearn soon incorporated the showmanship into his game call: "Fall back, baby," he would cry after a Barnett release. In his first season in L.A., Barnett made good on enough of his mini-prophecies to keep the coach off his back. In the twenty-first-century NBA, Barnett's antics would no doubt have set off a national debate, countless shouting matches on ESPN about etiquette and sportsmanship. Back then, Barnett figured if the game's most successful coach (Red Auerbach) could light up victory cigars, why couldn't he have a little fun? As Cal Ramsey said, it was the sixties, a decade devoted to shaking things up. Reporters and fans got a kick out of the man with the sleepy eyes and the gait so deliberate that Phil Jackson would later, in New York, give him yet another nickname: Molasses.

That the Lakers wound up trading him remains one of the more painful transactions in that franchise's history. West said the team was worried about Baylor's knees and the number of minutes he was playing, hence the need for Boozer. But during his three seasons in L.A., Barnett had helped the Lakers reach two Finals (they lost both) and developed all the trappings of a star—with the important exceptions of promoting and paying him as one.

West took issue with Barnett's assertions—made after he was gone—that there was no room on the team for another luminary, and especially a second black one, in addition to Baylor. He said Barnett was deployed as the sixth man because the Lakers needed a playmaker to start alongside him. "I loved Barnett," West told me. "Everybody did. I still don't know why we traded him. That day was one of the worst of my career." Not so much for Barnett: he was thrilled to go to the world's media capital. In the pre–Walt Frazier days, he was confident of becoming the Knicks' featured guard.

Barnett fit in well with the Knicks. Reed admired him for his fearlessness on the floor, the delight he took in challenging Wilt Chamberlain, craftily floating a runner or hook shot over the giant's high-altitude reach—and talking all the while: "Get this, you big motherfucker."

During the 2007 NBA All-Star weekend in Las Vegas, Willis Reed took part in a lunchtime panel at the ESPN Zone, with Bill Walton, Greg Anthony, and Spud

Webb. Most of the discussion was overwhelmed by a lively debate between Walton and Anthony about the state of the game. Both of them happened to be players whose careers had progressed from professional gaming to professional TV gabbing—Reed and Webb struggled to get a word in edgewise.

Eventually the floor was opened to the fans, and the program ended with the former players each shooting a trivia question at the crowd, with ESPN-brand prizes on hand for the winners. When Reed's turn came, he asked: "Who was the starting backcourt for the 1969–70 champion Knicks?" Several hands shot up. Reed called on one.

"Frazier and Monroe," the man said, proudly.

"Sorry," Reed said, disappointed.

Immediately, the other hands were lowered, all apparently having been prepared to give the same answer. Sitting at a table in the back, where Reed and the others couldn't see me, I gave my then–17-year-old son Alex a nudge.

"Frazier and Barnett," I whispered.

"Young man all the way in the back," Reed said when Alex raised a hand.

"Frazier and Barnett," he shouted with glee.

Reed smiled, looking relieved. Someone, thankfully, had remembered Dick Barnett.

Considering the totality of his career, a strong case could be made that Barnett—one of the most overlooked and underappreciated players in the history of the sport—should be enshrined in the Naismith Hall of Fame. After all, the other four starters from the 1970 champions—Reed, Frazier, DeBusschere, and Bradley—are found in Springfield. Why not the fifth? Barnett played in five championship series, winning two rings in New York. Playing under John McLendon at Tennessee A&I, he was the star of three consecutive NAIA champions—the first time that many were claimed in succession by any college team.

Barnett was vital to the success of a system predicated on the delicate melding of unique personalities. He was its cold-blooded gunslinger, lock-down backcourt defender, and most offbeat locker-room character.

When I asked him about the Hall, the subject evoked Barnett's typical cocksure charm and a suspicious, almost dismissive attitude about the establishment that kept the black athletes of his time way down, if not out. "Based on my ability, I know I should be in the Hall," he told me. "Even if I didn't play in the pros, we were the first team to win three national titles before UCLA. That whole team should be in the Hall. But now you're getting into a whole political construct. It's who you know. And you can say whatever you want, but what are you going to do?"

While those three NAIA titles may not sound like much based on college basketball's contemporary classifications, those were the days before the major southern universities were desegregated. Many NAIA teams reaped the benefits of the black talent that would eventually move on to big-conference powerhouses. Knowing how strong much of his competition in college really was, Barnett never doubted that he was as talented as any nationally celebrated All-American of the late fifties.

"In my mind, it came down to answering the question, Am I as good as that player from Kentucky or UCLA, who benefited from the promulgation of the media?" he said. "Do I accept the conspiracies and stereotypes that were designed to continue a corrupt system that was going to crumble and bring about major change in American society? In the pros, it was one-on-one—can you play at this level or not? But on my college team, we always believed that we could play with anyone in the country. We had no reason not to think that, unless we wanted to accept the greater deceit that we were also lesser human beings."

Barnett's teammates had to lobby the Knicks organization before they would retire his No. 12 jersey,

20 years after the first title was won. On the night of March 10, 1990, Barnett at least had good company. A banner was also raised for Holzman, with the number of his Knicks regular-season victories, 613 (the same as the number of commandments in the Torah).

Other than his backcourt mate, Walt Frazier, who called Barnett "the most exciting of us to watch when he got hot," nobody appreciated him more than Holzman, who had experienced the live phenomenon of Skull Barnett during his college career as a scout. "Red loved Barnett," Marv Albert said. "He always thought he was one of the most underrated players in the game."

"Barnett was a pain in the ass," Larry Pearlstein said. "But Red considered him a great player. He used to tell me that all the time."

When Holzman returned to the Knicks for a second coaching run, replacing Reed on the bench in 1978, he would reflect on his old guys, often with his assistant coach Butch Beard. "We'd stay up late on the road, a couple of drinks, and I'd get inside his head as a coach," Beard said. "He wanted to talk about Barnett all the time. See, by the time Red took over as coach, Barnett didn't care about getting his name in the paper, as long as his teammates and his coach knew what he was about."

And yes, Barnett was flaky, occasionally a pain in the aforementioned *tuchus*, with his streetwise needling and his incessant need for "action." During his Knicks days, he was well known for his gambling and for bumming dollar bills wherever he could get them. "Dick owed us and probably a lot of other people money," Reed said. "But I always figured, What the hell—he was winning us a lot of money on the court."

No one knew what value Barnett brought to the team more than Holzman. Years later, in reflective moments invariably fueled by his beloved scotch, Holzman would get misty-eyed while expressing his fondness for the old lefty. He would contend that Barnett was as much a student of the game as any Old Knick.

But even with the memory of Holzman's sly appreciative grin, it occurs to me now that this might well have been a tacit admission that Barnett, also a child of modest urban roots, somehow reminded Holzman of himself. He was feisty and uncompromising and in no particular hurry to say or do anything for the sake of promoting himself. Known for his outrageous commentary among teammates, Barnett dialed it down considerably as soon as reporters entered the room.

At bottom, he was a team-first insider, a coach's kind of guy. Following the second championship in 1973, Holzman made Barnett his first-ever bench assistant.

Barnett took the job to stay in the game and to keep some money coming in while he pursued his advanced degrees. He wasn't much interested in athletic achievement anymore. Flamboyant as he was on the floor, he never much cared for the limelight.

In 1978, Barnett was cited by the New York State Attorney General's office for "engaging in fraudulent business practices" related to monies invested in a magazine venture he had fronted. A report in the *New York Times* said that the DA's office was unable to locate Barnett to serve a restraining order. Friends told the DA they were accustomed to going months without seeing him.

Thirty-one years later he was still mysteriously elusive. Former teammates would cackle when I mentioned that even Zelda Spoelstra, the NBA's senior director of alumni relations, did not have a clue about how to contact Barnett. "You know, Dick's probably staying a couple of steps ahead of the law," Reed said jokingly. Such was the way most of Barnett's former teammates and friends spoke of him: as the most endearing rascal they'd ever shared a locker room with—but also a consummate professional. Phil Jackson called him an "all-time teammate, great storyteller, a hustler who never drank or smoked and was always looking for an angle."

After some old-fashioned telephone sleuthing, Cal Ramsey eventually produced a cell phone number for his onetime Syracuse Nationals roommate and Harlem

running partner. Ramsey, who'd wound up broadcasting Knicks games by 1972, called Barnett on my behalf,
and that initiated a series of conversations, always with
me leaving a message and Barnett phoning me back
minutes later.

"Barnett," he would say when I answered.

"Dr. Barnett," I made sure to address him.

This was no colorful sobriquet bestowed by sportswriters, no phony honorific. Cal Ramsey, for one, said
the metamorphosis from Skull Barnett to Dr. Barnett
had to be seen to be believed. "When I first got to
know Dick up in Syracuse, everything was 'motherfucker this, motherfucker that,' but that all changed in
New York," he said. "Dick was still a character, but at
some point he had this amazing transformation, like a
light went on in his head and he thought, 'I can be a lot
more than I am.'"

In New York, Eddie Donovan had told Barnett
that he would upgrade his paltry contract of "around
$20,000" if his performance merited a raise. Donovan
eventually made good on the promise, but Barnett was
already 29. He rightly suspected he would never make
serious money, or even what he really deserved by that
era's scale, which was notorious for paying black players less than whites of comparable ability. As the years
passed and the Knicks assembled their championship

cast, Barnett would come to a personal crossroads: he could be bitter about the money or he could play the hand he had been dealt.

"In New York, my vision was being altered not only as a player but as a person in a much broader sense," he said. "Being part of that team definitely had a major impact. There were extensive communications with Bradley, with Jackson and others, with this ongoing cultural transformation, probably the most tumultuous American decade since the Civil War. For me, it was a process of self-discovery, as an adult who was having considerable thoughts about what it all meant, where this was all going, the transition that would have to take place when I left the game. I really began to think in terms of moving forward."

Barnett sought out the advice of socially minded athletes he admired: Bill Russell, Jim Brown, and others. He forged a relationship with Eugene Callender, the Urban League leader who by then had gone to work for the Lindsay administration. He began browsing brochures for graduate school programs. By the early seventies he was ready to take the plunge, settling on an urban affairs program at New York University. He went to class with men and women a dozen years younger, most of them doing double takes when Dick Barnett, graduate student, walked into the room. He became immersed in the work, packing his texts when the Knicks hit the road. He earned his master's while playing, and after retiring from the game he went on to a doctorate program in urban and international affairs at Fordham.

In 1974, with input from Bradley and Jackson, Barnett launched a group called the Athletes for a Better Urban Society, to develop community-minded pros. He took it upon himself to set up meetings with New York's other professional sports teams to pitch his ideas for a greater social commitment. Much later, done with basketball, he would teach sports management at St. John's University. With the help of the activist Dr. Harry Edwards, he moved on to a similar adjunct post at the University of San Francisco. The man who had regularly dispensed profane pearls of wisdom during his playing days had become downright professorial.

He had long ceased measuring life by the number of points scored or dollars earned. He had little interest in rehashing or reliving the glory days, or distinguishing one clutch jumper from another game-winning drive. He was content to just say he had been there, done that. Rising from the ghetto, and that Nashville lunch counter, Barnett was a proud black man with championship rings and academic degrees. Nobody could diminish or take them away.

When I pointedly asked whether he ever felt overlooked as a basketball player and, more specifically, as an Old Knick, Barnett, barely missing a beat, startled me by responding in verse. It was from one of the many poems he had taken to writing over the previous decade, scribbling them during idle moments on a plane, on a porch, on a lake. He hoped to publish them, perhaps under the same umbrella—Fall Back Baby Productions Inc.—from which he had self-published his book *The Athlete Negro* in 2007:

After the cheering has ended
And the accolades begin descending,
What now, my brother?

Tell me, what happens to the hangers-on?
Did they leave you for another?
What now, my brother?

When the media and fans turn to others,
For their dose of entertainment,
When no one notices what happens to you,
And life turns real,
What now, my brother?

6

FROM MOTOWN TO MIDTOWN

D avid Albert DeBusschere was built like a Chrysler 300C. A rugged 6'6", 250-pound forward cast in the image of his blue-collar family, he starred in basketball and baseball at Austin Catholic Preparatory High School and the University of Detroit, commuting from home and working weekends in the family business. His father, Peter Marcel, had delivered beer during the Depression and later bought his own distributorship and a bar, the Lycaste, which sat on Jefferson Avenue in the shadow of a Chrysler plant's smokestacks.

DeBusschere signed a pitching contract with the Chicago White Sox in 1962, the same year he was drafted by the Pistons with a territorial pick. He pitched in 24 games in 1963, started 10, and went 3–4 with an excellent 3.09 earned run average. The next year he was sent down to the minors once hitters figured out he couldn't get them out with a curve ball, and after two more seasons he quit altogether, in favor of basketball. The Pistons kept him close to home, near his family, and he had come to prefer the physicality of the court to the solitude of the pitcher's mound.

"To be honest, it made life a lot easier for Dave to play one sport," his wife, Geri, said. "For the couple of years he did both, he would finish a basketball season totally exhausted because of how hard he played. He would have no time to relax, just pick up and get back to baseball. It was a crazy life. He told me that it just came down to picking the sport he believed he was better at and the one that he just enjoyed more because it was more of a team game. Pitching felt like an individual game for him."

By choosing basketball, he committed himself to a lousy team, but he was a big crowd favorite in Detroit, where the notion of the young DeBusschere as Old Reliable, as the ultimate guy's guy. "There was always something about Dave—the sort of easygoing nature—that made him appealing to men on a social basis," said John Andariese, the longtime Knicks announcer who also worked with DeBusschere in the communications business. "Everybody wanted to be his friend, have a drink with him."

The attraction, many believed, was less about celebrity than it was about DeBusschere's equanimity. "He always believed that if he hadn't played basketball, he would have been just another guy, walking down the street, going to work," his son, Peter, said. "He didn't think of himself as this special person and never really got the fuss people made over athletes. He never gloated about his accomplishments."

In 1965, after losing nine of their first eleven games, the Pistons fired Charles Wolf as their head coach and turned to their homegrown 24-year-old star.

"Dave would tell you he may have been one of the worst coaches of all time," said Bill Goldman, the Oscar-winning screenwriter who became a close friend of DeBusschere's during his Knick years. "He used to tell me all the time he had no control of the team, had one or two guys with guns in the locker room."

DeBusschere lasted three forgettable seasons in the dual role, wondering how to motivate men mostly older than him, never really understanding why he had been chosen in the first place. "He always thought the perception of him that people had was that he was older or more accomplished than he really was," Peter said. "When they wanted him to be coach, his attitude was, 'Why me?'"

As a player, DeBusschere was averaging a double double—points and rebounds—but as a coach he'd taken a .400 team and made it worse. Well into his third season, with an overall record of 79–143, DeBusschere gave up the coaching reins. In New York, GM Eddie Donovan, who always liked DeBusschere and had been monitoring his situation from a distance, wondered if the Pistons might be thinking of completely rebuilding their roster.

Born and raised in Elizabeth, New Jersey, Donovan had been a college coach at St. Bonaventure in upstate New York from 1953 to 1961. From there he made the jump to the pros as the Knicks' head coach, where he lasted for three-plus seasons that produced a sickly winning percentage of .302. In a demonstration that Ned Irish's decision making could occasionally defy logic, Donovan was rewarded with what appeared to be a promotion, moving up to the general manager's office while Harry Gallatin and, soon after, Dick McGuire took over on the bench.

After the Knicks' run to the playoffs under Holzman in 1968, Donovan began the following season with elevated expectations for his team. But as he stood in Lost Battalion Hall one day in November—the Knicks' practice site on Queens Boulevard in Rego Park—he shouted at the top of his lungs that the Knicks were "a fucking embarrassment." Supposed contenders in the Eastern Division, they had stumbled out of the gate, dropping home games to the Bulls and Lakers in mid-October and continuing their lackluster play right into that month. They were limping along at 5–11 when Donovan burst into Holzman's practice.

Lost Battalion Hall was a brick-faced building named for the 77th Division of the U.S. Army, which had fought the Battle of the Argonne Forest in World War I. The court had wooden backboards and a dull floor full of dead spots that could stop a ball just where it bounced. The players wore their practice gear under their coats when they arrived. "Guys would come in and just throw their stuff on the floor in the corner," said Mike Riordan, a rookie that season who was getting little time off Holzman's bench. "I never showered there. For the few guys who did, it was a race to get there, because there was only enough hot water for one or two guys."

Riordan chuckled at the memory of the dump, especially compared with the state-of-the-art facilities of the modern NBA. "On a scale of one to ten, that place might have gotten a one," he said.

Riordan had been drafted the previous year but was cut by McGuire and spent the season toiling in the Eastern League at Allentown. He'd made the team on his second try—not all that surprising, since it was Holzman who recommended drafting him— after staying connected to the team with a summer job barnstorming Catskills resorts and sleepaway camps with the Knicks. On those trips upstate—where he joined his idol Willis Reed, Butch Komives, and sometimes even Walt Frazier—Riordan would scrimmage overmatched kitchen staffers and pimple-faced camp counselors.

Holzman was convinced that Riordan, from a blue-collar Long Island family, was tough enough to play in the NBA. At the very least, he could be a dogged practice player, and a bench specialist who might simply check into a game for the purpose of fouling an opponent. Riordan embraced the cameo role; he was thrilled just to be at the Garden, where he had played in several high school games. He wasn't too proud to give a foul. "I would have jumped in the East River if Red had asked me to," he said.

But to Donovan's (and no doubt Holzman's) dismay, there were still players on the team not quite as committed or combative as Riordan who had personal agendas that both Donovan and Holzman believed were getting in the way of the team. The inability, for example, of Butch Komives and Cazzie Russell to get along on the court. Meanwhile, the big man known as Bells, Walter Bellamy, wasn't making Holzman swoon with his defensive effort in the newly installed team approach. So Donovan's tirade was clearly targeted, and the longer he went on, the redder his ruddy Irish mug got. "His speech was like something from Hollywood," Riordan said. "There was spittle coming out of his mouth."

When he finished, Donovan asked: "Any questions?"

Bellamy raised a hand.

Donovan glared at him.

"Yeah?" he snorted.

"What are we gonna do about the damn hot water in the shower?"

That's when Donovan really let loose, dropping F-bombs all over the place. A little more than a month later, Bellamy and Komives were gone from Lost Battalion Hall and Madison Square Garden. Less than a week before Christmas, they were traded to Detroit for the player who would complete the championship puzzle in New York. David DeBusschere became a Knick.

"I've never seen Red so happy as the day they made that trade," said Larry Pearlstein, Holzman's old friend from the Long Beach handball courts. "He used to say, 'Nobody realizes how good that DeBusschere is.'

They'd been trying to get him for a while. I remember Red saying, 'We finally did it; I'm going home to get drunk.'"

The least Holzman could do was raise a glass to the Pistons' GM, Ed Coil, and his coach, Paul Seymour, for sending DeBusschere to New York. Or go to the nearest synagogue and thank the Lord for a deal that was simply divine. For if DeBusschere's losing coin toss in the flip for Cazzie Russell wasn't enough of an omen in that it provided the Knicks a building block, consider what he was doing at the precise moment the telephone rang with news of the deal from Coil. As DeBusschere wrote in *The Open Man*, his book-form diary of the 1969–70 season:

"I was in my living room, hanging a painting, a gift from one of my fans. The painting showed me, in my Detroit uniform, driving toward the basket, and it showed me being guarded by a New York Knick wearing the number 8, their center, Walt Bellamy." The painting would always remind DeBusschere of the thrilling turn his life took at the mature basketball age of 28.

Quietly, DeBusschere had been hoping for a trade. He was tired of playing in a chaotic environment, of losing year in and year out, with a hapless cast of characters he was asked to coach (and play among, simultaneously). The chance to go to a developing, defensive-oriented team like the Knicks, in a basketball city like New York, represented a career rebirth. To make it sweeter, his wife, Geri, had grown up on Long Island—a cheerleader at Garden City High School, and a Knicks fan—and always hoped they might find a way back east.

They'd met when she was working in the sales department at American Airlines and DeBusschere came in for a promotional event. "He came over to me and started talking—about basketball, where I was from, just small talk," Geri DeBusschere told me. "He told me how much he always loved going to New York to play, because the fans really knew the game. I just think it was meant to be, but you know what? Happy as I was for him, I cried like a baby when the trade was made. I'd made a lot of friends in Detroit. It wasn't easy to leave. It should have been harder for Dave—he'd spent his whole life there. He was a part of that city."

Don May, a Knicks rookie swingman when DeBusschere joined the team, said he wished he were "half the man Dave was. I adored him. He was what I always wanted to be—a good Catholic boy from the Midwest, with that can-do mentality and that winning smile."

Ditto Bill Hosket. "When he joined the team, it was like I got another coach," Hosket said. "Red was coaching the team, and Dave was coaching me. He'd prep me for everything, especially defense, because he didn't want a guy like Chet Walker scoring a quick ten on me after he'd held him to two or four. All I can tell you is Dave DeBusschere was born a man. From the minute he joined us, it was if he'd been there all along."

As it turned out, the Knicks' first game after the trade was in Detroit. DeBusschere's family and former teammates witnessed for themselves his strange new uniform, blue and orange with NEW YORK across his chest. Cobo Hall was practically bursting at its decrepit seams. DeBusschere disappointed no one, except the people who had sent him to the Knicks. He dropped 21 points on his former team, grabbed 15 rebounds. It seemed as if he had been with the Knicks for months. The local fans gave him a standing ovation when Holzman removed him with the Knicks winning in a rout. Captain Reed gave him a hug.

DeBusschere told his wife that he was so moved by the experience, he almost cried. He wasn't the weepy type. The name itself—DeBusschere, of Belgian descent—had a polysyllabic sturdiness. You might say it suggested a man who was bent on giving an honest day's work in return only for a cold beer.

Dave DeBusschere was a dedicated company man. By all measurable criteria, he was the prototypical Holzman player. Basketball historians and Knicks loyalists would forever cite the addition of DeBusschere as the move that instantly upgraded Holzman's team from developing to contending—with one dissenting opinion.

"What I would like for you to write is that if—and it's a big if—Willis Reed had been completely healthy even during the last season I was there, we could have won the championship," Walt Bellamy told me. "But as you know, Willis was almost always hurt, playing on guts, even back then. So when they won the year after the trade, people had to say something, so it became, 'Well, it was all clogged up in the middle. Bellamy couldn't play with Reed. Bellamy had to go.' But when Willis wasn't hurt, he was a very mobile player. So, in theory, I believe it could have worked with the two of us."

Theories, however, could not trump titles. Beyond moving a happy Reed back to the pivot and inserting DeBusschere to open up the floor with his long-range shooting, there were other positional dividends to the deal. Already on his way to landing a spot on the first NBA All-Defensive Team that season (along with DeBusschere), Frazier flourished with Komives out of the way, and Russell didn't have anyone to feud with any-more. Adding to the team's sudden chemistry was the promotion of Riordan to third guard, the first off the bench.

The trade jolted the Knicks. They won ten games in a row, lost to the Bulls in Chicago, then won a half dozen more. By the turn of the year they were challenging Philadelphia and Baltimore (led by Earl Monroe and a burly rookie center named Wes Unseld) for Eastern Division supremacy. The Celtics, in Bill Russell's final season, struggled to keep up.

On the night of January 21, the Knicks won their 13th straight home game and 17th of 19 overall, de-feating Seattle 113–106. But the real news broke with Cazzie Russell's right ankle, just before the third quarter came to an end. Hustling for a loose ball, Rus-sell sprawled on the floor, only to have the Sonics' Joe Kennedy stumble and fall across his lower legs. Rus-sell suffered a fracture that would all but finish him for the season.

Bill Bradley became a starter, by default—or, as he said, "by total dumb luck." In replacing Russell at for-ward, he was not the same shaky novice of the previ-ous season, perhaps in part because he didn't have to guard opposing players on the perimeter. "I didn't have my back to the basket constantly on defense," he said, meaning he was no longer having to stop quicker guards. The positional change explained his increased comfort level but not his growing confidence.

For those who had already written off the Bradley phenomenon as media hype, he returned from his rookie season determined to change their minds. The man dubbed Dollar Bill by Leonard Lewin of the *New York Post* (because of his contract) had done his summer homework in Philadelphia and earned extra credit. The old-timers in the City of Brotherly Love still talk about the night Bradley showed up in the basement of the Bright Hope Baptist Church at Twelfth and Oxford in North Philly and had the audacity to lock himself into an old-fashioned duel with none other than Black Jesus himself, Earl Monroe.

"You'd walk into the building and go down these steps to a gym where there were no windows and they didn't have enough money to complete the floor, so we wound up playing on concrete," said Sonny Hill, who founded the Charles Baker Memorial Basketball League in 1960. "We had so many NBA players in those days, the cream of the cream. They'd play in unbelievable heat, so bad that they'd have to go up the stairs and outside at the half and wring out their shirts. The gym had stands on one side for 400 or 500 people, maybe. That night we had them standing all around the court, packed together, maybe 1,000. Here in Philly, it's like Wilt's 100-point game: 10,000 folks will tell you 'I was there.'

"Earl played for Gaddie's Realtors. Bradley played for my team, Jimmie Bates B Bar. I took him under my wing, helped him reconstruct his game, but mainly his confidence. He was down on himself after his first year. You have to understand the pressure Bill was under. Because he was the great white college basketball player, people expected him to come into the NBA and dominate. But Bill was not a selfish player. Once he was on a team with players as talented as him, his instincts were to sacrifice. I had him mostly at guard to help with his quickness, to force him to create. I wanted him to let loose, just play like he did in college."

Across his career, there was only one man Bradley had ever called Coach, and that was Arvel Popp, who mentored him when he was the reigning superstar for the Crystal City Fighting Hornets on the western bank of the Mississippi River, about 30 miles south of St. Louis. But that didn't mean he didn't have heartfelt respect and admiration for Holzman and the others who put in the hours, who cared about players and playing the game right. He had fond memories of his Baker League experience and especially of Hill, who encouraged him to shake loose of his proclivities to fit in and unleash his school-yard id.

Separately, Bradley and Monroe smiled sheepishly when I asked about their stranger-than-fiction showdown. It was if I had stumbled upon an old family secret they didn't mind me knowing. Bradley remembered Monroe's team winning in overtime, and that he scored "fifty-odd points and Earl had sixty-something." Monroe said it had been "back and forth all game long," but played down the notion of any racial subplot.

"What you have to realize is that the Baker League wasn't like the Rucker, because Philly basketball was different from New York," he said. "We prided ourselves a little more on the team aspect of the game, even though you had some unbelievable talent out there every summer. And there were a fair amount of white guys playing with us back then, too."

For the record, Sonny Hill said he was certain that Monroe had 63 points to Bradley's 54. But it was the way Bradley played, getting his shot whenever and however he chose. "People always said, 'Oh, Bradley is a great team player but he can't do this, can't do that,'" Hill said. "Well, let me tell you something: people in the NBA never saw the true Bill Bradley. They saw the player who reconfigured his game to be part of the

Knicks. That night he played against Earl? That wasn't a game; that was an event. And I'm telling you, that was the real Bill Bradley."

Back in the NBA, where summer league defense could get you benched—or fired—and where not even Dick Cheney could quiet the New York press, Bradley was suddenly tasked with even more. With Russell still recovering and with Bellamy and Komives gone, Holzman's team was thin. It needed Bradley to show something, and soon.

As a front line, Bradley (6'5"), DeBusschere (6'6"), and Reed (listed as 6'10") looked perilously small. Modern guards are as tall or taller (not to mention more athletic) than the Old Knicks' forwards. But even before conventional positioning by size was revolutionized by the likes of Bob McAdoo, Magic Johnson, and Dirk Nowitzki—all of them 6'9" or taller—it was clear that the Knicks were on the small side. People looked at Wilt Chamberlain and other behemoths of the day and wondered how this team could possibly contend. "If you saw them line up, it was easy to raise questions about how they would defend and rebound," said Jack Ramsay, who in 1969 was coaching a strong 76ers team in Philadelphia. "But after they threw the ball up, you would see how and might remember, Oh right, Russell and the Celtics aren't the biggest guys, either."

His point was this: somewhere along the way, the Old Knicks developed a cohesion that was impossible to plan for on paper, and some believed that Bradley was the key. "Not because he was a great scorer or a great defender," said Ramsay, who would coach Bill Walton and Portland to an NBA title in 1977 and later be known on radio and TV as Dr. Jack (for earning a doctorate in education from the University of Pennsylvania). "He was tough—you didn't get away with anything with Bill. But his ability to run the floor, run the baseline, move without the ball, keep the ball moving, knock down the open shot—I always thought it opened up everybody's game."

Others thought matching Bradley with DeBusschere at the forward positions was most responsible for the team's offensive cohesion, the improvisational genius that Holzman never claimed. Guards are presumed to be the players who see the floor, recognize the game's geometric spacing, but suddenly the Knicks' starting forwards were a Rhodes scholar and a player who had been made coach of a professional team two years removed from a college campus.

"The great Jack McMahon, who worked for me in Philadelphia, who was one of the great lifers and evaluators of talent in our game, had a passion for passing forwards and used to say that if you had them, you'll be good," said Pat Williams, who was the GM in Chicago as the Old Knicks coalesced in the late sixties. "And Jack always said the reason why the Knicks were so good was because DeBusschere and Bradley were such good passers and it made their team so difficult to defend everywhere on the floor."

Less interested in crediting any individual or tandem, Bradley suggested that the team's lack of depth created an accelerated bonding period among the starters and laid the foundation for what the unit would become.

"Rather than say, 'Gee, my movement was the key,' I'd say that the team jelled when five of us had to average about 40 minutes a game after Cazzie's injury," Bradley said. "For me, personally, I was freed, having moved to forward. It felt like I was back with van Breda Kolff at Princeton. I could almost hear him yell, 'Clear the goddamn floor, don't clog it up.' Everybody had a job. I felt that I created space for things to happen. You know, cut along the baseline, go back three steps. I'd play with my man, try to keep him guessing, get him a little exasperated. Sometimes you would get an oomph, a 'Slow down, man,' and then you ran even more. See, the movement was conscious, but a lot of the time I was just clearing out space, say, to give Frazier room to operate. He could work on his own or work with Willis, so it would become a two-on-two, rather than three-on-three. Offense for us really had to be a collaborative effort, because we did not have the best player in the league or the biggest scorer or the biggest team. So through this period, we were on the floor night after night, all these minutes, and began playing off each other."

Meanwhile, in the backcourt, Barnett ceded control of the ball to the younger Frazier, whose leadership had become clear. Fall-back flamboyance and all, Tricky Dick was just as adept at flooding passing lanes and wreaking havoc with his lightning-fast hands. All of them orbited the sturdy captain, Reed, who was just entering his prime and had developed into the rarest of NBA centers: smaller than most opponents, he was agile and strong enough to score at the rim. Benefiting from his otherwise frustrating time with Bellamy, trying to fit two natural centers into one lineup, he was also more comfortable than ever facing up for his excellent southpaw jumper.

"How many teams have there been where everyone could hurt you from almost anywhere on the floor?" Pat Williams asked rhetorically.

As the 1968–69 season progressed, the pain was administered league-wide. Between January 25 and

February 15, the Knicks went on yet another streak, reeling off 11 straight wins. They finished the regular season with a 54–28 record, third-best in the East behind Baltimore and Philadelphia, and steamed into the playoffs to face Earl Monroe and the Bullets in the first round. After finishing ten games under .500 the previous season, Baltimore had added Unseld's bruising defense and rebounding and climbed to 57 wins. Out of nowhere, the Bullets were the first seed in the East. Under coach Gene Shue, they wanted to believe they had eclipsed the Knicks.

"We actually wanted to play them instead of Philly in the first round, because we thought they would be an easier matchup for us," Monroe said. "But you know what happens when you're young and dumb; it was our first time in the playoffs, our first taste of success. We weren't ready, and they were a much better team than when the season started."

It was a humiliating sweep, four straight and the start of a miserable pro sports run for the city of Baltimore against New York. But before the Jets and Mets could chime in, the Big Apple was, rather suddenly, a pro basketball town. The Knicks were in the Eastern Division finals, one step away from another shot at their first NBA crown. Now all they had to do was find a way past the greatest winner in the history of the sport—a man who, just their luck, happened to be making his last championship stand.

No one ever accused Bill Russell of suffering from excessive modesty. There was a reason he and Red Auerbach got along so famously. Ego was always an important and arguably essential component of Boston's winning equation, even after it officially ended in 1970. As Russell said to Willis Reed sometime after the Knicks' first championship run, defining the ethos of Celtic Nation, "I guess you guys are glad I left."

Sipping coffee in a quiet hotel lounge in Midtown Manhattan, Russell recounted the quip and followed up with his familiar hearty laugh. He was there to talk about his new book, *Red and Me*, while I attempted to steer the conversation toward Russell's coaching showdown with the other Red in the 1969 division final.

That series turned out to be the biggest disappointment of Holzman's career. "That was supposed to be our year, not theirs," he confided to Pearlstein. In his final go-round as player-coach, Russell, not surprisingly, saw things differently. Holzman, he said, let six more regular-season victories delude him into thinking that the Knicks were the favorite. The Celtics, he argued, had merely been pacing themselves, not worried about playoff seeding; they were lying in wait among the divisional weeds.

"I think, in my mind, I outcoached the Knicks in that series," he said, before setting out, in surprising detail, to explain how.

"First off, I had a lot of respect for those guys, but I also knew what we had done," Russell said. "That was in the books, too. I had a team that knew how to play, okay? When people talk about the better team, they usually mean personnel, not team. I had one that knew how to play half-court, uptempo. Now, in making my plan for that series, I decided the best player they had was Walt Frazier, and I wanted to attack him. He was the only guy I thought who could guard Sam [Jones] without help. So in the first game, I looked at the stats—they had beaten us six out of seven times, and I had averaged like six points, about four or five shots. So Willis was able to help out, back up everybody. First game, I came out looking to score, not because I cared about scoring but to make Willis pay attention. I always felt that Wilt was the only guy who could guard me when I wanted to score. So Willis was over here with me, there was no trap over there. The flow of that defense was disrupted. We won the first game with relative ease, and the beauty of that today is that they still don't know what happened."

After so many games, so many years, and, yes, so much success, Russell could be excused if memory wasn't serving correctly. The record shows he scored only 10 points in Game 1, though his typically suffocating interior defense did spearhead the 108–100 Celtics victory at Madison Square Garden—a victory that erased the Knicks' hard-earned home-court advantage. But there was a strategic move by Russell that indeed made a documentable difference: inserting Emmette Bryant, the former Knick, into his starting backcourt.

The Knicks had lost Bryant to the expansion Phoenix team the previous spring, but he'd wound up in Boston after refusing to play for the Suns. Nowadays, it's rare that a player would reject an opportunity to play in sun-splashed Arizona. Bryant expressed his displeasure in no uncertain terms. "I said, 'The desert? Oh God, no, I'm an asphalt guy, from Chicago,'" he told me from his home in—where else?—Chicago. "I told them, 'I'll quit before I go there.' Then that summer, Auerbach approached me at Kutsher's [Country Club in the Catskills]. K. C. Jones had just retired. He told me, 'We'll try to work something out and bring you in, but you have to promise to shave off that beard.' I told him, 'No problem.' Those days, everyone wanted to go to Boston because of the playoff money."

As Bryant remembered it, Russell put him into the lineup just before the playoffs, replacing Larry Siegfried. This was a typically iconoclastic statement by Russell. Bryant, a black player, was bumping a popular white player in a city that was not exactly the stronghold of racial harmony and honor. Russell's reward was a near triple double by Bryant in Game 1 against the Knicks: 13 points, 11 rebounds, and 8 assists. In Game 4, with the Knicks making a strong bid to reclaim the home-court edge, Bryant iced a 97–96 Celtics victory with two free throws after Reed missed a jumper with eight seconds left.

"Then we got to the sixth game in Boston," Russell said, picking the narrative up with the Celtics leading 3–2.

Now, I watched the fifth game, and Frazier had figured it out, okay? So I watched the way he was playing Sam, the way he was moving his feet. The whole series, I had been low post. The sixth game, I went high post. All the adjustments they had made were useless to them. Every play that was for Sam, Frazier ran into three picks, and because I was a good passer, we had good prospects for a layup with Sam or John [Havlicek] or Satch [Sanders]. So Frazier says, "I'll go behind the pick and get him as he's coming by." Now Sam's catching and shooting that little bank shot. Now Frazier's thinking, "I'll flash and make Sam go wider." Now I've got the ball, and if you remember that cover photo in *Sports Illustrated*, I'd turn and take one dribble and have a layup. Now we're back where we started. And Sam killed them.

Jones piled up 29 points as the Celtics closed out the series with a 106–105 victory, and Boston went on to a stunning win on the Lakers' home floor in Game 7 of the Finals. It was Russell's 11th title in 13 years—and his last. Again, contrary to Russell's version of events, the point must be made that Frazier was suffering from a groin pull and by Game 6 was limited to 29 minutes. "I couldn't run, man," he said, dismissing Russell's claim that Holzman and the Knicks had been outfoxed.

But the tense and hard-fought series only convinced the Knicks that they really did have an opportunity to be the next big thing, Russell or no Russell. In its postgame report on the last game the following morning, the *New York Times* noted how Frazier and the Knicks had sat around the cramped Boston Garden locker room downing cans of beer. Rather than drowning their sorrows, it seemed as if they were toasting their future.

While Auerbach and Russell puffed away on victory cigars, there was at least one Celtic who wasn't about to bluster or blow smoke in the Knicks' faces. That was Bryant, who had more right to gloat than anyone after coming up big again in Game 6, scoring 19 points. Looking back, he said that no matter how ecstatic he was to be going to the NBA Finals, closing in on a title, he was too fond of his ex-teammates, Reed especially, not to keep his emotions in check as he made his way around their cramped, foul-smelling locker room, shaking hands, lingering finally by the dressing stall of his first pro roomie and friend.

"You guys played a beautiful series," he said.

Reed shook his head, in mock disgust.

"Can't believe you're getting a championship before me," he said.

Bryant gave the big man a hug.

"Be patient," he said. "You guys are next."

7

COURTSIDE PERSONAE

N ew York was on a hot streak. Two days after the Knicks opened the 1969–70 NBA season with a 25-point drubbing of Seattle at home, the Amazin' Mets won the World Series by polishing off the heavily favored Orioles. It was the second major sports championship of the calendar year. In the nine months after the Jets (then of the AFL) had won Super Bowl III, New York had attracted the eyes and ears of what seemed like every sports fan in the country. Beneath the celebration, though, the city was divided. Yankees fans, myself included, were humbled.

As a young child in the early sixties, I had rather enjoyed the Mets as cute expansionist puppies who couldn't stop peeing on the carpet and chasing their own tails. It was easy to fancy them as hopeless wonders while counting on my beloved Yankees to play baseball as God and Joe DiMaggio had intended. But by 1969 the Bronx Bombers were has-beens of the highest order and I was sick to my stomach watching this tinker-toy team ascend the throne typically occupied by my pre-adolescent heroes, Mickey Mantle and Whitey Ford.

Somewhat paradoxically, I had by then developed a boy crush on the inimitable Joe Willie Namath, who had pulled the toupee off the figurative head of the avuncular NFL, as he had famously predicted. In the case of the Jets, I believe my aversion to change was mitigated by the cultural divide between the two sports. Still in its formative years, not yet America's hierarchal kingpin with its original social networking system known as the tailgate, pro football did not unpack for an annual months-long residence in my brain. It was never a constant of daily life; the NFL Giants had no emotional hold on me.

Only the Knicks could unite the metropolis. Only the Knicks, with their home games limited to the earliest cable subscribers, could create their own buzz in bars all over Manhattan. Only they could link the lunch-pail commuters of the outer boroughs with downtown's wealthiest power brokers, the denizens of Harlem with those made famous by Hollywood.

As Bill Bradley pointed out to me, few Mets were seen around town once their season ended. Besides Namath, the Jets were largely unrecognizable, like most fully costumed football players. And the American Basketball Association's Nets (so named to rhyme with the Jets and Mets) weren't exactly the picture of glamour amid the flies and mice of Long Island. Phil Jackson, a Manhattan scene regular, argued that the Old Knicks were more visible, more tangible. "We had more personalities," he said, adding that they were city dwellers who took the train to work and interacted with fans in ways that today's NBA stars would not comprehend, or dare to mimic without HBO-worthy entourages.

"There were times I would get on the Long Island Rail Road at my stop in Little Neck in the morning and save seats for Phil, who lived in Bayside, and for Mike Riordan, who lived in Flushing," said Gwynne Bloomfield, Red Holzman's secretary. "People would say, 'You can't hold seats,' and I would tell them, 'But it's for Phil Jackson and Mike Riordan.' They'd say, 'Yeah, right,' but then they'd get on and you'd see their jaws just drop. Back then, it was so different. Those guys were really part of the community."

Rich, middle class, or poor, there wasn't a Manhattan neighborhood that wouldn't welcome the Old

Knicks. Long before '69–70, Reed would take the subway up to Harlem and put his reputation on the line against Rucker League legends like Earl "the Goat" Manigault and other school-yard rats eager to dunk in the face of the Knicks' main man. Bradley, too, hustled into the park on the occasional steamy summer evening, slipping into his basketball gear behind a tree, ready to risk being undressed as the foolhardy paleface.

On any court, and especially under the hot Madison Square Garden lights, these were grown-ups in skimpy shorts, playing with a raw competitiveness and without worry of injury. "What we were doing was taking place in the heart of the city, Midtown Manhattan," Dick Barnett said. "It felt like more of a cultural experience than the other sports. Basketball players are much closer to the fans. Because you can see the sweat coming off them, the expressions on their face, it was more of a personal experience."

More than most, Stanley Asofsky and Freddy Klein could vouch for how up close those player-fan relationships could become with the right connection or karma. The two basketball-mad New Yorkers, whose decades-long relationship began with a fistfight during a pickup game, had enjoyed the view from courtside at the Garden since the mid-sixties, retaining their seats with a written appeal to Ned Irish when the team switched from the old Garden to the new. It's likely that nobody has seen more Knicks games than Asofsky, at the time an inventory control executive for a CBS publishing division, or Klein, a Manhattan restaurateur.

"It all started with Cazzie Russell at the 92nd Street Y, early in his career," Asofsky said. "He wasn't getting enough minutes, and he wanted the workout. The guy was a workout freak. So I said, 'Come to our Y.' He said, 'Are there ballplayers there?'"

Mostly there were young and middle-age wannabes who were thrilled to have a professional athlete in their midst. "I used to feed Cazzie for jumpers," Asofsky said. "He was crazy about working on his shot. We'd go into the small gym at the 92nd Street Y and he'd hit 20 in a row. I'd tell him, 'That's bullshit, you're standing still.' So we'd go full-court, I'd hit him on the run, and he'd make another 20 in a row."

Before long, Asofsky had made himself a new friend. After the workout they would shower and walk down to Papaya King on 86th and Third, talking sports and life, even women. Asofsky likes telling the story of setting Russell up with a "gorgeous receptionist" who had been distracting the guys at the office.

"Cazzie was not only a very religious guy but a nut about his health and body," Asofsky said. Three weeks after he introduced them, the receptionist barged into his office. She told him she was willing to sleep with Russell but that he'd told her he couldn't waste energy during the season. "I think your friend must be crazy," she told him. Having had a daily look at the receptionist, Asofsky pretty much agreed.

But that was Cazzie, Asofsky said: a walking enigma, endearing but strange. Then his even stranger teammate started coming around. "Cazzie must have told Barnett about the Y, because after a while Dick showed up," Asofsky said. Freddy Klein remembered the workouts with Barnett being more like wrestling than basketball, with a drill that would make today's coaches, general managers, and owners apoplectic. "Barnett would get the ball and he'd want three guys around him," Klein said. "He'd count down—five, four, three, two, one—and then we were supposed to hit him. On the arm, the shoulder, wherever. He'd still make the shots."

How great a percentage Barnett really made was beside the point; it was the memory of the interaction that hit nothing but net. Asofsky, Klein, and the others believed they were doing their share as committed loyalists, as ultimate fans. They were pushing Barnett for those tense playoff battles when he would have to drive in heavy NBA traffic with the game and maybe the season on the line. They felt like Knicks themselves.

Back in the late sixties, a young attorney named David Stern, just a few years out of Columbia Law School, was working for a giant of the profession named George Gallantz at the New York firm Proskauer Rose. Among other clients, Gallantz had maintained a long association as outside general counsel of the NBA. It was a role that had originated in the late fifties when Gallantz represented the league in a $3 million suit filed by Jack Molinas, a onetime Columbia star banned by the NBA for betting on games when he played for the Fort Wayne Pistons. Stern idolized Gallantz and loved pro basketball. Within a few years, in the early seventies, he put up his hand when Gallantz needed someone to work exclusively on the struggling league's account. At the time, the players' union was mounting legal challenges to the league's labor practices. More than anything, the NBA commissioner, Larry O'Brien, needed a good lawyer.

But in the fall of 1969, with Stern still convinced that a partnership in a reputable New York firm was his life's ambition, his connection to basketball was more as a fan, an Old Knicks fan. Long before he would become commissioner (in 1984), Stern settled in at night with his young family, flipped on the television in his Teaneck, New Jersey, home, and witnessed Red Holzman's team ambling onto the floor, care of Channel 9.

On occasion he went to the Garden, which was filling up as never before. Before the '68–69 season, the Knicks had sold out their building a grand total of six times in 22 years. They packed the new Garden 14 times on the way to losing the division final to the Celtics. In 1969–70, that number almost doubled, to 26. Granted, that was no great achievement by contemporary measures: in the nineties, the Knicks would sell every Garden seat for nine consecutive seasons.

Even during our modern recessions, some NBA teams can count on regular capacity. But the sports ethos was very different in the late sixties. There was passion for sports, but not the rampant consumerism—triggered by the proliferation of 24-hour television coverage—that would create a wide-reaching industry boom.

Stern, who eventually made a career of studying the sports phenomenon, said:

We've built that Knicks era up over the decades to be something like the Jordan phenomenon, but it was all so New York. The NBA at the time was this tiny little league. The Knicks created a personality on and off the court and connected with a city in a way that professional basketball really hadn't seen before—not even with Boston, which had ownership changes and all those racial issues. I don't know exactly what was going on at the Fabulous Forum in those days, because I didn't live in Los Angeles. You certainly had great charismatic players out there, too, and having that on both coasts created early melodies for the symphony that hadn't been written.

It was one thing to inflame the passions of basketball junkies like Asofsky and Klein. Getting the attention of the Madison Avenue crowd, the people with the power to recast basketball's image from blue collar to white, amounted to a Jordanesque leap across the socioeconomic divide. That was the beauty of a potential powerhouse in New York City: all the corporate heavyweights were within walking distance or a short cab ride away.

"What happened with the Knicks was great for the NBA, because when the biggest media town in the country gets hot for a sport, that sends a message to the rest of the country," said George Lois, one of that generation's most celebrated mythmakers, a man who understood the art of selling better than anyone, David Stern included.

Long before he sprouted to an athletic 6'3", Lois played the city game. A Manhattan native and Bronx resident, he was enough of a prep standout while attending the High School of Music and Art to earn a basketball scholarship to Syracuse—which he promptly rejected to attend the Pratt Institute. He lasted a year, dropped out to work, and soon after, in the early fifties, took his New York–honed skills to the heartland after being drafted into the Army. He starred on a team that barnstormed through Texas and Louisiana and "beat the living shit" out of other Armed Forces clubs and even some college teams with a front line that averaged 6'5", or one inch below the cutoff for service.

The company team was so good, Lois said, that it kept him in Texas and out of harm's way in Korea—at least until he refused to play in a game at LSU in support of his lone black teammate, forbidden by the university to suit up. Lois took a stand by taking a seat next to his teammate in the bleachers. He was shipped out soon after. "I got back to the fort, and the sergeant walks up to me and tells me I'm going to fucking Korea," he said.

Lois survived a war he considered "almost as dumb as Vietnam," and returned home to New York to launch a storied career as an advertising and art director, a real-life Mad Man. He became an industry legend for his pithy television campaigns and for his groundbreaking conceptual *Esquire* magazine covers, which frequently featured popular and controversial athletes. In 1963, Lois put the fearsome Sonny Liston in a Santa hat. Five years later, he depicted Muhammad Ali as a crucified Saint Sebastian. For an August 1972 cover story on the 10 Best-Dressed Jocks, Lois photographed the most stylish Knick, Walt Frazier, in a white suit and a wide-brimmed Clyde Barrow hat, hovering over the palest white player Lois could find, Philadelphia 76er Kevin Loughery.

This social statement apparently went over better with the hip magazine audience than it had with his Army superiors.

"Frazier was up in the air, literally hung on wires," Lois said. "And you know what? We did the shoot on the day before they were flying to the West Coast to play the Lakers in a playoff game that spring. He's hanging in the air and I'm thinking, If this guy ever falls and even stubs his toe, I'm totally fucked. People in this town will want to kill me."

Lois's use of athletes in commercials, like his "I Want My Maypo" cereal campaign, was an early har-

COURTSIDE PERSONAE · 167

binger of Nike Nation, laying the groundwork for what ultimately would become a jackpot for celebrity jocks. He hired the likes of Mickey Mantle, Johnny Unitas, and Oscar Robertson. He had Yogi Berra talk to a cat, whose voice, unbeknownst to Yogi, happened to be Whitey Ford's.

"Do you recognize that voice?" Lois asked Berra.

"No, who is it?" Berra said.

"It's the Chairman of the Board."

Berra replied, "What company?"

Away from the office, Lois was friendly with the biggest names in sports, Mantle and Namath, to name New York's top two. It made perfect sense to him to use them in campaigns, most of all because he got them dirt cheap. "Holy shit, I've got the most famous guys of the time and they're getting $100 apiece," he said. "They just wanted to do it for the fun of it. Wilt was in my office one day for some reason and I showed him a Mantle spot. He said, 'Man, I'd love to do that.' I said, 'I can only give you $100.' He said, 'I don't care about the money.'"

Lois was a fan of several sports, but he said there was nothing, ever, like experiencing the Old Knicks as they came of age. "Of course, we had all been jealous of the Celtics and couldn't even imagine that kind of team in New York," he said. "But all of a sudden, there they were, above and beyond basketball intelligence."

In 1969, with the championship cast assembled and rolling, Lois got a call from a friend who worked at the Garden as the head of ticket sales, asking if he might want a full-season plan. Lois rushed to the box office and asked for four seats on the baseline. "The guy says, 'On the baseline? Are you sure?' I said, 'Yeah, baseline. Half the game is right in your lap.'"

He was close to the action but would get even closer by befriending several players through Larry Fleisher, the agent and players' union power broker. Soon enough, some of the players were dropping by Lois's regular pickup game at the 23rd Street Y (which later moved to 14th Street, where Lois was still getting in a run at age 78). This was the downtown version of what Asofsky and Klein had going on 92nd Street.

"We'd play eight-basket games," said Lois, "and usually, when those guys first came, they tended not to play very hard." But these were also hard-core competitors, unaccustomed to being embarrassed, even when no one was watching. "Bill Bradley's playing against this guy, who's a really good jump shooter, and I'm screening him," Lois said. "The guy hits one from 17 or 18 feet, then another, and before Bradley knows what's going on, the guy's hit five in a row. Oh, shit. Suddenly Bill's climbing over me, hitting me in the face with his elbow. It was so fucking great."

Back at the Garden, Lois brought the same profane intensity to rooting, accompanied by three equally crazed ref-baiters in the seats next to him. He seldom wasted his tickets on clients or people who didn't have a similar passion for the game. "I gave the tickets to the guys I played ball with," he said. "We'd bust balls the entire game, get all over the refs." Mendy Rudolph, one of the hard-bitten vets, would give Lois and his buddies the once-over during time-outs, occasionally with his hand over his crotch. The byplay with the refs would reach the point where the Knicks regulars would look at Lois and friends in disbelief while the other guys were shooting their free throws. "We were real New York assholes," Lois said with pride.

Dick Schaap, one of the city's leading print and broadcasting sports journalists, anointed Lois "Super Fan" as the crescendo of Knicks coverage grew during the '69–70 season. Schaap would stop by his seat from time to time for a few colorful quotes, which Lois was always willing to produce. No doubt Asofsky and Klein would have fought for the title; Klein, in fact, insisted that he'd once tangled with Lois in a pickup game and, when Uptown met Downtown, had "knocked him on his ass." But all internecine hostilities ceased once the Old Knicks hit the floor, making comrades of all. And as they reached full-blown championship contention, the Garden became the hottest hangout in town.

Adam Clayton Powell Jr., who represented Harlem in the House of Representatives from 1945 until shortly before his death in 1972, appointed himself the team's unofficial chaplain. He had access, and he wasn't the only mover and shaker who wanted to get inside the emerging New York phenomenon. Ira Berkow, my friend and former *Times* colleague, recalled sitting in Red Holzman's office one night before a game that season, conducting an interview, when the coach was distracted by a commotion inside the locker room.

"What the hell's going on in there?" Holzman asked his trusty aide, Frankie Blauschild.

"Oh, Sargent Shriver stopped in," Blauschild said, referring to the Kennedy family loyalist and activist, who wound up as the Democratic candidate for vice president in the doomed 1972 bid to remove Richard Nixon from the White House.

Holzman's face reddened. "I don't care if it's fucking General Shriver: no one in the locker room before a game!"

Besides being politically ignorant, Holzman apparently wasn't too sure how to deal with the sudden fuss people were making over his team, the likes of which he had never seen at the basketball backwaters in Rochester, Milwaukee, and St. Louis. But there was no turning back, no stopping the stampede of stars.

George Lois was soon bumping into Zero Mostel near the concession stand before games, neither one wanting to go to his seat for the national anthem. (Mostel was one of many entertainers who were suspected of being Communists during the fifties and blacklisted.) They would talk the game, Mostel arguing that Russell should be starting over Bradley and Lois telling him he was seriously full of shit.

On the other baseline, Asofsky was amazed by the transformation the courtside neighborhood was undergoing as the Knicks appeared to be revving up for a championship run. Steve Lawrence and Eydie Gormé. The radio personality William B. Williams. Jerry Stiller and Anne Meara would score different seats around the lower bowl and occasionally leave little Ben on Freddy Klein's lap so the future comic actor could get the premier courtside view. Dustin Hoffman had a fairly regular perch behind the Knicks' bench, where the players—having seen *Midnight Cowboy*, like most people in the country—would address him as Ratso.

Stern was right: here were the earliest indicators that professional basketball players could actually blur the lines between athlete and entertainer, become crossover celebrities and walk alongside America's most popular.

"They had that quality because of how unique they were as individuals but also because of what they were doing as a team," Bill Goldman, another regular, told me. Goldman grew up in Chicago, a diehard Bears fan, before moving to New York to meet the everlasting love of his sports life, the Knicks. After the trade for Dave DeBusschere, he fell so hard that he took an entire West Coast road trip with the team during the '69–70 season, following the guys from city to city like the most devout groupie. He claimed that he didn't attend the Academy Awards during the playoffs that season—where he won Best Original Screenplay for *Butch Cassidy and the Sundance Kid*—because it interfered with the Knicks' playoff schedule.

Goldman and his wife dined frequently with the DeBusscheres, forever arguing that his good friend was the one player the team could not do without. Robert Redford, who would ring Lois for a ticket when he was in town, had DeBusschere and Bradley to his place in Park City, Utah, for a little snowmobiling during the '69–70 season—though Bradley would tell me that the notion of the Knicks forwards taking a wild ride was way overblown. "We went about 25 to 50 feet, that was about it," he said. "We were in the middle of a season and we weren't going to take any risks."

The actor Elliott Gould—who by 1970 had risen to stardom in *The Night They Raided Minsky's* (1968) and *Bob & Carol & Ted & Alice* (1969) and could have made the case for being more famous than anyone— tried to get Dick Barnett a cameo role in his 1971 film *Little Murders*. The film's director, Alan Arkin, nixed the casting idea because the only acting Barnett had ever done was flopping for the refs in the act of taking a charge.

"I once asked him, 'What do you do when you're not playing basketball?'" Gould said. "He told me, 'I'm in public relations without a telethon.' I didn't know what the hell he was talking about. But I thought, 'This guy's a real character.'" Gould, a character in his own right, was another celebrity friend of the Knicks. At various times he hosted Bradley and Phil Jackson at his Greenwich Village apartment. He played Frazier one-on-one at the Garden and would boast for decades that he had managed to pick Clyde's pocket and lost only 10–7.

At the very least, Gould talked a good game, and no one could accuse him of jumping on the Old

Knicks' bandwagon. He'd been going to the Garden for years. His father, Bernard Goldstein, took him by subway from their home in the Bensonhurst section of Brooklyn. They rooted for Dick McGuire, Ernie Vandeweghe and especially Max Zaslofsky, a Jewish player. "Those were good blue-collar teams," he said of the Very Old Knicks, who were coached by the legendary Joe Lapchick and lost three straight championship series between 1951 and 1953.

Gould's passion for the game was a source of pride. He loved it so much that when he presented the Oscar for Best Film Editing at the 1976 Academy Awards, held the same night as the NCAA championship game, he tore open the envelope and said, "And the winner is . . . Indiana, 86–78." You couldn't find famous fans like that anymore, he argued. The modern industry of sports has become too superficial. The be-seen spectacle that began to flourish in New York during the Ewing years in the nineties offended the old hands like Lois, Goldman, and Gould, who compared everything to 1969–70.

"To us, the Knicks represented everything—our hopes, our ambitions, our dreams," Gould said. "It was not about glamour, about being seen."

Early in his acting career, Gould was as addicted to gambling as he was to the game, once rushing out of a

Broadway rehearsal—in costume and makeup—to see Oscar Robertson take on the spread. But by the beginning of 1969, he said, he had beaten his bad habit, even as the big Hollywood bucks rolled in.

"I'd had a major breakthrough," said Gould, who added *M*A*S*H* and *Getting Straight* in 1970 to his growing list of credits. He was also married to Barbra Streisand, forming a dream paparazzi union that lasted all of eight years before they divorced in Santo Domingo in 1971. In Los Angeles, Gould also spent a fair amount of time at the Forum watching the Lakers. With all due respect to Elgin Baylor and Jerry West, he said, L.A.'s team didn't have the intrinsic appeal of the Old Knicks.

"Someone once asked me the difference between Bergman and Altman," Gould said, of the famous directors. "I said, 'Altman knows who Dave DeBusschere is.'"

By 1969, most hip New Yorkers had some idea of who Woody Allen was. He was on the cover of *Life* magazine and was starring on Broadway with Diane Keaton in *Play It Again, Sam*. He was on the rise, along with the Knicks, who became a prime source of entertainment and one for which he didn't have to leave his beloved island of Manhattan.

"It was in the heart of the city, you didn't have to drive," Allen said. "I would go every single night, every home game for the entire season."

Allen had grown up a huge fan of the New York baseball Giants. (Gould said he once gave him a Whitey Lockman card, one native Brooklynite to another.) But with basketball he discovered a very different athletic dynamic—sheer performance could actually blunt the power of partisanship. During a telephone interview on break while filming on location in London, Allen admitted to me, almost sheepishly, that he always preferred to see the opposition win a great game over an insipid Knicks blowout. "I'm not a must-win kind of person," he said. "When Reggie Miller comes in and scores eight points in the last however many seconds"—16.4, to be exact—"that's exciting for me. If Earl Monroe came in with the Bullets and scored 100 points and the Knicks lost, that also made me happy," he said.

Allen was one celebrity fan who wanted nothing more from the players than to sit and admire them, legs crossed, watching impassively, never letting loose.

"I never socialized," he said. "I never wanted to do any of those Knicks commercials. I preferred to go to the game, watch quietly, and leave. We'd go out afterward—Frankie & Johnnie's, Elaine's. Everyone was obsessed with what happened at the game. The whole town was tripping over the Knicks." If confronted by the Knicks' public relations folks wanting a halftime interview, Allen typically refused. He was there for the game, nothing more. For him, the Knicks were as much great theater as anything on Broadway or off. The only question was whether Red Holzman could direct them to the ending that the swelling legion of faithful—those famous or not—had in mind.

At the Garden, the players felt the surge of excitement as the 1968–69 playoff run raised hopes for '69–70 and the team's collective identity grew behind a wave of media attention and applause. "You began to hear the fans applaud the pass that led to the pass that led to the basket," Bill Bradley said. "You could hear the anticipation as the ball moved around the perimeter that something they would appreciate was about to occur. From a basketball point of view, it was always a knowledgeable audience, but now there was electricity every night, the belief that we all were headed somewhere special."

Only those paying close attention could have seen the Old Knicks coming, building like a tidal wave of good character and cheer. Jim Trecker was one of them, having typed play-by-play at the Garden beginning in the mid-sixties, a role he also had for the Jets as they moved into the Namath years. The other regulars at courtside were John F. X. Condon on public address, Jim Bukata as the statistician, Tommy Kenville as the official scorer, and, on the clock, Nat "Feets" Broudy—a sweet, diminutive man who also worked at the league office. Broudy handed out root beer candies to reporters, and his selective finger on the game-clock switch infuriated suspicious visiting coaches, who often charged that he, more than any fan or Minuteman, was the Knicks' sixth man.

None of the crew, Trecker said, made any bones about the fact that they loved the Knicks. They felt like part of the team. "People really took to the Knicks in the late sixties because they were such a pleasurable team to watch, but I think there's a strong possibility that they wanted to feel psychologically connected," Trecker said. "Because everything else was blowing up all around us, because it was a tough time to feel good about life in America, there was a yearning for togetherness, a sense of universal family. After the Jets and Mets, there was a strong atmosphere of achievement in the city, and as the Knicks developed, there was the feeling that this was where it was all happening. There was a tremendous sense of pride in the building, from the fans upstairs to the little people working the table. We saw that all coming out of a guy like Red, sitting there every night yelling, 'See the ball, see the ball.' We took it as a message that we all needed to see our ball."

While a generation of Knicks fans came to believe they had invented the chant "Dee-fense! Dee-fense!" many sports historians actually trace it to the 1950s and Yankee Stadium, when the Sam Huff–led Giants defense terrorized NFL offenses. Nevertheless, the Garden adopted it as its own. In a time before Jumbo-Trons and recorded bass thumps, the sound of 20,000 fans shouting as one proved demoralizing, galvanizing, and deafening.

"You always knew that when they started their run, here came that damn chant," said Butch Beard, the Louisville All-America guard who played nine years in the NBA, the last four with the Knicks. "Not only did it get them up, I thought it intimidated the officials. Many games, Clyde would strip me four or five times, and foul me half the time, but if it happened on one of those runs, with the crowd going crazy, forget it. The refs weren't calling anything."

Jake O'Donnell, one of the league's premier refs for 28 years, agreed that the Garden crowd affected him and his colleagues, but not in the way Beard believed. "The crowd was unbelievable in that place," he said.

"They were more rabid, more knowledgeable, than any other arena. When they started that chant, the game would come alive and would actually make you a better referee, get you really into the game, bring you to a higher level."

Years into retirement, O'Donnell would ask if "those Carnegie guys"—he meant Asofsky and Klein—were still around. "They raised hell a lot and got you going a little bit, not that they ever swayed a call," he said. "But it was all in good fun, never vicious, which actually was kind of how those Old Knicks were. Red, he got his T's, he said what he had to say, but he wasn't mean-spirited, didn't whine all night. All those guys, except maybe Phil Jackson, never had too much to say; they just played."

As a rookie during the '69–70 season, Beard came into the Garden with the Atlanta Hawks and discovered just what DeBusschere meant when he would implore the refs to "Just let us play." The two of them chased a loose ball near the Knicks' bench. "I'm telling you, that fucker hit me harder than a truck, knocked me right into the stands," Beard said. "In most cases, you get a quick look, maybe a 'You okay?' Not a word— nothing. Right then, even as a dumb-ass rookie, I could understand their focus, where they were trying to get to."

The view wasn't as good from the affordable blue seats, the nosebleed section, where I considered myself lucky to be on many a glorious night. Only the famous and lucky folks below, however indistinguishable they were to us from up high, could see the perspiration on the players' brows. But the game was our common denominator. We all had a voice and knew when to howl. We were all onto the fresh scent of success in the air. New York was a city of champions. Why couldn't our Knicks win one, too?

8

BLOWING IN THE WIND

Cazzie Russell said grace. At a long dinner table in a downtown Cleveland hotel on Thanksgiving Day 1969, the New York Knicks bowed their heads in common prayer. They were scheduled to play Oscar Robertson and the Cincinnati Royals the following night—one of several games since 1967 that the Royals had scheduled for upstate Ohio. In a deal with Cleveland Browns owner Art Modell, Cleveland would get a glimpse of the NBA action that was to arrive with their own team, the Cavaliers, in the league's 1970 expansion.

There was much for the Knicks to give thanks for. The previous night, in Atlanta, they had dazzled the Hawks with a 38–12 third-quarter exhibition that left Richie Guerin, the Atlanta coach and onetime Knicks star, in as much awe as agony. "In all my years in pro basketball, I've never felt so embarrassed," he said. Even Red Holzman, not given to self-congratulation, was struck by how helpless the Hawks were against the Knicks' defensive heat. "Frazier stole everything but the clock," he said.

That game was not atypical of their first 23. They sat down to Thanksgiving dinner with a ridiculous 22–1 record, riding a 17-game win streak, which tied the record held by two Red Auerbach–coached teams (Boston in 1959–60 and the Washington Capitols in 1946–47).

This was an added bonus, as the Knicks had no love for Auerbach and his bombastic ways. True to form, Auerbach cautioned the media not to overreact to the havoc the Knicks were wreaking. New York was good, he conceded, but greatness could only be measured by continuous success over a long period—for example, the 11 titles in 13 years the Celtics had won during the Bill Russell era. That, he'd say, was success. It was a fair point, but Auerbach, as usual, was too bullish to let someone else make it. The Celtics, meanwhile, were in utter free fall, en route to a 34-win season and their worst record since the 1949–50 team went 22–46.

Russell was gone, and, for the time being, so was the league's other goliath of the pivot. In early November, the Lakers' Wilt Chamberlain had torn up his knee, an injury that the team thought would be season-ending and possibly even career-threatening for a man of Chamberlain's size and age (34). The only issue with the Knicks was the loss of Phil Jackson, who had landed on the injured reserve list after herniating two disks in a game against the Warriors, an injury that would require spinal fusion surgery. Action Jackson became Traction Jackson. . . .

But even with the Celtics down, the Knicks knew the East was formidable. The Baltimore Bullets had a nice balance of experience and youth, along with the mercurial Earl Monroe. And Lew Alcindor, the slender rookie giant out of UCLA, had landed with fanfare and his unstoppable sky hook shot in Milwaukee.

The loss of Jackson aside, the Knicks were still deeper than they'd been for the '69 playoffs. Russell's ankle was healed, giving them another bona fide scorer. Within months, Mike Riordan had gone from hired hack to a valued member of the bench, a brigade Cazzie had dubbed the Minutemen. The reemergence of another bench player was arguably the best evidence yet that an authority even higher than Auerbach was smiling on New York. Dave Stallworth, having missed the two previous seasons with what doctors had diagnosed as a mild heart attack, was back—healthier than ever.

ABOVE: *When the Garden was on 49th Street:* Where Nedick's was all the rage, and Marilyn Monroe sang "Happy Birthday" to JFK.

RIGHT: *Irish farewell:* Knicks founder Ned Irish leaves the court of the old Garden for the last time.

BELOW: *Curtain raiser:* Walt Frazier (10) takes, and makes, the first shot at the new Garden on Valentine's Day 1968, amid a sea of business suits.

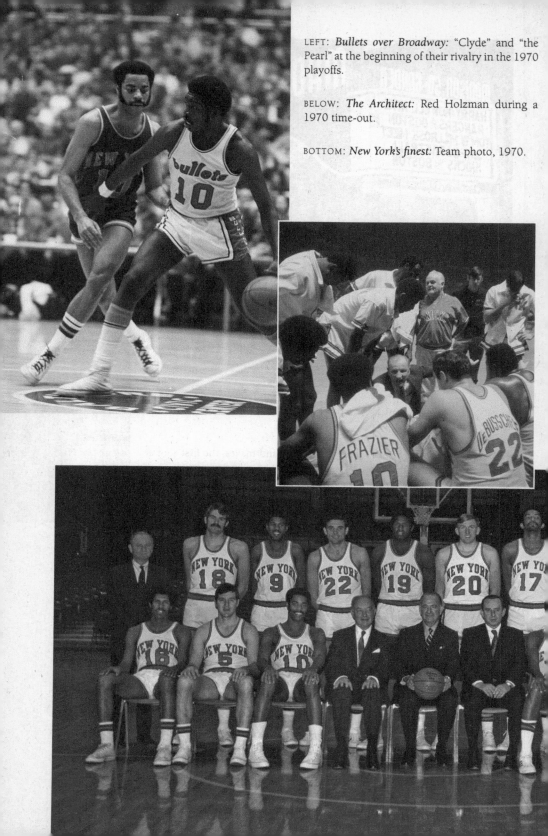

LEFT: *Bullets over Broadway:* "Clyde" and "the Pearl" at the beginning of their rivalry in the 1970 playoffs.

BELOW: *The Architect:* Red Holzman during a 1970 time-out.

BOTTOM: *New York's finest:* Team photo, 1970.

Pass me the ball, Coach!: Dave DeBusschere, in his dual role as player-coach for Detroit, circa 1966.

Yelling himself Red: Holzman on the bench.

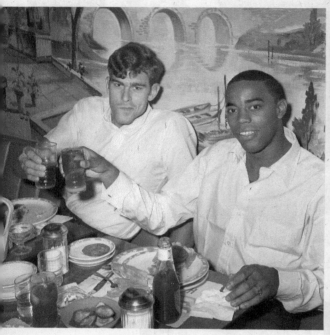

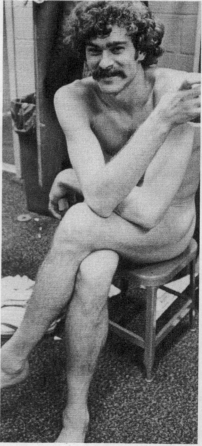

TOP RIGHT: *The photo that made the man:* George Kalinsky poses Walt "Clyde" Frazier for a celebrated portrait outside the Garden.

ABOVE: *A couple of country boys:* Pre-hirsute Frazier and Phil Jackson at a diner in 1967.

RIGHT: *South Dakota stud:* Phil Jackson cooling off after a game, circa 1973.

LEFT: *Fall back, baby!:* Dick Barnett gets off his patented jumper.

BELOW: *From Motown to Midtown:* DeBusschere fights for position in 1968.

BOTTOM: *A National Guard:* Cazzie Russell in 1970.

TOP LEFT: *The Stilt wilts:* Willis Reed got the best of Wilt Chamberlain in the 1970 Finals.

BOTTOM LEFT: *Down goes Reed:* After tearing his right tensor muscle, Reed grimaces on the floor, while Game 5 proceeds without him.

ABOVE: *Last man out of the tunnel:* Willis Reed makes his storied entrance to Game 7. The boy below the basket (*circled*) is George Lois's son, Harry.

Telling it like it is: Bill Bradley *(left)* and Dave DeBusschere *(right)* celebrate their championship with Howard Cosell.

From his high school days in Dallas to his All-America years at Wichita State and now in New York, basketball had been the flame of Stallworth's life, and it burned the brightest with the Knicks. In 1965, with Bradley in England, he'd hit New York with a colorful nickname, Dave the Rave. Along with Russell, he brought loud taped music to the locker room and an extrovert's spirit. But it all dissipated one March 1967 night in Fresno, California, in a game against the San Francisco Warriors. Stallworth clutched at a sharp pain in his chest and got so dizzy he couldn't play. When the Knicks returned home, he was told by doctors that he'd suffered a minor heart attack. He'd be fine—but no ball.

The game, unfortunately, was all he knew. He had grown up in a Dallas ghetto, raised by his mother, Doris, who worked at a local hotel to support him and a younger sister. He did not have a college degree, and like everyone else in the NBA had been playing on a one-year contract. Eddie Donovan paid him as a scout, but the money didn't compare.

"I couldn't go back to Dallas—life was tough there, a lot of killings, poverty, the whole works," Stallworth said when I reached him in Wichita, where he was retired after putting in 25 years at the local Boeing affiliate. By the time of his heart attack, his mother had moved to Compton, California, but there was nothing for him to do there, either. "I came back to Wichita and got my degree," he said. "I coached kids and played some pickup, even though the doctors told me not to." Almost two years later, during a routine checkup with a Wichita specialist, Stallworth was given the opinion that his heart was strong and there was no reason he couldn't play pro ball again. He traveled to New York to see the team doctor, who concurred.

It was, he said, "like fate. Like I was supposed to be back there in 1970."

So even without Jackson, the Knicks' bench was strong. If there was any cause for concern, it was in the middle, where Reed was showing early signs of breaking down. He didn't like seeing Nate Bowman, Stallworth's old teammate at Wichita State, playing in his place, and his minutes were piling up. Insiders worried that his knees were starting to go, even at what should have been the prime of his career. He was all of 27. No one wanted to think what might happen if they squandered yet another season.

On October 15, 1969, a Wednesday, an estimated one million antiwar protesters gathered on college campuses around the country for what was known as Vietnam Moratorium Day. Across the Atlantic, a young

Rhodes scholar named Bill Clinton organized a demonstration at Oxford. The Knicks won a game against the Royals.

Before the game, Bradley talked DeBusschere into joining him at a downtown rally against the war, staged mostly by students from the University of Cincinnati and Xavier University. The two forwards had quickly become constant dinner companions on the road, dissimilar men from vastly different backgrounds who were forging a very special friendship. In Cincinnati, Bradley took the opportunity to chat up some of the students, listen to their complaints about the immorality of the war. DeBusschere wasn't quite sure what to do. He was far less political than Bradley and not all that certain that he agreed with the protesters. But he listened to the chants and the speeches, impressed by the orderly and peaceful demonstrations.

The pacifism didn't last. Once the game started that night, DeBusschere got into a shoving match with the Royals' Tom Van Arsdale, a player he'd coached in Detroit and the identical twin of a former Knick, Dick. From the Royals' bench, a rookie coach named Bob Cousy yelled to his man, "Next time DeBusschere shoves you, take his head off."

DeBusschere shot back, "Why don't *you* come out of retirement and try it?"

Cousy must have liked the idea. A month later, six years after quitting at the age of 41, he activated himself for spot duty just in time to try and keep New York from winning its 18th game in a row, a record held by Boston. In the *New York Times* on the morning of the game, in Cleveland, reporter Thomas Rogers noted that Cousy "was a member of Boston's record-sharing team and having been reactivated as a player may put in some playing time in an effort to stop the New York charge."

Cousy or no Cousy, Holzman's team should have been stoked for the game, given its implications: the chance to snatch a line in history as if it were a cigar dangling from the jaws of Red Auerbach himself. It felt like "the seventh game of the playoffs," Bill Bradley said.

Surprisingly, the Knicks came out flat and played what Bradley called a "lousy" first quarter, trailing by seven. DeBusschere was particularly unproductive, on the way to a 2-for-8 shooting night, the same numbers posted by Dick Barnett. Reed would take 22 shots and make only 8. Fortunately for Holzman, the Minutemen—Russell, Riordan, Stallworth, and even Nate Bowman—picked up the starters with a 32–22 second quarter. The game seesawed down the stretch, with the Royals led by Oscar Robertson's 33 points and

10 assists and by ex-Knick Jumpin' Johnny Green's 19 points and 20 rebounds.

Since the last game between the two teams, Cousy had quickly recast Cincinnati from a team dominated by Robertson and Jerry Lucas into one that played tougher defense, ran a more uptempo offense, and shared the ball as though it couldn't hit the ground. In other words, he had modeled his new team on the Celtics. But in trading Lucas, a gifted outside shooter and rebounder, to the San Francisco Warriors, Cousy had created some locker-room tension, if only because the deal didn't sit well with Robertson. Lucas had been his costar and sidekick. Who the hell was Cousy to walk through the door *four games into the season* and send a mainstay like Lucas packing? All these Celtics acted like they had invented the damn game. Now the coach was *playing*?

Cousy spent the game in his sweat suit, for the most part letting Robertson do his thing. But with 1:49 left in the fourth quarter and the Royals clinging to a 3-point lead, Robertson fouled out. Enter the Cooz: here came the passing and ball-handling wizard to the scorer's table, ready to roll.

"He was in his forties, hadn't played in six years, and he put himself in—can you imagine that?" Robertson told me. He still couldn't, bristling four decades later at the sheer audacity, waiting for the chance to sound off, if someone would just call and poke the scar from the old wound.

Cousy got to work right away. He found Norm Van Lier, a rookie guard, on the wing for a jumper. He made two free throws to give the Royals a 105–100 lead. To a man, the Knicks thought their streak and their chance to break the record were over. But the Royals gave them hope when Van Arsdale fouled Reed with 16 seconds to play, mercifully stopping the clock. Reed sank both free throws. And Coach Cousy, somewhere around midcourt, called his final time-out.

When play resumed, Cousy selected himself to inbound, hemmed in along the sideline near midcourt. "He put himself in because he didn't trust anyone else, like he was trying to make a point: 'I'll show you how it's done,'" Robertson said. "And then he was the one who turned the ball over—not once but twice in, like, ten seconds."

The miracle began in Cousy's eyes. On the inbounds play, the Knicks extended their defense to midcourt to challenge the pass—except for DeBusschere, who deliberately held back a step and a half from his man, Van Arsdale, while counting down from five. He knew Cousy had left himself without any remaining time-outs and would have to find someone open. With an instinctive feel for how much space he needed between himself and Van Arsdale, DeBusschere anticipated the release and angled his way between passer and receiver. The ball came to him like a lovesick puppy; he bounded downcourt and dropped in a layup for his second basket of the night, the biggest of the game. The score was 105–104, and those among the 10,438 fans at the Cleveland Arena who'd started moving toward the exit reconsidered.

From Robertson's courtside view, the Royals were still in control. The NBA had no three-point line yet, so all they had to do was inbound, let the Knicks foul, and make two free throws for a 3-point lead. "Everyone knows you make the shortest pass and hold the ball," he said. "But what does he do? He puts the ball up in the air. Man, this is a sore subject."

Cousy risked a heave for Van Arsdale, beyond half-court. The pass was on target, but because the ball was in the air so long, the Knicks were able to swarm the receiver, like free safeties. Van Arsdale was what the Old Knicks liked to call their pigeon. He came down with Cousy's pass, ripe to be plucked. Reed knocked the ball loose and Walt Frazier picked it up. He barreled downcourt, pulled up from about ten feet, and threw up a brick but had the presence of mind to follow his shot. At the rim, he was fouled by the hapless Van Arsdale.

Under long-abandoned penalty rules on shooting fouls, Frazier had three chances to make two. He didn't need the third.

"They never touched the net," he said. "I had ice water in my veins." There were two seconds left. The Royals tried another inbounds pass, but that, too, was picked off, this time by Reed. The game-ending sequence was like something out of *Hoosiers*. The Knicks triumphantly ran off, their streak having reached a record-breaking 18.

On the one-hour delayed telecast back to New York via WOR Channel 9, the broadcaster Bob Wolff, who had called Don Larsen's perfect game in the 1956 World Series and the groundbreaking Giants-Colts sudden death overtime NFL championship game in 1958, called it "one of the miracles of basketball . . . Folks, I've never seen anything like it."

Looking back, the gentlemanly Wolff was less critical than Robertson of Cousy's decision to put himself in. He chalked it up to the mind-set of a man who stubbornly believed in his Hall of Fame basketball IQ. To him, the moral of the story was that five great basketball minds had outwitted one. "In my opinion, the Knicks were the smartest team ever assembled," Wolff said. "Their ability to anticipate on the floor was amazing."

Robertson, conversely, wondered whether Cousy was just selfish. Was he too eager to protect the Celtics' share of the record that he had helped set? Did he have Auerbach—the mentor he always affectionately addressed by his given name, Arnold—in mind? It still annoyed Oscar that nobody back then had dared question the tactic, at least not that he recalled. "No alarm, no criticism in the media about how a guy at that age could do that," he said.

Such was the license of a Celtic after Boston's despotic rule, those 11 championships in 13 years. But in the end, Cousy's comeuppance was really no more than a subplot to what had transpired in Cleveland. The real story was much bigger than one man's hurried passes or hubris. To the Knicks and their followers, the 18th straight victory was more than a milestone or even a miracle; it was symbolic of what Holzman had been preaching—team defense—from the day he took over. "The game in Cleveland pretty much convinced us that we were capable of anything," Frazier said.

The next night, back home against the Detroit Pistons, the Knicks were promptly outscored 35–20 in the fourth quarter and lost by 12, a measure of redemption and revenge for the departed duo of Bellamy and Komives.

It didn't matter. The Knicks had breached the record books, and not for the last time. The team left the court while a Garden crowd stood in an uproarious ovation still echoing throughout New York City.

Easy as it is to characterize the Old Knicks as the perfect blend of basketball brainpower and abilities, even they weren't immune to internal conflict. It is the nature of all teams to be challenged from within, said Bradley. Only the best of them can ensure that those "conflicts never turned to bitterness."

They beat the Phoenix Suns in a neutral-site game in Salt Lake City, where DeBusschere and Bradley had done their snowmobiling with Robert Redford, then the Knicks moved on to Detroit to play the Pistons again during the second week of January. In their previous meeting, on Christmas night in New York, the Knicks had produced another of those revelatory moments. Down a point with one second left, Frazier inbounding the ball from the sideline, Dick Barnett shook Reed loose with a back screen on Bellamy, and Frazier delivered a perfect looping pass that Reed laid in off glass for the game winner.

They pulled into Detroit with a 30–10 record. With three days off between the Suns and Pistons games, the players had a chance to get away from one another, have some room to breathe. Russell spent some time in Ann Arbor, where he had attended college. On that Thursday afternoon, January 15, he barged into practice—late and full of road rage.

A few minutes outside Ann Arbor, he had been stopped by police and ordered out of the car with a gun pointed at his head. The explanation he was given—after producing a driver's license and only then being recognized as the beloved Wolverine—was that an African American male had broken out of prison in the vicinity. There were roadblocks everywhere. All law enforcement personnel in the area were under orders to look for a black man with a mustache. Russell had a mustache.

Russell's teammates were appalled by the blatant profiling and were naturally sympathetic when they heard his story—at least until Russell continued to vent with his elbows and forearms during a scrimmage. He especially made a target of Don May, the second-year forward and one of five white teammates (excluding the injured Phil Jackson) on the racially mixed team.

It was no secret that Russell believed he had lost his starting position unfairly to Bradley while he was injured. "I kill [that] white boy in practice," his friend Stan Asofsky recalls him complaining. He missed the theatrical grandeur of being introduced with the starters. Sometimes he didn't feel like much of a contributor. Asofsky and others felt for Russell but didn't agree with him. The team was playing too well with Russell coming off the bench.

No one wanted to believe there was anything deep-seated like racial animus between Russell and Bradley—least of all Bradley.

"In that whole drama, I don't think race was very relevant," he said. "It was people with certain talent, and the year when Cazzie came back, he and I were in this competition that Holzman orchestrated. I always thought that Red got the best out of both of us." Inside the locker room, Russell's likability was evidenced by the fact that he was a constant target of teasing for his prodigious workout regimen (though Frazier dryly noted that Russell mostly worked on the one phase of his game that was already formidable: his shot). There was no discussion of the subject between Bradley and Russell, just a spirited daily competition that was fraught with implication. Perception or reality, Bradley knew it posed a threat to the team. "I always tried to never say anything or do anything that didn't show full respect for him and his abilities and, quite frankly, for his character," he said.

As delicate as things were in the real world, one might expect the controversy to have splintered the locker room across racial lines. But people—his team-mates included—looked at Bradley differently than the average white player. No team outsider identified with and befriended the black players more than Cal Ramsey, but he also vouched wholeheartedly for Brad-ley, having worked with him in community service programs. He knew Bradley would show up whenever anyone asked him to spend time with at-risk kids, or to speak at a rally for their sports teams.

"One time there was a game in Philadelphia the night before and they got back about three o'clock in the morning," Ramsey said. "I remember it vividly: the weather was bad, a big rainstorm that lasted into the next day. The rally was at eight A.M. at the school. I'm walking down the street on my way, thinking there is no way he's coming, figuring out what I'm going to say at the rally." Ramsey turned a corner and there was Bradley, tucked under an umbrella, wearing his tat-tered fatigues jacket. "How could anyone make a racial issue out of the thing with Cazzie when you had a guy like that?" Ramsey said.

Frazier called Bradley "the least prejudiced player I've ever met." Still, there was a divide among the team, at least socially. "He seemed to be on the out-side looking in," Frazier said. Bradley didn't disagree, saying that he never acted as if he understood the black experience and tried to make sure other white players didn't make such pretenses, either.

"If I detected that a white player had an attitude, I would designate myself to talk to him," he said. "I would say that we don't do this or that on this team." He only had to make that speech a couple of times, but he remained vigilant. "You always had to try to figure out what you could try to do on and off the court to try and help the team," he said. "Sometimes it was in the playing of the game, sometimes it was psychological, sometimes it was who's got what role, who's going to talk to the press, who's going to do this or that, so you have that meshing."

To many around the league, especially opposing coaches, it was obvious that the Knicks were better with Bradley as the starter. "He wasn't a great scorer or defender, but there were intangibles—especially his movement and toughness—which opened up everybody's game," Jack Ramsay said. "Cazzie was a great shot maker, but they had a lot of guys that could score. They needed Cazzie, but as a spark plug. Not as a guy playing 40 minutes and taking 20 shots, even though that's what he'd always done."

Russell's identity had been forged from raw production. Now his minutes had dropped to 18.3 per game from 32.9 before his injury the previous season. His scoring average was down from 18.3 points a game to 11.5. In Detroit, his feelings of highway victimization crashed head-on with his frustration at playing second fiddle to Bradley. Their history was vast and tumultuous, from their college showdown at the Garden to the unequal pay upon being drafted by the Knicks to their perceived standing on a team that was soaring in the nation's imagination.

If there was anyone on the team with a platform to speak out on sensitive racial matters, it wasn't Russell but Dick Barnett. Everyone knew how much he had suffered and sacrificed as a player, given his age and ability and how little he'd earned in part because he was black. Barnett being Barnett, whatever he said came out in droll, often hilarious, and sometimes painfully honest sound bites of sobering reality.

"Cazzie was the better player individually, that much was obvious," he said matter-of-factly. "The team members understood the 'white hope' thing was there when Bradley came in—that's part of sports. But it's always going to come down to the question, Can you play? Bradley proved he could, and it was up to the coach to recognize which player fit in better. In fairness to Cazzie, it wasn't easy, that situation, and I would to a great extent call him very accommodating and diplomatic, except for that one time."

· · ·

Holzman wasn't above barking at or needling players when they blew assignments or played badly. He would say to Bradley, "How the fuck did you become a Rhodes scholar?" Disgusted after a blowout loss, he would bark, "Go get laid tomorrow, don't even come to practice." But when he sensed the need for a tender mediation, he preferred that it come from a fellow player. When he saw Russell sulking, disconnecting, he would pull Reed aside. "Talk to Cazzie," he would say. "See what he's thinking."

This time, Cazzie's anger was obvious—he was playing like he wanted to hurt everyone around him—and Reed already had a pretty good idea what it was about. Russell had every right to be mad at the world, as long as his teammates were excluded.

He stepped toward Russell and threw up his hands.

"What the hell are you doing, throwing elbows at your teammates?" Reed said. The gym fell quiet. Reed's expression demanded an answer. Before Russell could rewrite the thought, it spilled out, angrily and regrettably.

"Be quiet, Uncle Tom," he snapped.

Shut the fuck up, Adolf Hitler, would have landed better. But to say what he'd said—a black man from

Chicago to another from the Jim Crow South—was a mind-bending betrayal, even if it was behind the team's closed doors (as opposed to Muhammad Ali's very public slandering of Joe Frazier several years later).

"I thought he was going to kill me," Russell told a friend afterward. Those most familiar with Reed's history had to know that the possibility of violence was not beyond the realm. As early as the start of his third pro season, Reed had demonstrated that he was no one to fool or fuck with. On October 18, 1966, in the Knicks' home opener against the Lakers, Reed was involved in a fracas at the old Garden that was downright shocking—not so much because it broke out in the typically combative theater of an NBA game but for what transpired after the first punch was thrown.

It was the third quarter, and Elgin Baylor was at the free-throw line at the side of the court nearest to the Lakers bench. Reed had been complaining about the physical play of Rudy LaRusso, a 6'7", 220-pound All-Star-caliber forward out of Madison High School in Brooklyn and Dartmouth College. The famed refs Richie Powers and Mendy Rudolph told him to shut up and play ball. Reed decided he would have to send LaRusso his own message—and chose an elbow to the side of the head as they jockeyed for position. On his way upcourt, LaRusso threw a right cross. Everything after that was a blur of Reed beating on men in blue (the color of the Lakers' uniforms at the time).

"It all happened fast," said Gail Goodrich, who was in his second year with the Lakers. "Rudy threw a punch and Willis went off. Rudy backed up. Willis started swinging. It was all right in front of me on the bench, and I can tell you that Willis was a menacing-looking guy when he was mad." Goodrich gave himself the best advice of his life: " 'Do not get up!' "

As Reed recalled, the 6'10" Darrall Imhoff tried to grab him in a bear hug—so LaRusso could nail him, or so he feared. Reed responded by sending Imhoff to the floor with a punch that drew blood from a cut above the eye. Next, a 6'9" rookie named John Block made the tactical mistake of stepping inside Reed's punching range. He took a blow to the face that broke his nose and bloodied Reed's fist. With Imhoff and Block stretched out, fans streamed onto the court for a closer inspection of the damage. Police scrambled to restore order.

It was a scene that, in the contemporary NBA, would have had David Stern meting out draconian suspensions and fines and holding spin-control press conferences. On multiple ESPN channels, every angle and aspect of a black man's evisceration of three white players would have been rewound and dissected, frame by frame. But news traveled much slower in 1966, and the NBA did not have much of a national image to uphold. Reed and LaRusso were ejected but shrugged off the brawl. Reed mostly wondered where the hell his teammates had been. "Man, you were winning," the newly acquired Dick Barnett told him.

Barnett was one of three Knicks in uniform that night who would still be around when Russell crossed a line that neither LaRusso nor any other player ever would. Dave Stallworth was another. The third was Russell, a rookie who was making his NBA debut after missing the season opener on the road with a sprained ankle and who was asked after the game where he had been while Reed was taking on all comers. "Right in the middle, observing," he said. Hence, Russell was well aware of what the otherwise affable Reed was capable of when someone challenged him. He also knew why Reed, at 24, was named captain of the Knicks not long after the L.A. fight.

Reed had held the same title for his high school football team and for Grambling during his junior and senior years. He proudly accepted the Knicks' honor when Dick McGuire made the announcement one day at practice that management had made the decision. He had been under the impression that captain was a position that players voted on.

"I guess I had showed them I was a guy who wasn't going to get pushed around," he said. Yes, Reed had demonstrated how much of a one-man wrecking crew he could be, but more important was his total commitment to doing whatever it took to make teams respect the longtime doormat Knicks. "The guy was an unbelievable teammate, the absolute best," McGuire said, calling Reed his favorite player ever. "Winning was all he ever cared about."

Reed did not view his position as ceremonial. He wanted his teammates to expect him to lead in every way possible. He wanted their respect. When Bradley joined the team, for instance, it troubled him that Reed, of all people, would address teammates on a first-name basis— "Hey, Cazzie," "Hey, Dave"—except him. "I would always think: Why is he always calling me Bradley?" he said. In the Cleveland airport one day, he finally mustered up the nerve to ask, "Why don't you call me Bill?"

Reed looked at him, considering the request.

He nodded, finally, and said: "Okay, Bradley."

Flustered, Bradley dropped the subject but eventually caught on to the ways of the Captain.

"It was his way of saying, 'I'm in charge,'" Bradley said.

There were times when Reed wanted the ball in the post and wasn't shy with his feelings when it didn't come.

But he always gave back, in ways that were surprising and incalculable. "Willis did so many things for guys on the team that no one even knew about," Frazier said. Sometimes the help was financial—Barnett, according to Frazier, was the biggest beneficiary—and sometimes it took other forms, like when Reed set Frazier up on his first date in New York.

By the late sixties, Reed had set a tradition of rooming with a rookie, whether white (Bill Hosket in '68–69) or black (John Warren in '69–70), to demonstrate firsthand how to conduct oneself as a pro. "He filled you in on all the dos and don'ts—and there were many," said Warren, who honed his dribble and jumper on the same Far Rockaway courts at 108th Street that had produced the McGuire brothers, and, like Dick, he then went on to St. John's.

In that one season, Reed made a lasting impact on Warren's life, promising his parents—who were from Georgia, with deep southern roots, and could relate well to Reed—that he would look after their self-described mama's boy. Reed did that and more, even trying his hand as an unlicensed social worker.

"At some point that season, I pissed off my girlfriend and was in a bad way," Warren said. "We got back into Newark Airport after a game in Cincinnati the night before, and Willis says, 'Rook, what's wrong?' I said,

'Willis, you gotta help me out.' I knew he was dead tired, but he got right in the car with me and drove out to Westbury in Long Island." There, Reed rang the doorbell of the girlfriend's parents' home. Naturally, they were delighted to see him. While Reed charmed the parents, Warren slipped away to plead with his girl for forgiveness. They married and had a son, John Warren III. "Whenever we see Willis, he'll say, 'Hey, I put this together,'" Warren said. "He's right about that. We're like his children."

The man from Bernice knew that the fabric of a team had to be as strong as the familial ties that bind, and especially for challenges like the one in Detroit. Russell had thrown down the existential gauntlet, from the color of Reed's skin to his innermost core. And why? Was it because Reed was not an outspoken man on political or social matters? Was it because he roomed with a white player? Or that his most pressing cause was the behavioral well-being of his basketball team?

Even as his teammates recoiled and prepared for the worst, Reed was instantly calculating his options in the line of fire: he could take the slur personally and teach Russell a lesson he would never forget, or he could put the welfare of the team first. The Knicks, he knew, could not afford to lose Russell's concentration and offense, a distinct possibility if Reed vilified him to the point of alienation. On top of that, everything he had been taught in college by Fred Hobdy had been centered around shielding the team from the corrosive issue of race.

Reed stepped in Russell's space, looked him in the eye.

"This Uncle Tom is gonna be whuppin' some ass in a minute if you don't keep quiet," he said.

If I'm an Uncle Tom for calling you out for abusing a white teammate, so be it. We play basketball here and we play it together.

How many men in the corner Reed was backed into would have been able to resist punching their way out? How many would have had the restraint to give Russell even five seconds to back down? How truer a test could there be of character and leadership? "I was telling him, 'Hey, throw those damn elbows at other people, not us, and *us* includes everyone wearing the uniform,'" Reed explained. "I mean, basketball-wise, we're in the same war. You can't hurt one of our guys. You can't hurt me. Take it out on the Pistons tomorrow."

Of course he was hurt. But he knew he couldn't let his teammates recognize the pain. "That story," Bradley said, "was the essence of Willis."

In the end, nobody appreciated Reed's restrained leadership more than Russell. When we spoke, he had just finished a 13-year run as the head basketball coach at the Savannah College of Art and Design, which had ended its men's and women's programs. Was he interested in another coaching job? I asked. No, he said, he had finally moved on from basketball to his higher calling. He was the new head pastor of a 287-member nondenominational church in Savannah.

I asked the preacher about the episode with police in Michigan and those two terrible words he had spat at Reed. There was a long pause. "How do you know about that?" he asked. I said there was a very brief accounting of it—without context—in DeBusschere's book. But it had also come up in a couple of interviews, referenced primarily as a pivotal moment for that team.

Russell took a deep breath, seemed to relax and let his guard down. Those years leading into what transpired in Detroit had been bewildering for a young black basketball star, he said. He wondered how it was that even as he was feted as college basketball's player of the year in 1966, "those kids at Texas Western couldn't eat in a restaurant."

After two Final Four appearances, Russell and Michigan were beaten that year by Kentucky in the regional final. He had come to believe that this was all part of some master plan from the head coach upstairs. Adolph Rupp's team was in the national spotlight and in the NCAA title game against Texas Western's all-black starting five, so the country could witness the deconstruction of the white superiority myth. Unwittingly and involuntarily, Russell considered himself an agent of change.

"It would have been nice to have gone back to the Final Four again, but then what Pat Riley always calls basketball's Emancipation Proclamation wouldn't have happened," Russell said. "So I'm happy to have taken part, done my share, in that piece of history."

The racial climate and profiling did not excuse "the worst thing that had ever come out" of his mouth, he said. He was ashamed and worried about what his teammates would think going forward. He had never had problems with white players or white people at large; he had taken several white Michigan students home with him to Chicago on school breaks, to sample his mother's southern-style cooking. But above all, Russell had to square things with the Captain. He apologized and asked Reed's forgiveness, and not just once.

"It was something I learned from," Russell said. "I came to see it as a character-building situation, not just for me but for us as a team. No matter what I had personally experienced, I think we all understood how important it was to keep a situation, and especially one like that, from getting in the way—to keep things in perspective, focused on our job."

He couldn't say whether Reed, at the height of the fast-moving drama, really had had enough time to ponder the best way to defuse it. As much as he'd replayed it all in his mind, Russell had long ago settled on the belief that the right thing to say had just come naturally to Reed. It was just who he was, a natural-born leader.

"Willis Reed," Russell said, "is an amazing man."

The most unconventional loss the Knicks suffered during the 1969–70 season was not a game. Before the playoffs, Eddie Donovan, their general manager, departed the organization for a similar position in Buffalo, where the expansion Braves would debut the following season, along with teams in Cleveland and Portland. Donovan's departure left Holzman pretty much in charge to make a shrewd personnel decision: a recovered Phil Jackson was kept inactive to protect him from the expansion draft—and in all likelihood Donovan. Based on the regular season, Holzman determined that he had enough talent to win it all.

Despite a late-season swoon in which the Knicks lost their focus and dropped seven of their last ten, they finished with a 60–22 record, best in the league and four games ahead of Milwaukee in the East. Reed was the league's Most Valuable Player, despite being its 15th-highest scorer (21.7) and fifth-best rebounder (13.9). He was joined on the all-NBA first team by Frazier. Holzman was named Coach of the Year, but most gratifying to him was the inclusion of three Knicks—Reed, Frazier, and DeBusschere—on the All-Defensive first team. The Knicks played the stingiest D in the league (at a time when allowing 105.0 points per game counted as such). Their point differential was 9.1, almost five full points better than anyone else.

They began the playoffs against a Baltimore Bullets team they seemed to own, having won nine of the past ten games, including the playoff sweep the year before. Their five regular-season victories came by an average margin of 19 points. But like all of Baltimore, the Bullets were tired of being a piñata for New York. They came into the Garden for Game 1 with a chip on their shoulder the size of Wes Unseld's biceps. With the improving Unseld grabbing 31 rebounds and Earl Monroe scoring 39 points, the Bullets pushed the Knicks into a second overtime before losing, 120–117, in Game 1 at the Garden. "You could see a difference in them, like they knew they belonged," Frazier said.

Reed had to play 54 of the 58 minutes, about 10 more than Holzman would have preferred and way too many for a man with barking knees matched against a younger opponent, Unseld, who was built like a brick shithouse. Reed's performance was uneven as the series dragged up and down the coast, on the way to a nerve-racking seventh game. On the night of April 6, 19,500 packed the Garden, wondering for the first time if the Knicks really were of championship timber. But the Knicks took charge early behind DeBusschere and Barnett. They built a 62–47 halftime lead. And when the Bullets made a run to within 88–82 after three quarters, the Knicks had a none-too-secret weapon to unleash. They had Cazzie Russell.

With Bradley in foul trouble and the Bullets forcing the Knicks to play at Baltimore's freewheeling pace, Holzman turned to his most explosive and highest-paid Minuteman. And here, with the magnificent season hanging in the balance, Russell came on to play the role he so dearly wanted. He hit clutch fourth-quarter shots, the kind that halt rallies and break spirits. In January, Reed had given Russell seconds to compose himself, and he had. In Game 7, Holzman gave him 21 minutes to redeem himself, and he did. On the strength of his 18 points overall, the Knicks won by 13, a sweet epilogue to the saga of Cazzie and the Captain and a buoyant prologue of better things to come.

9

DOWN GOES REED

Willis Reed sat peacefully in the great room of his Grambling home. After a morning of chores outside, or fishing with a pal, he loved cracking open a grape soda and settling into the recliner in the middle of the room, in front of his flat-screen television and surrounded by the vacant stares of his hunting conquests. But at age 68, lowering himself into his easy chair was no effortless exercise. The maneuver unfolded in stages, like a sequence of snapshots. Knees too acquainted with the touch of a scalpel do not bend as they once could.

"This one's been replaced," he said, tapping the right one, safely ensconced. We had just finished touring the property during my visit in the steamy summer of 2009, concluding the walkabout in a garage filled with every fishing tool imaginable.

The left knee, stretched out, was also going to need a replacement, Reed said, but doctors had advised him to hold out for as long as possible because surgical techniques were constantly improving. In the meantime, he took a daily anti-inflammatory pill and tried not to put undue stress on the leg.

Funny, he said, but that was exactly how the whole storied medical drama of 1970 had begun.

The minutes had piled up in the opening playoff series with the Bullets, and then came the ballyhooed challenge of the Milwaukee Bucks and Lew Alcindor (who wouldn't change his name to Kareem Abdul-Jabbar until 1971) in the division finals. The rookie from New York (a high school legend at Power Memorial on 61st Street) was already a handful in the post. He possessed an unstoppable sky hook, but Reed was much stronger and could muscle him just enough to disrupt his flow. Making Alcindor's playoff homecoming even worse was the booing he endured at the Garden. Maybe the city's basketball fans still harbored a civic contempt for Alcindor's attending UCLA instead of staying home and making St. John's an instant title contender. Stanley Asofsky called that theory "a lot of bullshit." The razzing, he said, was more about the young Alcindor being the enemy of the Old Knicks, plain and simple.

"I don't think he ever liked playing in New York, and it probably was because the fans gave him such a hard time that first year," Reed said. "He was just young, and we were really good."

Offensively, Reed was a nightmare for the UCLA grad. The young Alcindor was loath to switch on screens, and against a team with as many shooters and willing passers as the Knicks, that sort of immobility amounted to playing too long on the railroad tracks. Reed would step outside for jumpers, and when Alcindor deigned to challenge him, he would fake the jumper and go hard to his left.

New York won in five unremarkable games, a welcome breather after the close encounter with mortality in the Bullets series.

Reed's approach against the young Kareem—camp out on the perimeter and dare him to come out—would go double for Wilt Chamberlain in the Finals. After playing in only 12 regular-season games, the man known as Wilt the Stilt or the Big Dipper had made a surprisingly effective recovery from his own knee injury. He had helped the Lakers survive a seven-game challenge from Phoenix in the first round and to sweep Atlanta in the second.

And—unlike the Bucks—the Lakers had superstars in the backcourt and on the front line to offer

Chamberlain support. Nearing his 32nd birthday, Jerry West averaged 31.2 points that season while Elgin Baylor, though no longer the NBA's preeminent high-flier at 35 years old, was still good for 24 points and 10 rebounds a game. They also had abundant NBA Finals experience, having played all seven games the previous spring, in Russell's farewell with the Celtics. But in contrast to the Knicks, the Lakers were not the purest blend of personality and talent. With their top-heavy star system of West, Chamberlain, and Baylor, they more resembled a twenty-first-century NBA team: big names in an uneasy and sometimes fragile coexistence. Production-wise, there was a yawning gap between the haves and have-nots. A rookie guard—Dick Garrett, Frazier's college teammate at Southern Illinois—started alongside West in the backcourt.

In Game 1, for reasons that were related to his health, his head, or both, Chamberlain refused to move away from the basket to contest Reed's midrange jump shot. Reed scored 25 points—in the first half.

The teams split the first two games in New York, but Reed erupted again for 38 points in Game 3, the majority of which put the Knicks in position to win on a possession with the score knotted at 100. They ran one of their staple half-court sets, Bradley on the baseline, moving right to left around screens set by

DeBusschere and Reed. It was the play they called 2-3-F, with DeBusschere drifting out to the free-throw line as a second option while Reed positioned himself in the lane for a rebound.

"Nine out of ten times, Bill would be open, but for some reason, both guys went with Bill and they left Dave alone," Reed said.

Baylor was just a second late hustling after DeBusschere, who caught a pass from Frazier at the free-throw line. He had just enough space to rise and can a 16-foot jumper. Three seconds remained. Joe Mullaney, the Lakers' coach, was out of time-outs.

Chamberlain inbounded to West, not even bothering to make sure both feet were out of bounds. West took three dribbles in the backcourt and, with Reed in his shadow, launched a running one-hander that swished cleanly through the net, sending the L.A. fans into spasms of delirium. Under the basket, a disbelieving DeBusschere put his hands on his head. Chamberlain, heading toward the locker room, apparently thinking the Lakers had won, had to be called back.

A decade later, that shot would have been worth three points, a game winner (though Reed argues that the Knicks' long-range marksmen would have been comfortably ahead had the three-point rule been in effect back then). In 1970, the 55-foot shot simply spelled overtime. The Knicks had to gather themselves for another five wrenching minutes.

"Most teams in that situation, you'd have bet anything they'd lose in the OT. We killed them," DeBusschere would say years later, with imprecise recall. Reed had to break a tie at 108 with a free throw. Dick Barnett, the former Laker, had to pump in the clincher with four seconds left. But DeBusschere's point is well taken. The Knicks defied the natural tendency in that situation to deflate, especially on the road. By winning, they further convinced themselves and their followers that Destiny—having already urged the Jets and Mets to victory—was indeed a New York fan.

West's 37-point, 18-assist masterpiece two nights later evened the series in another overtime classic, though both games in Los Angeles were historically diminished due to the lateness back east; this was long before the NBA fixed Finals start times. The Game 4 loss did not dampen New York's conviction. Nothing could, except one nagging caveat: Willis Reed's health.

The Knicks all knew that the Captain's left knee was barking as the team returned to New York for Game 5. It had been an issue for months and was aggravated earlier in the series when Reed was accidentally kicked there, suffering a bruise.

The team doctor asked him if he wanted a shot to dull the pain.

"No," came the reply. Reed had already taken his share of cortisone and had been warned that the pain-numbing drug could soften the tissue and lead to permanent damage. Reed's threshold was high to begin with, and he figured, or hoped, that the adrenaline of a crucial game would see him through. But with his declining the injection, unseen forces were set in motion, creating a narrative that would stretch the realm of plausibility and define Reed as an exemplar of athletic heroism, the one-legged wonder who stared down the goliath named Wilt.

Even before the sellout crowd of 19,500 filed into the Garden for Game 5, that day—May 4, 1970—had already become a historic day in America; that is, historically bleak. Hours earlier, the National Guard had fired on Kent State University students after several tense days of protest in the Ohio college town. During an afternoon rally on the school's Commons against a Vietnam War that had just been expanded into Cambodia by President Nixon, a multitude of National Guardsmen unleashed 67 rounds into a crowd of students. Four were killed, including two who were merely walking to class.

The tragedy was a defining moment for the antiwar movement and a disaster for America's war hawks. The loss of innocent life could not be ignored, even by professional athletes in the middle of the most important games they'd ever played.

"Up until Kent State, you had to worry about long hair and being against the war," Phil Jackson said. "Then it turned, and people were asking, 'How can this be happening, and all for a war that most people don't know why we're in?' You had to be paying attention to what was going on."

Jackson had already publicly expressed his views on the war, if only by his choice of clothes and length of hair. But he could afford to be distracted by what was going on outside the basketball cocoon. Still on the injured list thanks to Holzman's determination to protect him from the expansion draft, he wasn't playing. And Jackson had an expanding cabal of liberal friends who were shocked by the images they saw that night on the evening news. In the ensuing days, students nationwide would boycott classes. But the rest of the Knicks and Lakers were like millions of others on the night shift who had to go to work.

Steve Albert, brother of Marv, was a college sophomore at Kent State when the shootings occurred, and had fled campus as soon as he could. He caught a late-afternoon flight to Newark and walked into his home on Kensington Street in Brooklyn's Manhattan Beach section while Walter Cronkite was solemnly sharing the horror of what had happened on the evening news.

"I saw it all for the first time that night: the rock throwing, the guns firing," Albert said. "I guess I was in a state of shock." Safe at home, the family exhaled and soon after flipped on the radio for Marv's broadcast of Game 5.

The night before the Kent State shootings, Steve had walked out of the library—the campus already in lockdown, curfew in place—with an armful of books and had a national guardsman's bayonet pointed at his nose.

"What are you doing?" the guard asked.

"A paper, on broadcasting," Albert responded. He was escorted back to his dorm.

Studying to follow Marv into the business that would eventually employ three Albert brothers and later Marv's son, Kenny, Steve was no campus radical. He was not involved in the next day's demonstrations, which formed while he was in a child psychology class that ran from 11 to 1. "We were watching a film, and in it a baby was crying—so we never actually heard the gunshots," Albert said. But a voice thundered on the public address for students to grab whatever belongings they could and exit campus pronto.

Outside, wailing ambulances rolled by—Albert recalled counting nine—and smoke from the guns and tear gas choked the air.

"It was like one of those scenes in a Godzilla movie, where people are fleeing the city," he said. He rushed to his dorm, gathered some things, and hitchhiked to Akron with a friend. The airport was in chaos. He didn't have time to call home, where his parents had already heard that one of the dead students was from Long Island. At the WHN radio studio, Marv scoured the wires, hoping no news was good news, before heading to the Garden. By game time he'd been informed that his brother was home. Naturally, his family's involvement in the debacle was part of the pregame chatter.

In high school, Steve had been a ball boy for the Knicks, like Marv, working special occasions like Bill Bradley's debut and the opening of the new Garden. He missed one game in three years on the job. It was a Tuesday night, and he wanted to watch an episode of *The Fugitive*. "I gave them an excuse that I was sick," he said. Danny Whelan, the irascible trainer, didn't hold it against him. An old wisecracking Navy guy out of San Francisco who had been with the Pittsburgh Pirates when they beat the Yankees in the 1960 World Series, Whelan had a heart of gold. He always liked Steve, felt for what he'd been through after hearing about it from Marv.

Whelan would eventually come up with an idea to soothe Steve Albert's pain. But first there was a Game 5 to play, with home court to desperately defend.

I had tickets to the game that night, courtesy of a friend's relative. My high school graduation was weeks away, and my interest in the antiwar movement was intensifying. I had attended protests in Central Park and sung the angry anthems of the folk singer Phil Ochs. Still, news of the shootings was almost overwhelming. My friends and I were a year away from college ourselves, and some of us had relatives—my cousin Stan, who was like an older brother to me—in Vietnam.

There was a scary, surreal nature to the shootings and a palpable tension in Midtown that evening as my friend and I stepped out of the subway at Penn Station. The late-afternoon editions of the *Post* screamed bloody murder from its front page while we walked into the arena. Upstairs, in the blue seats, the shootings dominated the pregame chatter, especially among the younger fans. As usual, the smell of marijuana wafted through our section. There was a feeling of restlessness in the crowd, an air of pessimism and fear that came close to resignation. With the first quarter under way, it didn't feel appropriate to be expending so much emotion on a basketball game, even one that was billed as the most important ever played at Madison Square Garden.

Game 5 began with a road rush for the Lakers. Eight minutes into the first quarter, they opened a 23–13 lead behind Chamberlain and West. Reed had scored the Knicks' first basket on a soft jumper from the left side of the lane and soon after nearly gave Chamberlain a facial after a strong drive, only to miss the dunk off the back rim. But Reed was persistent: he scored the Knicks' 14th and 15th points by cleverly ball-faking Chamberlain, spinning off his pivot foot, and shielding the ball with his body as he laid it up with his back to the basket.

The problem was that the Lakers were dominating the Knicks at the other end of the floor, looking strong despite their own nagging injuries—a groin pull that Baylor had suffered in practice and a jammed thumb that made gripping the ball a chore for West. After Reed's basket, they promptly scored again to lead 25–15. On the Knicks' next possession, Bradley hit Reed in the middle with a two-hand pass, and Reed immediately drove left as the Lakers' Keith Erickson dropped off Bradley to help. Reed had a step on Chamberlain, and there didn't appear to be contact when Reed suddenly lurched forward and down. The ball squirted loose, into Chamberlain's hands. He shuffled a pass to West. DeBusschere saw Reed hit the floor, writhing in pain, and blurted out, "Oh my God." But the Lakers were off in transition and the four upright Knicks followed, leaving Reed alone and crumpled.

How and why he tore his right tensor muscle, which originates around the hip and extends into the upper thigh, remains something of a mystery. Reed always had his suspicion about what went wrong.

"I think because of the pain in my left knee, I may have instinctively shifted all the weight to my right side as I made my move around Wilt," he said. The one thing there was never any doubt about was the excruciating pain he was in as he lay on the floor. It was etched unforgettably on his face and was captured magnificently by the lens of George Kalinsky.

As it happened, the Garden photographer had just switched courtside positions, as he often would during the course of a game. Call it journalistic savvy, random intuition, or just dumb luck, but Reed crashed not more than a minute later, right in front of him.

Kalinsky was more than a fan of Reed's; he was a friend. Consequently, the photo, while one of his greatest, was also one of the most painful he would ever take. In the *New York Times* the following morning, a grimacing Reed would be captured sitting up, struggling to stand. But in this shot, the *Times* had either missed or not published the most gut-wrenching frame. Working for the Garden, Kalinsky had the much tighter and superior close-up of Reed stretched out, eyes shut, facial muscles contorted, head resting on his right arm.

The Captain was down. For the time being, the horror of Kent State was forgotten. The Knicks were in trouble.

All over the Garden, including along the Knicks' bench and even with the players on the floor, there was the dread of impending defeat. "We thought it was over," Frazier said.

With the season suddenly dangling on the edge of disaster, Holzman sent Nate Bowman into the game. Nate the Snake was something of a foul machine, accumulating more personals during his five NBA seasons than field goals. To no one's surprise, he quickly hacked Chamberlain twice. The Knicks fell further behind and trailed by 16 late in the second quarter. Fearing that Bowman would foul out before the break, Holzman reached deeper into his bench. Several seats away, Bill Hosket was minding his own business when he felt a poke in the ribs from Cazzie Russell.

"Red wants you," Russell said.

Hosket was dumbfounded. He hadn't played a minute in the first four games.

"*Me?*" he implored.

He looked down at Holzman to make sure Russell wasn't mistaken or pulling his leg. Holzman waved him over and put his arm around the strapping blond kid's shoulder. "I knew something was up, because he had never done that before," Hosket said. Only 6'8" and 225 pounds, Hosket would be giving away at least 50 pounds and 5 inches to Wilt. What the hell could he do to stop him? He peeled away his warm-ups to check in. On the way, a pained voice called to him from behind.

"Wilmer . . . Wilmer."

Hosket turned and there was Reed, still on the bench with an ice pack attached to his waist, motioning him over. When they had roomed together during Hosket's rookie year, Reed had taken to calling him by his real name. Around the team, they became known as a tandem, Willis and Wilmer.

"Yeah, Will?"

"Lean on him, Wilmer," Reed said. "Just lean on him."

"Okay, Cap."

When the Lakers set up their half-court offense, Hosket did exactly as he was told. At least he tried. He lowered his left shoulder into Chamberlain's back, affixed his right hand to his waist, and pushed with every muscle he could muster. Chamberlain took one step back as he received the entry pass. Oh my God, I can't believe how strong this guy is, Hosket thought. Chamberlain dribbled, backed in some more, and thrust his behind into Hosket's stomach, literally knocking him out of bounds. In his sweet spot, Chamberlain went up for a trademark finger roll, only, instead of floating through the net, the ball danced off the rim. The Knicks rebounded and took off upcourt. Trailing the play, Hosket gave a quick look to the bench, hoping for a nod of approval from the league's MVP, but Reed was already gone.

Cooling off in the great room, Reed's eyes widened when I casually mentioned that I had come upon a DVD of what Old Knicks loyalists have come to simply call Game 5. It appeared to be a scouting video, incomplete, in black-and-white and with some of Marv Albert's radio play-by-play dubbed in. Given the scarcity of NBA video from those years, Reed was delighted to learn that some form of Game 5 even existed.

"No kidding!" he said. "You know what? I never actually have sat down and watched that game." Not on the night in question—when he remained in the locker room for the second half, listening to Albert's classic call on the radio—or any other night, which amazed me, considering that Game 5 is one of the Knicks' all-time classics.

Once he had pressed PLAY, the first thing he noticed was his limp: faint and unnoticeable to a layman like me. He was certain now that the injury had occurred because he had favored his left knee and leaned too heavily to the right.

When Reed went down, naturally all eyes were on him, but the camera followed the play as it advanced up the court. The ball moved from Chamberlain to West to Baylor on the left side. For a moment it appeared that Baylor would launch a jump shot, until Chamberlain, following the play, lumbered into the picture and the paint. Baylor fed him the ball. A dunk seemed imminent, but before Chamberlain could lift, he was surrounded by DeBusschere and Bradley. They tied him up: jump ball.

This one play, so easy to overlook in the tumult of the moment, spoke forcefully and symbolically about how the masters of improvisation were already banding together, compensating for the loss of their leader before he'd even left the court. "I guess you could say that's what our team was about," Reed beamed as the camera found him again, being helped off by the trainer, Whelan.

The screen went dark for a few seconds. When the players reappeared, DeBusschere was jumping center against Chamberlain to begin the third quarter. The hole-plugging with Bowman and Hosket had ended with about four minutes left in the first half. DeBusschere shifted over from Baylor to play Chamberlain, leaning on the big man for all he was worth, having to peer over his shoulder or around him to keep tabs on the ball. Holzman had realized that no backup center or power forward was going to bail the Knicks out of their dire situation. This was no time to be fighting fire with convention. The Knicks needed a different strategy to challenge Chamberlain, physically and mentally.

Reed had waited in the locker room for the team to come in at halftime. Now the Captain had a ringside seat for the Knicks' halftime discussion. According to Reed, it was Bradley who devised the strategy that would change the course of basketball history.

Old Knicks huddles were always known to be studies in democracy. Holzman's ego never got in the way. He would look around at his players' faces, wanting them to be part of the process. He had no problem asking, "What do you think we ought to do?"

His coaching philosophy was to teach the players, in effect, to coach themselves. He had no interest in being dictatorial, calling every play, or clinging to a particular style because it was his MO. To Holzman, a coach with a so-called system was mostly interested in maximizing his job security, of trying to have it both ways. If the team won, the system was brilliant. If it didn't, the players didn't fit the system. A coach, he believed, could program his players to the point of paralysis. The best of them would invariably figure out the game and make their own decisions.

Holzman didn't burden his teams with an abundance of half-court sets, and his players couldn't recall him ever diagramming a play, but that didn't mean his offense was shallow or predictable. Every play had multiple options, to which Holzman would dedicate entire preseason games in order to make sure his players could execute each and every one in their sleep. As the team grew better, and tighter, often there was no play called at all, just fundamental screen-and-roll movement. The players would communicate with their eyes and body language, five men linked to the central nervous system of the coach, who believed in their basketball IQ and allowed them freedom as long as they followed the scripture: *Make the extra pass, find the open man.*

So Bradley didn't have to twist Holzman's arm, exactly, to rewrite the Game 5 plan. He was never much interested in taking credit for figuring out how the Knicks would approach the second half without their center and most important player. Reed remembered it as essentially a zone offense. Others called it a 3-2 or 1-3-1, but whatever it was, Reed dismissed Bradley's revisionist spin that it was a consensus scheme.

"It was Bradley's idea all the way," he said. In summary, it called for spreading the floor with five players who could all shoot or drive and force Chamberlain to guard someone. Instead of Bowman or Hosket, he would have to pay close attention to the jump-shooting DeBusschere or the athletic Dave Stallworth.

His teammates—and especially Dave DeBusschere—promised that they would somehow make it a game. Years later, in fact, Frazier would contend that if the Lakers had gone on a minor run to start the quarter, the Knicks would likely have psychologically collapsed and surrendered the game, the series, and probably their place in history. But it was the Knicks who came out fast. The team that took the court was no bigger than an average-size college team, but their defensive pressure bothered the Lakers; it unhinged them, really. When they weren't throwing the ball away or having it stolen amid the full-court press, they tried to force-feed

Chamberlain, who was swarmed asunder. More shocking, West disappeared along with the big man. The Lakers maintained a lead throughout the quarter, but the Knicks chipped away.

With less than two minutes remaining, Frazier stripped West at midcourt and cruised in for a layup. The lead was just six, 78–72. As if slipped a massive dose of mood-altering medication, the crowd awoke from its nightlong melancholia.

The Knicks tied the game at 87 on a 20-foot jumper by Bradley and took the lead on the Oxford man's next shot. DeBusschere was in foul trouble, having accumulated five by wrestling with Chamberlain in the low post. Holzman replaced him with Stallworth, who presented a different problem for the tiring giant. At 6'7", Stallworth was longer and more athletic than DeBusschere. Plus he was fresh. He stepped in front of Chamberlain and tapped the rebound of a missed West shot to Frazier, who returned the favor by finding Stallworth on the right side for a driving banker and a 95–91 lead.

There was bedlam in the Garden, an air of insurgency and defiance. Continuing to make good on his vow to redeem himself in the eyes of the Captain, Russell scored the Knicks' next three baskets—including one at the rim, over a flat-footed Chamberlain—as they extended the lead to 101–94. On this signature night for the Minutemen, Russell had 20 points off the bench and Stallworth added 17. But there was one basket by Stallworth that, more than any other, would provide the lasting memory of Game 5 for those who witnessed it live or through the illustrative, auditory magic of Marv Albert.

Russell gave him the ball on the right side, about 17 feet away, with Chamberlain holding his position just outside the lane. Given room, Stallworth had already knocked down two jumpers in the period. The Lakers were desperate for a defensive stop. Chamberlain had no choice but to lug his big body to the last place he wanted to be. Stallworth gave an up fake and put the ball on the floor, already by Chamberlain's hip. One dribble . . . a second . . . and he was in the air, under the backboard, with Chamberlain's left hand up and West dropping down to help. Levitating to the far side of the rim, gripping the ball in his right hand, Stallworth turned in midair and banked in the layup, falling away.

As the years passed and his health waned, Stallworth wouldn't remember much about the shot, or give a damn that he didn't. He just came to believe it was all part of God's plan for him to be back in basketball and with the ball when Chamberlain came out to challenge.

After seeing it for the first time, Reed, smiling like a man who had just opened up a vault of treasure, emphatically called it "the shot of Stallworth's life."

And after Stallworth's basket killed the Lakers' hopes of turning the game back around on the way to a 107–100 victory, Reed dressed in the jubilant Knicks locker room and then hobbled into the team's administrative offices to pick up his mail. While there, he tossed his Game 5 sneakers into the trash. "These weren't very lucky, were they?" he said to the secretary, Gwynne Bloomfield. But she had the good sense to retrieve one of the shoes, place it on her desk, and use it as a plant holder for the rest of her days at the Garden. She took it with her when she left, and Reed signed it for her 25 years later, her lasting souvenir.

Given the benefit of 40 years of reflection and his first Game 5 viewing, Reed had to admit that the night was worthy of keepsakes. He raved about the Knicks' team defense, marveled at how they held Chamberlain to three field goals in the second half and West to 4 points after 16 in the first. He was amazed by how they'd forced 19 turnovers in one half (and 30 for the game) against a team as formidable as the Lakers. Reed was so energized by the ancient video that he had to call Bradley to congratulate him on the effort, as if the game had been played the previous night.

"Senator," he said, "I'm here watching Game 5, 1970, on an old tape. You know what, you guys did a hell of a job that night without me."

He waited as Bradley figured out what the hell he was talking about—it took a few seconds—and had a good laugh.

What it all proved, he said, was that Holzman had been absolutely right to harp all season long on his team to play hard every night, because who knew when that extra home game was going to mean the difference between ecstasy and misery?

"If we hadn't, and I had gotten injured in Game 5 on the road, there is no way we come back to win this game without the Garden fans," he said.

Weeks later, he returned the DVD by mail and sent along a note.

"Thanks for Game 5—our greatest victory," Reed wrote, man enough to acknowledge that what was arguably the most thrilling game—if not the most climactic—in Knicks history was achieved, by and large, without him.

On the morning of Game 6 in Los Angeles, Reed awoke and deluded himself for a few minutes into thinking that a medical miracle had occurred. After getting out of bed and taking a few relatively pain-free steps, he became excited, anticipating that he might be able to play after all. He stood between his bed and John Warren's.

"Hey, Rook, I think I can go tonight," he said.

A groggy Warren, head on the pillow, opened his eyes.

"Really, Cap?"

"Yeah," Reed said. "Watch this."

He jumped up and touched the ceiling, landing with the force of his 240 pounds on his right side. That's when the pain hit him like a comet out of the sky. He fell back onto his bed, grimacing as he had when he first took the Game 5 fall, almost to the point of tears. Warren didn't know which was worse for Reed: the physical distress or the psychic pain of knowing he wouldn't join the team that night.

With Reed still stretched out in agony, the rookie was suddenly the mentor in the room.

"No, you can't play tonight, Cap. You just can't," Warren told him. "Save what you have for Game 7."

10

GAME 7

All day long, New York held its breath, waiting for word. There was no 24-hour sports television or talk radio to consult. No Facebook or Twitter to leak the news. On Friday, May 8, the Garden switchboard was jammed by fans clamoring for medical updates. *O captain, our captain.* At Reed's Rego Park apartment, his high school coach, Lendon Stone, checked in. Fred Hobdy called from Grambling, imploring Reed to give it a try, just as he'd prodded him years earlier to attend the Olympic trials in New York. Again history beckoned.

Reed had flown back to New York with the team's orthopedic surgeon, Dr. James Parkes, after the Knicks took a beating in Game 6. The rookie Dick Garrett took seven shots in the first quarter and made them all, embarrassing his old Salukis teammate Frazier and helping stake the Lakers to a 20-point lead. West had a brilliant night with 33 points, and Chamberlain the best of all of them: 45 points and 27 rebounds. The Knicks didn't play a lick of defense; at the end of the game, their 113 points—robust by twenty-first-century standards—were still 22 short of the Lakers' 135. All the while, Reed rested.

"Doc," Reed told Parkes on the long ride east, "you've got to get me out there. This is the pinnacle of my life."

On Friday, Reed arrived at the Garden at around two o'clock to meet the trainer, Danny Whelan, for 90 minutes of heat treatment. They had lunch in the Garden's Penn Plaza Club, and then Reed called home and told his mother not to worry. He was feeling better and would probably play. He returned to the locker room, which Holzman—fearing a mob—had cordoned off strictly for players and coaches. Reporters gathered on a bench outside and remained for most of the pre-game period. George Kalinsky, loitering nearby with his camera, tried peeking into the Knicks' locker room, hoping for a glimpse of Reed. Instead he kept bumping into Chamberlain, lurking around corners. "I knew Wilt well," Kalinsky said. "He saw me standing out there waiting and kept coming over to ask, 'Is Willis playing?'" It took Jerry West, exasperated, to come and lead Chamberlain away.

Nearing six o'clock, Reed decided to move around a bit, hoist a few shots. Don May was already dressed and agreed to fetch rebounds. Reed walked past reporters, divulging nothing. The reporters—not quite the mob that would have hounded him in the New Media age— gave Reed his space. On the court, he worked cautiously around the perimeter, May feeding him the ball. While under the basket, May noticed an interested observer, a head towering above a row of empty seats. Once again, it was Chamberlain. He stood there, inexplicably, and watched until Reed was finished. Even Reed found the behavior strange, and revealing. On his way back into the locker room, he walked right past Chamberlain and complained lamely to his opponent: "I can't go to my right that well." The truth was, he never could.

By the time he was out of sight, a knowing grin flickered past the pain on Reed's face. The mind game was on, if not already won. "I'll crawl out there if I have to," he told PR man Jimmy Wergeles.

There was still a long way to go to Game 7, and Reed would be spending all of it in the trainer's room. Now it was his teammates who moved in and out of the cramped quarters, inquiring about his condition. Soon Holzman had seen and heard enough. He shut the door, growling that the Knicks had a game to play, Reed or no Reed. Order restored, the team prepared to take the floor while Reed braced himself for three injections of Carbocaine, a powerful derivative of novocaine, administered by Dr. Parkes.

As a child, Reed had hated the sight of a needle, and this one looked like it could do more damage than good. He sat up and put his hands on the back of the training table. He bit his lip. He grimaced but did not howl.

While this was happening, Reed's idled teammate Phil Jackson—working that night as a photographer for a book he would later co-publish with George Kalinsky—had the insider position that even Kalinsky, a Garden employee, didn't have. From just beyond the bare soles of Reed's feet, Jackson snapped a portrait of the injection that has been kept secret ever since. Years later, Spike Lee would offer Jackson thousands of dollars for the negatives. But at Holzman's request— the coach cited Reed's privacy, and he didn't think it was fair that Jackson had access denied the regular shooters—the photo would remain buried among Jackson's treasured possessions.

Reed sat for a moment to let the drug take effect. After a while he swung his legs to the floor, took a deep breath, and tentatively put weight on his leg. He was hurting, there was no doubt about that. But it was just past 7:30 on May 6, minutes from tip-off. Game 7 awaited him, along with his teammates. He stood up and said, "Let's go."

Reporting to Madison Square Garden on a cold winter afternoon in early 2010, a broadcaster named Walt Frazier wore an olive green suit, a pink tie, and a look of Caribbean nonchalance to match his apparent indifference to the occasion for which he'd been summoned. As the person who had requested he report for duty an hour and a half early, I felt slightly embarrassed asking him to review a piece of four-decade-old history, even though Frazier proved the star in what we were about to watch. Game 7. *The* game.

Based on that night alone, my younger version would have been holding out a pad and pen to the Hall of Fame guard, hoping for an autograph. As the longtime New York newspaper basketball commentator, I had found the Garden's legend-in-residence to be gracious and friendly, though often difficult to read. The serpentine Clyde, still with a magnificent mask of cool. In 13 NBA seasons, the man never so much as incurred a technical foul. A financial conservative, it never made pecuniary sense to him to endure a fine for the briefest of outbursts. When the more emotive Phil Jackson wondered how he could have an Imelda Marcos–size budget for footwear, Frazier asked him how he justified the standard cost for unloading on a ref. "At least when I open my closet, I can see where my money went," he replied.

A Garden public relations official had agreed to vacate his office for our viewing of Game 7. While the DVD loaded, Frazier and I sat side by side in front of a flat-screen television, chatting about the dismal state of the Knicks as they continued, in the wake of the Isiah Thomas debacle, a two-year roster purge in anticipation of a free-agent bonanza in the summer of 2010. In the meantime, it was his job to analyze on television the dreck that passed for the beautiful game he and the Old Knicks had played. In calling the games, he still prided himself on never revealing his emotions, or disgust, at what he saw. But he admitted to me, "Man, sometimes it's like watching a different sport."

On the subject of his emotions, Frazier could also admit, years after the fact, that when Willis Reed was named MVP of the 1970 Finals, he was sacrilegiously teed off. "I told everyone it was bullshit," Frazier said. "I was still a young guy, trying to get where West and Oscar were. I remember saying, 'You know, momentum can only carry you so far . . .'"

Still, an incipient smile creased the corner of his mouth as the ABC broadcast began, with Howard

Cosell quizzing Red Holzman on the condition of Reed. His body language changed—he sat up straighter in his chair—and watched raptly. He had not seen Game 7 in years.

It always began the same, with Cosell sending it back to the play-by-play man, Chris Schenkel, for a pregame exchange with the analyst and former Royals star Jack Twyman, while the teams warmed up, waiting for a sign of Reed.

Minutes earlier there had been a false alarm when Cazzie Russell came through the tunnel after receiving treatment for a thigh bruise sustained in Game 6. The crowd erupted—a six-foot-something black man, in uniform, making his way! ("I was always told I resembled Cap—I didn't know what that meant," Russell told me, chuckling at his little white lie about an old black stereotype. He wasn't insulted when the crowd abruptly shut up. "It was like, 'We love you, Cazzie. You're just not who we're looking for,' " he said.)

In the middle of his conversation with Schenkel, Twyman picked up a frantic voice in his earpiece. It was the ABC director Chet Forte, relaying information that Reed had received the Carbocaine injections and was on his way. (When Twyman mistakenly reported that Reed had taken 200 ccs, enough to kill a couple of elephants, the switchboard lit up with incredulous callers.)

So while Twyman continued setting the scene with Schenkel, he kept an eye trained on the tunnel. The Lakers were apparently waiting on Reed as well. When he finally appeared, Chamberlain took a walk in the direction of midcourt to see what was happening for himself. Watching the replay on the television screen next to me, Frazier chuckled at the big man's obvious inability to stay focused on his side of the floor. After all these years, no matter how indifferent he tried to be, the pregame drama remained spellbinding. It was the greatest single moment in the history of the Knicks.

George Lois was driving himself crazy in the first row behind the basket where the Knicks were warming up. If the Knicks won their first championship, it would be akin to the consummation of a first love. It would be achieved with a heroic Willis Reed or without him, either way under extraordinary circumstances.

And what if the Knicks were to lose? Unthinkable as that was, then West and Baylor would finally have their championships and Chamberlain would get to celebrate his second, this time on the Madison Square Garden floor. Much as the Knicks were his guys, Lois worked with and worshipped celebrity athletes nationwide.

Above all, the renowned adman, the darling of Madison Avenue, was a basketball junkie. Whatever the outcome, the spectacle would be one to remember.

Intuitively, Lois knew this was no night to share exclusively with the ref-baiting YMCA ballers. He had to bring his son Harry, who was a few months short of his 12th birthday. Already a huge Knicks fan, he was certainly old enough to appreciate and remember the magnitude of the occasion.

"The whole day, it was, 'Do you think Willis is playing?'" Lois said. He didn't know what to tell his son. He was hoping—no, praying—like everyone else who had watched this team come together piece by piece over the previous six years, who all season long had anticipated its crowning glory, that it was just meant to be. And now this unfathomably shitty luck and interminably torturous wait, made even more agonizing by that uncertainty that attended the Knicks hitting the floor without their center and leader. "We're all standing around thinking, He's not fucking coming," Lois said. "And they destroyed us without him in Los Angeles."

What were the odds, realistically, of the Knicks staging another miracle like the one they'd pulled off in Game 5? "What the hell, you play the game," Lois said.

His seats were on the east end of the arena, first-row courtside, where the Knicks were warming up, the crowd already on the verge of a nervous breakdown. As young fans gifted with tickets in the lower bowl often do, Harry Lois wandered away from his seat and stood inches from the court, watching, waiting, and all wide-eyed as the Knicks shot around.

Jim McMillian was a basketball child of New York City by way of rural North Carolina. "It's not where you're born, it's where you learn the game," he said, proud of where and how he cut his teeth—on the cement playgrounds of East New York, Brooklyn. "I started playing in the eighth grade," he said. "In those days, when you grew up in Brooklyn, you didn't have to leave to go very far to find great competition."

In the early sixties, the neighborhood was a middle- and working-class melting pot. Racially speaking, the basketball courts were a harbinger of the area's rapidly developing white flight, the proprietary sanctuary of the rising black player.

Before long, the new kid from Carolina, Jimmy Mac, was running full-court with the budding playground legends Rodney Parker and James "Fly" Williams, along with a future St. John's star and Knick,

Mel "Killer" Davis. McMillian became a court and classroom star at Thomas Jefferson High. He rejected a scholarship offer to play with Lew Alcindor at UCLA and even spurned the University of North Carolina and its impressive young coach, Dean Smith. All to embrace his adopted city and to play Ivy League ball at Columbia University.

"Being in the city, being near Harlem, you could really pick up a tremendous education that goes way beyond your years here in college," he said. That was never more the case than in 1968, when the campus was roiled by war protests and racial strife ignited by the university's expansion plans, and basketball games became a de facto demilitarized zone. Fortuitously, the '67–68 season, McMillian's sophomore year, happened to be the best in Columbia's history.

A 6'5" forward with a jump shot to die for, he teamed with Heyward Dotson, a Staten Islander out of Stuyvesant High, who, like Bill Bradley, would become a Rhodes scholar. Columbia went 23–5 and was one missed free throw from the regional final.

"Fucking Bruce Metz," I said to McMillian when he picked up the phone, back in his native Carolina, in the Greensboro area.

"You remember that?" he said. "You know, it happened right down here in Raleigh."

"Vividly," I said. Heyward Dotson had come from my West Brighton neighborhood on Staten Island. His sister was in my high school class. Before the Old Knicks, Columbia was the first basketball team we all lived and died with, perishing most painfully in the '68 NCAA tournament when Metz, a guard, missed a free throw against Lefty Driesell's Davidson team in a 55–55 game with two seconds left in regulation. On a transistor radio, I listened disconsolately as the Lions lost in overtime before spanking a very good St. Bonaventure team with Bob Lanier in the regional consolation game.

Still, Columbia finished the season as the sixth-ranked team in America, far and away the number-one basketball story in town. But the Knicks were a play-off team that spring, too, and McMillian occasionally would ride the subway from Morningside Heights to check them out. He was intrigued. "I liked the way they played the game, as a team, because that's the way I learned it—moving without the ball, backdoor, setting screens," he said.

Team player that he was, McMillian was also a three-time winner of the Haggerty Award—given annually to the best college player in New York—and one of three Ivy Leaguers destined for the pros via the first round. (Princeton's John Hummer and Geoff Petrie were the others.)

On March 23, 1970, the Lakers took McMillian with the 13th pick of the NBA draft, which was then held right after the college season and before the professional season had ended. The next day, he attended a banquet to receive his third Haggerty, on the same day the New York Nets of the ABA acquired his rights in a trade after that league's own draft.

Willis Reed, also being honored as the pro player of the year, chatted with McMillian, wondering which league he was leaning toward. McMillian wasn't sure. He thought of himself as an NBA player, but the Nets offered an opportunity to play pro ball in New York. Reed told him—just his opinion—that there was only one place to play, and that was with the best, against the best.

The following week, McMillian signed a three-year deal with the Lakers and was heralded as Elgin Baylor's eventual heir.

As he concluded his senior year, earning his degree, McMillian suddenly had NBA rooting interests on two coasts. "I had been a Knicks fan from the time I started playing," he said. "But now I was a member of the Lakers." To make matters worse, he met Chamberlain, West, and Baylor and they all treated him like a kid brother.

By the time the Finals began, McMillian was on a figurative fence, invested in both teams. By the night of Game 7, he had a ticket that had been provided by the Lakers and a sick feeling in the pit of his stomach. "Who am I rooting for?" he asked himself. He went to the Garden without a clue.

He sat in the lower stands and watched the Lakers jog out, followed by the Knicks, without Reed. The tension was building, along with his discomfort. His head told him that he was an L.A. man now. His heart bled for New York. He reasoned that if the Lakers won the title, he would be joining the NBA champions in the fall, a much healthier environment—he assumed—than the aftermath of another agonizing finish for West and Baylor.

Then Reed appeared.

The fans on the opposite side of the court spotted him coming through the tunnel and rose as if it were the Messiah himself. "It felt like the building rose off the ground 20 feet," George Lois said. "It was like an out-of-body experience."

The line that would be repeated ad infinitum across the decades—*the night Willis limped onto the court*—was a distortion. He didn't limp. Just past the press table, a step onto the court, he brushed past a man in a burgundy sport coat—Sam Goldaper of the *New York Times*. Feeling playful, in control of his emotions, he bumped Goldaper deliberately as the exhilarated crowd came unhinged.

When John Warren turned and saw his roommate seemingly propelled by the roar of the crowd, tears filled his eyes. Chills washed over Bill Bradley. Bill Hosket's heart beat so fast he feared he might have a stroke. Ever pragmatic, emotions in check, DeBusschere sidled up to Russell and casually thrust his chin toward the other side of the floor. "Watch those guys," DeBusschere said. Russell gazed at the Lakers' faces, specifically those of Chamberlain, Baylor, and West. He saw what DeBusschere saw. DeBusschere laughed and said: "We got 'em."

Fans with the benefit of a courtside view would swear on a stack of 1969–70 Knicks yearbooks that they also had turned instinctively to look at the Lakers' side as Reed came out. They would make the same claim as Russell, Frazier, and the others: the Lakers were mesmerized. Chamberlain was stricken. Knicks loyalists would never believe that Chamberlain might merely have been stretching his legs when he took his little stroll. The Lakers were simply whipped by the magnitude of the moment. This aspect of the night would become as much a part of the legend as Willis limping out.

Yet Dick Garrett protested, "I didn't even see him. That stuff was so overrated."

The mere thought was insulting, West said. "I never believed that for a second," he told me. "I actually felt we had an advantage against an injured player. I knew he would play, and I wanted him to." His longtime teammate Elgin Baylor would have no doubt agreed.

The ballad of West and Baylor begins with an interlude of loss. By 1970 they had suffered through a total of seven different NBA Finals (six of them together) that all had one thing in common. As a rookie averaging almost 25 points a game, Baylor's Minneapolis Lakers were swept by Bill Russell's Celtics in the 1959 Finals. After the team moved to Los Angeles and West joined, they did the same dance six more times through the 1960s, the last of which brought the additional ignominy of an MVP trophy granted in a staggering home defeat in Game 7, balloons tied to the rafters above. "You think, By God, will it ever work out?" said West. "It's too painful; I can't go through this again."

While Baylor was in career twilight, West had grown into a giant of the game. Sports pages around the country hailed him as Mr. Clutch (imagine that, without a ring), and the attention only soured him. All he could show for six championship series was "a lot of scar tissue."

And then there was the enigmatic Chamberlain, who was acquired for the '68–69 season to neutralize Russell and instead finished the Finals on the bench, feuding with the coach, Butch van Breda Kolff. Chamberlain had asked out of the final minutes, with the Celtics comfortably ahead, claiming to be in some form of physical discomfort. The Lakers rallied, only to fall excruciatingly short when Don Nelson made a jump shot off a broken play late in the shot clock that bounced high off the rim and back through—"the luckiest shot of my life," he said.

As in most NBA cases pitting coach against star, Chamberlain outlasted van Breda Kolff. But here he was, one year later, facing yet another left-handed Louisianan, another smaller man who, like Bill Russell, was celebrated for his big heart—in this case for just walking onto the floor. The circumstances surrounding Reed were enough to test the most resolute of players—and Chamberlain was not that. From the moment he stationed himself near the court to observe Reed warming up, Chamberlain's body language seemed to ask: Could a basketball game really be this important?

Consider the plight of the Stilt: he'd made his own accelerated and thoroughly commendable rehabilitation and comeback from the torn knee tendons, working hard at the end of the regular season to get into game shape for the playoffs. But who would extol him now for beating up a virtual cripple? It was another in a career of no-win situations. Chamberlain was always supposed to win it all but most often didn't, even back when he centered a Kansas team that was considered a sure national champion—until Chamberlain and the Jayhawks were edged by North Carolina in the 1957 title game. For much of his career, Wilt seemed trapped in a basketball purgatory between the roles of unstoppable force and committed—or Russellesque—team player.

Chamberlain intensely disliked mind games within the game and especially what he considered to be simplistic media typecasting of him as Goliath in short pants. Many people who knew him and were genuinely fond of him believed that his boastful side had more to do with deep-seated insecurities than self-confidence. He was sensitive and quixotic and disinclined to appear consumed by basketball. He wanted to be where the action was. The day before Martin Luther King's August 28, 1963, speech at the Lincoln Memorial, he called his friend Cal Ramsey. "We've got to go to Washington tomorrow," he said, and so they did, with Chamberlain rising above 200,000 civil rights supporters, while Mahalia Jackson and Joan Baez, unmistakable to the masses, sang songs of peace and love.

Unable to string titles together like his rival, Chamberlain went out of his way to convince people that basketball did not define him. He took the opportunity to lecture reporters on the dangers of fueling America's obsession with winning at all costs—a worthy discussion, then and now, but made at a rather questionable juncture: soon after his 45-point, 27-rebound performance in Game 6. Teammates rolled their eyes, chagrined at the latest iteration of Wilt being Wilt. Was he already making excuses for what he feared or expected would happen in New York? One of his teammates told *Sports Illustrated*: "You play the whole season to win, don't you? Isn't that what competition is all about?" Another one, requesting anonymity for fear of coming off disrespectful to a deceased man, told me, "We were dumbfounded. For the second year in a row, it was as if he was saying, 'It doesn't really matter.' After we all—Wilt included—had worked so damn hard to get there."

Long before there was Mars Blackmon or Reggie Miller, before he commanded a row of seats priced by the thousands, Spike Lee, at the age of 13, had the most prized Knicks ticket ever . . . and it was free.

"My father's lawyer—a Mr. Eichelberry—lived down the street from us in Fort Greene and he had season tickets," Lee said. "He knew how much I loved the Knicks, and he promised me that if there was a Game 7, I would get one."

Shelton Jackson Lee was born in Atlanta but moved to Brooklyn as a young child. His mother, a teacher, nicknamed him Spike. His father, a jazz bassist who played for the likes of Bob Dylan and Aretha Franklin, got him his first autograph when Walt Frazier wandered into a club he was performing in. "You're my son's favorite," Bill Lee told the Knicks' stylish guard.

Mr. Eichelberry's tickets were in the yellow section, third level, a marked improvement from the nosebleed seats of blue, where the young Spike typically sat after scraping together the money for a student-discounted ticket.

"At that age I'd go to about ten games a year," Lee said. He would continue going into adolescence, often showing up alone as a teenager and endearing himself to Holzman's secretary, Gwynne Bloomfield. "He'd literally be the first one in the building when the doors opened, this sweet skinny kid who kept talking about how much he loved the Knicks," she said. "After a while, we'd try to find him a seat downstairs, give him the stats. He'd be sitting there an hour before the game and Red would come out and say, 'Who the hell is this kid?' I'd say, 'He's okay, he's here every night.'"

Getting to courtside became more difficult as he got older, when a determined and already media-savvy Lee would work his way down to the baseline during warm-ups and shout out to the likes of Bernard King and the young Patrick Ewing. He'd chat up reporters before being shooed away by security personnel. He came to the next home game and the one after that, promoting himself as a New York University–trained film student, soon to debut his first full-length feature.

Walking down Broadway on the Upper West Side with my wife one afternoon in 1986, there it was: *She's Gotta Have It*, by that Spike guy from the Garden. We joined the line that had formed outside.

Within the movie, the world was introduced to the Mars Blackmon character, soon to be Michael Jordan's commercial foil in a series of Nike commercials. Several years after attaching himself to His Airness, Lee would become ingloriously entangled with the mouthy Miller. During an unforgettable playoff night in 1994, Indiana Bones erupted for 25 fourth-quarter points and turned on Lee, his courtside tormentor, in demonstrative and vulgar retribution. Lee instantly replaced the Lakers loyalist Jack Nicholson as the nation's most conspicuously famous hoops fan.

But he swears he would trade all the notoriety and perhaps the courtside proximity for another Knicks championship sometime in his adult lifetime, though he believes nothing will ever match Game 7.

"I've only been to one other game like that—the first one in New Orleans after Katrina, Saints versus Falcons," he said. "It's one of those things where you can see it in the body language of a team: 'Why do we have to be the one scheduled to play here this game? Why us?' That's where the Lakers were that night. They knew there was no way they were going to beat the Knicks in the Garden."

Lee was one of the many who claimed to have "instinctively turned" to look at the Lakers and seen them transfixed, with expressions of despair, after Reed walked on. How that was possible from the yellow seats or any beyond those in the first few rows is another story, one about the repetitive and hypnotic powers of legend.

While Lee's films have often brazenly confronted race in America, he said it wasn't a black-white thing that night, even though West had largely been the media's sole focus. Rooting for the Old Knicks was, for Lee, largely a color-blind experience (though don't get him started on how the Knicks organization and the basketball world at large shortchanged Dick Barnett).

"In Fort Greene, most of the kids thought that Cazzie should start over Bradley," he said. "I used to argue with them that Bradley deserved to start because he fit in better and that Cazzie was better coming off the bench. I love Bill Bradley. He's my man. I had a fund-raiser for him at my house. But I loved Walt Frazier more. I mean, I don't care who the Lakers put on him that night: no one was going to stop him."

Also a Mets fan back in the day, Lee said he ran onto the field in celebration three times during the 1969 season and that he skipped school three days in a row to attend Games 3, 4, and 5 of the World Series. He relished Joe Namath and the Jets. But in terms of shaping his lifelong sports addiction and his willingness to go anywhere for a fix, nothing made an impression on him like those Knicks, and especially Game 7.

"Of all the sports teams in New York, they may be the most beloved, the one we can be most proud of," he said. "I mean, look at the kind of game they played—it was great to have that kind of sharing, especially in those days. But it wasn't just how they played; it was who they were, all the things they all went on to do.

"That whole year or so seemed like a dream, and by the time we got to the Knicks, you just believed they had to win, that it was fate. That night, it was pandemonium. And I think it meant something more than it would now, because in those days you were a fan of your home team. Today, you see every team on television every night. You can follow any team or player. It's just different."

Not for him, he said, though the sight of Lee fraternizing with visiting superstars, the shoe-company chosen ones, has become part of the Garden scenery and show—and a self-promotional career score. But when we spoke during the 2009–10 season—another miserable one for the Knicks—Lee was still ruing the missed opportunities of the Patrick Ewing era, when he had to watch Hakeem Olajuwon and the Houston Rockets snatch a championship away in Houston (he was there) and the San Antonio Spurs win their first NBA title on the Garden floor five years later.

By the end of the first decade of the twenty-first century, Lee had already spent a not-so-small fortune on his two Knicks season tickets but come away with little more than an aching heart. He was still waiting for another night like the one with Mr. Eichelberry.

"When you're a kid and something like that happens," he said, "you really think life is always going to be that good."

There is a classic shot of Reed's dramatic appearance, striding toward his teammates before they have even looked up to see him coming. You can see it blown up in the Garden lobby, on a wall of its chosen "Great

Moments." Just like the Game 5 shot of him stretched out in agony, the photograph was taken by the persistent George Kalinsky, who never strayed from his pregame post and trailed Reed as he made his way onto the floor.

Once again, thanks to judicious positioning, Kalinsky's photo was a gem, an angle all his own. "I walked out behind him—never heard such passion in a crowd," Kalinsky said. "Of course, I didn't know what the photo would mean in terms of the game and history, because if the Knicks had lost, it wouldn't have meant as much."

Still, he'd had the presence of mind to wide-frame the shot to show Reed on the way to joining his teammates as they were getting on with their business—without him, for all they knew. In Kalinsky's photo were other photographers in their conventional positions on the baseline, shooting Reed straight-on but failing to capture the profound symbolism of Reed to the rescue. And of course, Kalinsky's photo included the fans, most on their feet, a roaring welcoming committee that included a dark-haired boy near the basket, in a white shirt, hands spread apart in mid-clap. Little Harry Lois.

Familiar with many of the courtside regulars and naturally those more full-throated and famous,

Kalinsky had previously shot George Lois and sons—Luke was the younger one, seven years old at the time and, for reasons neither he nor his father could recall or explain, not present for Game 7. When Kalinsky developed his photo of Reed's entrance, he recognized the very conspicuous Harry, made a copy, and gave it to Lois, who took the photo home. It rests quietly now in the drawers of family lore, a keepsake from one of the most famous sports occasions in the history of the city.

Eight years later, it would come to represent something else entirely, a tribute to a life tragically cut short.

Harry Lois went on from Game 7 to become an excellent basketball player in his own right at the McBurney School on the Upper West Side. He left Franklin & Marshall after a year to pursue his dream of producing in television shows and movies. He was 16 days past his 20th birthday when his heart gave out, a victim of arrhythmia, on September 21, 1978.

"He was gone before he hit the floor," Luke Lois said. In the conventional mold, his big brother had been his "abuser and protector . . . but we had also reached the point where we had found things in common—and going to the Knicks games was one of them. We'd become really good friends. Then, boom, everything was destroyed. It was devastating."

"It was like the Hank Gathers thing," George Lois said, referring to the Loyola Marymount basketball player who collapsed and died during a 1990 game. "But how do you make any fucking sense of it?"

Who so cruelly fated to lose a child ever has? But the cliché born of fact is that life goes on, grief wanes, and it becomes possible to smile again while gazing at a snapshot of long-lost boy in a state of unadulterated and unchanged joy.

"I have this photo," George Lois says. "And all you can see is this young kid clapping as Willis comes out, the happiest fucking guy in the world."

While the crowd went bananas, Reed was dealing with his own anxieties. "I'm trying to play against the greatest big man, only guy to score 100, average 50," he said. "I'm playing on one leg." As he warmed up, he refused to look at the Lakers, because he didn't want to share his emotions or doubts. He already knew how limited he would be when he'd warmed up with May. While his teammates fired up practice jumpers, he flexed his right leg, and soon went to the bench for the player introductions. When he followed DeBusschere and Bradley, the fans stood and cheered for about a minute while John Condon on the public address mic had the strategic good sense to let the ovation build while the Lakers fidgeted on the other side of the floor.

Surrounded by his teammates, Reed trudged to center court for the opening tap and shook hands with Chamberlain. Game 7 began with Reed conceding the game's first possession, too tender to jump.

Chamberlain sent the ball to Baylor, who found himself open at the free-throw line. Air ball. The action moved to the other end, with Bradley giving to Frazier, who spotted Reed just inside the key, about 18 feet out. In the lane, Chamberlain made no attempt to move out and contest the jump shot, even after Joe Mullaney had begged him beforehand to not give Reed the room to do the one thing at the offensive end he still could. Reed's quick release gave the Knicks a 2–0 lead, but more important, the basket gave everyone in the building more reason to believe something special was playing out before them. "Look at him limp," Chris Schenkel told the national audience, playing up the angle of the wounded warrior as Reed moved back on defense with a wooden-legged gait.

After Chamberlain tied the game with a put-back basket and Bradley hit a free throw, the Knicks again moved into a half-court set. Frazier passed to DeBusschere out front. On the right side this time, Reed again was open, and Chamberlain was too late stepping forward. With the familiar follow-through of the left hand, Reed launched his second shot and hit nothing but net. The fans were beside themselves, standing, jumping, stamping their feet. "You're five stories above the ground and I swear you could feel the vibrations," Reed said. "For a minute I thought, This is what an earthquake must feel like."

Forty years later, watching Reed come out again, Frazier was still amazed by how the scene played like a Hollywood script, except that it was perfectly real.

"It was like a giant wave that came out of nowhere," he said. "We always believed Willis would play, but until he was out there . . ."

On the screen, Reed was crossing the press table, bumping the *Times* reporter Goldaper. "You get goose bumps, even though you know what's going to happen," Frazier said. Years of reflection and the maturity of a man nearing his 65th birthday had also given him a clearer picture, a greater perspective. Reed, Frazier could admit now, had to be the MVP.

"He made it all happen by setting the atmosphere, the ambience," Frazier said. "I watch this now and I see that if Willis didn't do what he did, I would never have had the kind of game I had. When he made those shots, there was no way we were going to lose. For me, it was as if a veil was removed and everything in front of me was crystal clear. I became the open man."

A couple of months earlier, I had tracked down Dick Garrett at his Milwaukee home, called, and said that I wanted to talk about Frazier and Southern Illinois and, inevitably, Game 7. He laughed and said, with no detectable ruefulness, "Oh, *that* game. Yeah, I remember that one."

Through the years, when Garrett wanted to relive his days at Southern Illinois, educate his now grown sons on the marvel that was Walt Frazier, his teammate, he would turn to a VHS tape of their double-overtime victory at Louisville with its All-Americans Wes Unseld and Butch Beard. "There's the point in that game when we just give the ball to Walt and get out of the way," Garrett said. "A beautiful thing to watch."

But that was college ball. As a second-round draft pick who wound up starting alongside West, Garrett quickly developed an appreciation for what it took to be an NBA superstar. West was a different breed from Frazier, he said, more self-made, a striver. "I never saw a guy with the drive that Jerry had. Never took a day off. He made a young guy like me work so much harder." Years later, trying to instill that ethic in his sons, Garrett would explain to them how, in following the West Virginian's lead, he would run so hard that he'd eventually have to make a mad dash to the bathroom to throw up.

Frazier took an antithetical approach, his intensity locked away in a biological vault to rival Tim Duncan's. But as much as anyone, Garrett could speak to the presence Frazier had just by stepping onto the floor and going about his business with the gliding grace of a dancer.

"Back then, it was cool to be cool," Garrett said. "With Walt, there was no rah-rah, no trash talk. He just played." Garrett, a loyalist, considers Frazier to have been every bit as good as Oscar and West on any given night, even if his career statistics suggested otherwise. "You don't think Walt could have scored 30 points a game if he'd needed to or wanted to?" Garrett said.

In the first six games of the '70 Finals, Frazier averaged less than half that, 14.5, a shade better than Garrett's 13.8, while heeding Holzman's wishes. "Hit the open man, Clyde," the coach had reminded him throughout the playoffs, and especially during the Finals. The game plan had been to spread the floor, make everyone on the Lakers labor defensively, and exploit Chamberlain's unwillingness to move out of the lane. Forced to tail Frazier one-on-one, Garrett took pride in the fact that Frazier, to that point, hadn't broken loose.

"Going into the seventh game, I thought I'd had pretty good success, held my own," Garrett said. In fact, at the top of the ABC telecast, Twyman noted that Garrett's perfect first-quarter shooting had been the key to the Lakers' Game 6 blowout. With Dick Barnett on West, he said, Frazier probably believed he could roam free for steals with impunity, but the rookie had made him pay.

Frazier had a slight size advantage on Garrett, an inch taller at 6'4" and 15 extra pounds at 200. "But he was really strong," Garrett said. "The last thing you wanted to let him do was back you down. I was trying to pick him up full-court, just be in his jock as much as possible. A lot of times he wouldn't start off trying to score. But in Game 7, I knew when he began hitting jump shots and looking for the basket it would be a long night. With Willis hurt, it was as if he came out with the idea of saying, 'Here is the true Walt Frazier.'"

Frazier, meanwhile, hated that a friend stood in the way of his championship ring. He never wanted to like anyone he was playing against. He preferred being matched up with West (who would eventually take a turn guarding him that night to no avail).

"Dick was one of the nicest guys you'd ever want on your team," Frazier said as the action picked up following Reed's game-opening jumpers. "When things started going my way, I really had to concentrate on not thinking about what I was doing to him. That's why I never wanted to be friends with any of our opponents, because stuff like that can get inside your head."

Early on, Frazier used the move he'd copied from Barnett, up-faking Keith Erickson in transition, then timing his own leap to get the shot off while trying to draw a foul. He nailed a jumper for a 7–2 lead. Next he went to the defensive glass, dribbled out of the pack, and hit DeBusschere, who in turn found Bradley for a 15-footer. It was 9–2 Knicks, and the Lakers called time-out.

Switching to his commentator persona, it struck Frazier that we were watching a game largely antithetical to the one he would be covering from his broadcasting chair later that night. "The first thing you notice right away is the ball movement—much more dishing before the swishing," he said. "I mean, we're not doing anything out there that's so complicated: screen, backdoor, move the ball, look for some options if they overplay." But something else was about to become clear. As well as the Knicks had collectively started the game, Frazier was on fire, in all facets.

His two free throws gave the Knicks a 13–6 lead. A left-side jumper was followed by a spin move on Garrett, who fouled him: basket good, 3-point play, 24–14. He dribbled behind a DeBusschere screen and hit another jumper, 28–15. With the Knicks leading 32–23, Reed set a high screen. Frazier took one dribble and pulled up behind it.

"See there?" he said. "Garrett went under." And, predictably, Chamberlain made no effort to help. So Frazier calmly stepped back and sank another jumper. When the first quarter ended—38–24, New York— Frazier had 15 points on 5-for-5 shooting from the floor, 4 rebounds, and 4 assists. Twyman was no longer raving about the Dick Garrett effect.

For his part, Frazier insisted that he made no conscious decision to dominate the ball or the game. "By this point I was just happy that everyone was into it and we didn't feel like we had to bug Willis anymore about how he felt," he said. "Red kept asking, but that was just to see how much he could play."

Reed was persevering, not scoring after those first two baskets, shooting only three more times in the game, but contributing with rebounds and picks and by willing his numbing hip to move laterally as a defensive shield. After his Game 6 eruption, Chamberlain's meager 21 points in Game 7 would baffle historians.

In our telephone conversation, even Garrett wondered why the Lakers hadn't gone to him more. But a close inspection of the video suggested that they did run much of their offense through the low post—17 times in the first half alone.

The problem was that Chamberlain wasn't doing much of anything with the ball, not that the Knicks were making that great a collective effort to stop him. "We weren't doubling him," Frazier said. "Red kept telling us, 'Stick with your man.' If he got hot, yeah, but Wilt hadn't done anything." With Reed pressing him, a strangely reticent Chamberlain would take a dribble or two into the paint before turning back, looking to pass, or settling for a contested finger roll. On nine first-half shot attempts, he scored the grand total of two field goals.

Did Chamberlain's lack of aggression have anything to do with his pregame preoccupation with Reed? Garrett recalled Mullaney exhorting his big man during time-outs to pick up the pace before it was too late. But, as Frazier said, he was feeling it now, on a fantasy roll. For the Lakers, it already was too late.

Early in the second quarter, in a free-flowing and gambling mood, Frazier swiped a pass headed for Chamberlain, broke upcourt, and fed Bradley for a layup. Twyman noted that the Knicks, now leading

42–25, were shooting 72 percent. "They had to be thinking that wouldn't last," Frazier drolly noted. But Mike Riordan came off the bench to bang home a long jumper, and then came a virtual backbreaker, a microcosm of the Lakers' game-long misery.

West was dribbling at midcourt, guarded by Riordan, when Frazier suddenly appeared like a thief on a darkened street. He poked a hand into West's midsection and pried the ball loose, and went on his way. Red-faced, West gave chase. Frazier went in from the left side and up with the right hand. West raked him across the shoulder. The ball rolled in. With the free throw, the lead reached 20, 51–31. "Don't even know how I got that one," Frazier said, marveling at himself.

Pressured by Riordan, again at midcourt, West turned the ball over yet again, stepping back across the line. "See how tentative they are?" Frazier said, pointing to the Lakers on the screen. "That's where I knew we had them. West was out of it, all discombobulated. They had no leader. And the rest of them are just standing around, watching West and Wilt. It looks like Baylor's not even out there. Wilt killed him, man, clogging up the lane. You could feel the tension between them."

The performance by West was particularly baffling, with most of his 28 points and 6 assists coming after the Knicks' early deluge. "I don't know, it looks like kind of a halfhearted effort, like he already knew they were going to lose," Frazier said. When he followed up a jumper with another smooth drive to the rim just before the half, Frazier had 23 of his eventual 36 points in what would become, with 19 assists and 5 steals when it was all over, arguably the greatest Finals Game 7 performance ever.

Now the lead was 67–38, and then 69–42 as the teams left for intermission. You didn't have to be Walt Frazier—or a basketball history buff—to know the Lakers were whipped. "I've seen enough," Frazier said. Work beckoned, but he still managed a parting shot: "It's amazing: when they got Wilt, I remember thinking, How will they ever lose a game? You watch this and think, How the heck did they ever win one?"

On the night of Game 7, ABC delayed its telecast in the New York City area until after the late-night news, as part of an agreement with the NBA. These were the embryonic days of cable television, and the deal was mainly a concession to the league's big-market owners—especially Jack Kent Cooke of the Lakers— who were already afraid that television broadcasts would hinder their attendance. So it was that the eyes that bore witness to the championship for most Knicks fans in the New York metropolitan area belonged to Marv Albert, who was calling the game on the radio.

Born Marvin Philip Aufrichtig in 1941, Albert was the oldest of three brothers growing up in Brooklyn's Manhattan Beach section. By the time he attended Lincoln High School and Syracuse University, he had already glimpsed his future, having served as a Knicks ball boy while spending hours in his bedroom filling tapes with play-by-play calls of imaginary games and those he watched on television with the sound turned down.

He knew the game, having played some as a kid. He honed his skills with a microphone under the tutelage of Marty Glickman, the onetime track star and Albert's predecessor on Knicks radiocasts for 21 years. The timing of his career could not have been better. By 1970, Albert's most famous call—"Yes!" for a basket—was a school-yard staple all over New York, but he had lifted it from a ref. "There was an official in the NBA in the fifties named Sid Borgia," he told me. "He was very animated and would go through gyrations when someone scored a basket. He would say, 'Yes!' and if a guy was fouled, 'And it counts.'" Early in his Knicks broadcasting career, during a playoff game, Dick Barnett hit one of his patented fallback jumpers that banked in at the end of a quarter. Excited, Albert blurted out, "Yes!" It seemed like a natural call for such a moment. He incorporated it into his repertoire, and soon people began acknowledging him as the Knicks' Yes Man. Later, he would add "And it counts" to his call of a basket and a foul. Albert became a New York institution destined for national network popularity.

"Game 7 was the largest radio audience at the time for a sports event," he said. "People were sitting around their kitchen table, listening to the radio, just like the old days."

Nervous, biting my nails, and unwilling to deal with even the most serious familial interruptions, I locked myself in my 1961 Mercury Comet, purchased the previous summer for $500 and parked in the resident lot of the West Brighton Houses on Staten Island's north shore, waiting for word on Willis. If I could relive the experience, I wouldn't want it any other way. Wouldn't want the 24-hour *SportsCenter* updates, the continuous sports-radio white noise, the Twitter updates from the sportswriters camped out in the locker room corridor. Just Marv and me, with my chips and Royal Crown cola, the engine not running to save the little gas I had in the tank.

The car battery had burned out by halftime, but so had the Lakers. Nine days shy of my 18th birthday—at that time the legal drinking age in New York City—I met up with friends to get a head start. We shared our various radio locations and adventures. "Walt Frazier," I remember someone saying, several sheets to the wind, "is God."

Once again, the city was relishing the result of another sports event on a day when one needed 200 ccs of Carbocaine to the brain to get good and numbed to the harsh political reality. Much earlier, at a noontime student antiwar protest in the city's Financial District, construction workers had started a melee that resulted in about 70 injuries. The hard-hats didn't stop there, rushing City Hall, where they forced officials to raise the American flag to full staff from half, where it had been since the shooting deaths of the four Kent State students. Police offered no resistance. With war protests raging, President Nixon planned a nationally televised news conference to defend the troop movement into Cambodia, during which he would promise to conclude the incursion by June.

Those days, I cast my own wary eye on the draft lottery while waiting for precious dispatches from my cousin and surrogate big brother in Vietnam. But to step inside Madison Square Garden was to grab hold of a lifeline to an alternate world of harmonic order and balance. Black men and white men from north and south, east and west, worked together for the common good, with purpose, commitment, and intelligence. It was a time in

America when the generation gap may have never been wider but a Knicks game could bridge even the widest. It was Broadway's rendition of what the country aspired to be but obviously, and painfully, was not.

"In life, it's very difficult to get to the mountaintop, because one day leads to another day and leads to another day," Bradley would tell me years later. "There are small wins and losses in the process. You win an election or lose an election. You can close a deal or not close a deal. But in sports, what you can do as a team, and with your fans feeling part of it, is show what's possible for human beings to achieve if they work together, if they care about each other. Winning the title gave resolution to people who didn't have much resolution in their lives, at a time when resolution was something they really needed."

Late in the ABC broadcast, which was live in Los Angeles, Schenkel told his audience to stand by after the telecast for the president's address. But Knicks fans were to be forgiven if they preferred to savor every last second before letting the real world intrude on their triumph. Like me, they were likely reliving the whole thing in an inebriated state of euphoria.

As he sat alone in his apartment, a University of Denver grad student glued to his television and the

Game 7 massacre at Madison Square Garden, Richard Lapchick was filled with warmth in a way that far
transcended the meaning of any one game. More than
the manner in which his team was winning, his joy was
tethered to the gratification of knowing that his father
was there watching.

Joe Lapchick, who had already suffered multiple
heart attacks, had survived to see his beloved Knicks—
the team he had coached to the NBA Finals three times
in the early fifties—finally win a championship. How
well they played made the man who had also put St.
John's University on the basketball map "want to rip
out the mooring of my seat," as he told the author Pete
Axthelm for his book *The City Game*, in 1970.

"They are the meeting point of the old and new in
the sport," Joe Lapchick said. "You really have to know
and understand basketball to enjoy some of the things
they are doing out there. This is the greatest basketball
team I have ever seen."

Such gushing from the impassioned or the provincial
had to be taken with at least a tacit nod to Russell and the
rest of the Boston cast, but in the case of Joe Lapchick,
one of the sport's first iconic figures, who was going to
tell him he didn't know preeminence when he saw it?

He was a Celtic in his own right, a member of the
Original Celtics, barnstormers out of New York City

in the 1920s and 1930s, often with the all-black New York Rens. In most places, the Rens would have to take their meals and slumber on the bus. One time, a gas station owner shooed the whole traveling squad off with a rifle. In places where a riot was entirely plausible at the sighting of a white man hugging a black, Lapchick, who jumped center at 6'5", would embrace his Rens counterpart, Charles "Tarzan" Cooper, prior to tip-off. Later, his contributions to basketball's integration would go far beyond mere demonstrations of racial comity.

As far back as 1947, Lapchick made a presentation to the league to have the Rens crash its color line by entering intact. No, thank you, he was told. Undeterred, Lapchick three years later, in his role as Knicks coach, put a contract in front of Nat "Sweetwater" Clifton, a former member of the Rens. Clifton became the first African American to sign with the NBA. The news was not universally welcomed, even in Lapchick's hometown of Yonkers. Young Richard awoke one morning to look out the window to find his father hung in effigy from a tree in the family's front yard. People called only to sneer "nigger lover" and hang up.

Richard's values were admittedly shaped by his father's acts of virtue. An aspiring player, he went off to basketball camp one summer and befriended a towering, skinny kid named Lew Alcindor. One day a problem arose between Alcindor and another boy. A racial epithet fouled the air. Lapchick objected, took a pummeling for his trouble, and made a friend for life. In 2009, when Jesse Jackson's Rainbow Coalition was preparing to honor Lapchick as a human rights activist and for his relentless efforts in promoting racial equity in sports, Kareem Abdul-Jabbar called. "Please let me be your presenter," he said.

On his desk at the University of Central Florida, where Lapchick was named endowed chair of the DeVos Sport Business Management program in 2001, is a keepsake one of his father's trainers gave him after finding it in a pawn shop in Detroit: a blue-and-white street sign, Eighth Avenue and 50th Street, site of the old Garden, where Joe Lapchick coached and where Richard went religiously to watch Clifton and others forever change a game that kept getting better. By 1969–70, it couldn't get any better in New York.

"Symbolically, for me, that Knicks team definitely represented the attitudes I developed growing up," Richard Lapchick said. "As someone who thinks about race almost every day of my life, I would say that a major allure of that team, looking back, was that it was so mixed, black and white working so well together, and so beloved at a time and place when it was important for people to see that. I think that has been one of the beautiful things about sports: it has allowed African Americans to be embraced for their qualities, contrary to the stereotypes many Americans believed in. Willis, especially, smashed a lot of that with his courage and sacrifice."

Three decades after Reed walked out of the tunnel and the Knicks owned the town, Richard Lapchick would think of them not long after terrorists forever scarred the downtown skyline on 9/11. Weeks later, New York turned to a baseball team to help it cope and move forward.

"I hated the Yankees all my life, but at that moment after the twin towers were destroyed, I was rooting for them because they were helping," he said. "Sports teams can do that. A football team at Virginia Tech helped that community after the shootings just by bringing people together. I have always believed the Knicks had that effect on New York during a difficult period in the country."

Having followed the Knicks from the time he could bounce a ball, Richard Lapchick had watched Reed and the others take their first toddler steps and grow into a team he would always relish, respect, and remember. Receiving the live broadcast on May 8, 1970, in the Mountain Time Zone, he smiled at the thought of the old coach witnessing the summary essence of his lifetime intentions.

"I'm so glad my father lived long enough to see it," he said.

Joe Lapchick, 70, died of a heart attack in Monticello, New York, on August 10, 1970, three months after the Knicks beat the Lakers in Game 7.

Competitively speaking, the second half of the Knicks' 113–99 victory was as anticlimactic as a clock counting downward.

With the Knicks coasting, Schenkel and Twyman sounded particularly stricken for West, though not so much for Baylor, who arguably deserved more pity as the older player less likely to have another chance at a title. They avoided the observation that West had not exactly risen to the occasion of this Game 7 in his seventh losing championship series—or Game 5, for that matter. West had been the third best guard on the floor, behind Frazier and Barnett, who scored 21 points and played solid defense against him.

"I was there, sitting with Larry Fleisher," said Kevin Loughery, the Bullets guard, referring to the legal muscle behind the players' union, whom Loughery was serving as vice president. "In all honesty, the Lakers quit in that game. Even Jerry didn't play hard, I'd have to say."

For an NBA colleague to offer such an indictment of the proud legend —who a year later would become the model for the league's silhouetted logo—was almost unthinkable. Teammates like Mel Counts and Garrett were quick to defend West—and Chamberlain and Baylor. They would point out that with all the attention on Reed, the Lakers' own medical woes were grossly overlooked. Chamberlain was not in peak condition after rushing back from surgery. Baylor's groin was groaning. While Reed was taking the most celebrated injections in NBA history, West was given shots in both aching hands—not the most ideal conditions for a man who was expected to shoot the ball 25 times and handle the ball on the majority of possessions.

West was not one to dwell on injuries or excuses. To him, the '70 Finals was another botched opportunity, another swift kick where it hurt the most. "I look back on that Knicks series and what I remember is that we'd get in position and everything that could go wrong would," he said. "People shooting the ball who shouldn't have been, turnovers, missed free throws."

Over the decades, the miscues had blurred with the misery, but if there was one lasting impression, one haunting echo, it was the collective voice of the Madison Square Garden fans. "I could not hear that well for a few days after that seventh game; that's how loud that crowd was," he said.

In the final minutes, the Garden faithful chanted, "It's all over now" and "We're number one," quaint and tame sendoffs compared with more contemporary taunts. Still, Jim Trecker, the Garden's play-by-play typist at the scorer's table, knew a New York mob was nothing to trifle with. With about 90 seconds to go, he picked up his typewriter—the gig required he bring his own—and wedged himself between the edge of the table and Holzman.

Working a college game, Trecker had already had one machine ruined when a young Army coach named Bobby Knight furiously kicked the table and sent his Royal portable flying. The Garden replaced it, but Trecker wasn't about to lose another. During a lull in the action, he made a dash for the tunnel on the opposite side of the floor. Kneeling against a wall, he watched as the 19,500 fans were treated to the final home-team basket—one last study in sharing, and one that was as distinctively Old Knicks as any in the franchise's first championship season.

Reed had already left the floor, but the other four starters remained to finish the job. Now the ball moved around the perimeter in a game of keep-away—DeBusschere to Bradley to DeBusschere to Frazier to

Bradley to Frazier. With the shot clock winding down, Frazier drove along the left baseline as Barnett slipped into the lane just below the free-throw line. Frazier delivered the ball. Barnett's kick-back jumper from 13 feet registered Frazier's 19th assist.

Game and season ended soon after, with the ball in DeBusschere's hands. The players dashed for the tunnel, trying to beat the crowd surging onto the court. Inside, DeBusschere went straight for Reed and planted a kiss on the big man's cheek.

When the Knicks triumphantly reached the locker room after Game 7, the first person they saw was Steve Albert, who had been invited by Danny Whelan to "help out with things" on the bench and in the locker room for the night, to distract him from the Kent State nightmare. But beyond Reed's first jumpers, and the mind's highlight reel of Frazier's excellence, the game nevertheless remains a blur. "I've watched it on tape and see myself running back and forth, picking up the warm-ups," he said. "And that's what I really remember most: Danny telling me near the end of the game to collect them and get them into the locker room because it's going to be a madhouse at the final buzzer. So that's what I did. I never actually saw the end."

In a development that would be unfathomable in the twenty-first century and that bespoke a nobler time before television had seized sports in its iron grip, ABC was refused entry to the Knicks' celebration. Howard Cosell set up camp nearby, informing viewers that he was in the "quietude" of the Rangers' locker room due to the "diminution" of the Knicks' champagne-soaked quarters.

The players were funneled in, Frazier first, with his muttonchop smile. When Cosell told him he and the Knicks were finally champions, Frazier added: "Of all the world." When Cosell asked Barnett how he'd managed to float his driving shots over Chamberlain's elastic reach, Barnett responded as only he could: "I see dollar signs up there on the basket." (The Knicks' collective take for winning the title would be $118,000, or less than $10,000 per man.)

Bradley came in with DeBusschere, Cosell several times fawning over Bradley's verbal acumen—which in Cosell's mind was second only to his own. DeBusschere flashed his dimpled smile and said the title was "a long time coming." Finally, Reed appeared after having been preoccupied by a ringing telephone in the locker room that was answered by Phil Jackson. It was the White House calling: even as Nixon prepared for his televised address, he found a few moments to congratulate the series MVP. To no one's surprise, and Frazier's chagrin, it was Reed.

The party moved uptown to the Four Seasons on East 52nd Street—Reed's favorite restaurant. "DeBusschere was putting them down, I do remember that," Reed said. In pain, Reed stayed for about an hour before hailing a cab. He eased himself into the backseat, went home to his apartment in Rego Park and straight to bed. With the Carbocaine still coursing through him, he fell into a strange, fitful sleep.

Did those first two shots really fall? Did it all really happen? Reed might have slept for a week after all he'd been through, but sometime after ten the next morning—Saturday, May 9—a car pulled up in front of his building. Holzman was inside, and so was Marv Albert. The appearances at a chain of toy stores had been prearranged—win or lose. At the various outlets in Queens and Long Island, thousands would line up for autographs. Reed was aching and exhausted—"really out of it," according to Albert. But duty called. The Captain of the newly crowned NBA champions showed.

He was feeling better several days later when he went to Leone's restaurant to be honored as the Finals MVP, an award from the old *Sport* magazine that came with a new car, a Dodge Charger. The joint was jammed with reporters, including *The Boys of Summer* author Roger Kahn, and a buddy who had tagged along, Zero Mostel.

"Mostel was the first guy on the Upper West Side we knew with cable TV, and he used to have people over to his place on 86th and Riverside to watch some games," Kahn told me. "Entertainers, writers. So I tell him I'm going to see Reed get his award and he says, 'Can I come?' I said I doubted they'd mind. We walk in and the basketball people spot him right away and ask him to sit on the dais and say a few words. He gives me a look and he says, 'Can you write me something quick?'"

Kahn told him to be serious, get up and ad-lib like the paid professional he was. When the time came, the once-blacklisted actor stood up, looked out at the roomful of reporters and various sports heavyweights, and said that he, like the late Martin Luther King, had a dream: "That there will eventually be a day when a man like Willis Reed can not only be captain of the Knicks . . . but president of the United States."

PART III

Fallout

11

BULLETS OVER BROADWAY

Two weeks after the shootings, Kent State students returned to collect their possessions. The retrieval was done alphabetically, which meant Steve Albert was among the first to go. He got a ride with his roommate's father, packed up in one day, and did not return until the following fall.

"It was a changed campus, very somber," he said. "On the other hand, this horrible thing had put the school on the map. Who had ever heard of Kent State? Suddenly we were a symbol. The Crosby, Stills, Nash and Young song—which still makes me emotional every time I hear it—was everywhere. And all these entertainers wanted to come—George Carlin, Bob Hope, Sinatra."

Albert went to a few events, all of them haunted and spiritually numbing. For him, nothing could match the gift he'd been given by Whelan: the chore of running warm-ups and towels to and from players, of being inside Madison Square Garden on the night it was also united by pain—just not enough to keep a man like Willis Reed down.

Steve Albert had seen Game 7 with his own eyes. For him, even more than Sinatra could vocalize, that would always characterize the recuperative powers of New York, New York, and the night his college town blues began melting away.

"To experience that after what had happened at school was the best medicine I could have gotten. In the midst of all the tumult in the country, all the unrest, I think there was some poetic justice to having that feel-good story in the media capital and having it end as dramatically and inspirationally as it did after Willis came out."

As defending champions, the Knicks were officially the darlings of New York City, regularly drawing packed houses of 19,000-plus to Madison Square Garden. But the crowning glory of the New York franchise—what Ned Irish had strived for seemingly from the beginning of time—also unearthed an issue that would plague the NBA for decades: the profit disparity between large- and small-market teams.

Owners like the Bullets' Abe Pollin, a Washington builder who purchased the team with two partners for

$1.1 million in 1964 and gained full control four years later, believed teams like the Knicks and Lakers should be forced by the league to share home gate receipts. (Founded in 1961 as the Chicago Packers and soon after renamed the Zephyrs, the Bullets moved to Baltimore in 1963. They played in the Baltimore Civic Center, opened in 1962—often far short of its 12,500 capacity.) That socialist notion, which had also been championed by the smaller markets when the league set sail in 1946, was quashed, largely by Irish.

When Irish made his presentation for league membership, the first words out of his mouth were that he represented a corporation worth $3.5 million. Most of the others, virtual paupers by comparison, resented Irish and his braggadocio. But he got his way. The league would base itself in New York and be driven by large urban centers and their handsomely compensated stars, and as a result would forever be vulnerable to charges of favoritism—even conspiracy—for the sake of higher TV ratings. The notion of lucrative paydays in New York for owners like Pollin would remain a fantasy, with one conciliatory exception: in the deciding game of a playoff series, gate receipts were shared.

But beyond the dollar signs, for a team like the Bullets, a visit to a packed Madison Square Garden was "extraordinarily charged," as Jack Marin, the Bullets' small forward, said. Even the hired help seemed sprinkled with stardust. "You had that great John Condon voice on the PA, a character like Feets Broudy on the clock, Marv Albert broadcasting the games. Who even knew the people who did these jobs in other places?"

Trips to New York were also marked by an unmistakable connection to the prevailing social upheaval of the times, as the sixties gave way to the seventies. For players who didn't quite relate, the Garden could be a bewildering, disorienting place. For his part, Marin sometimes felt as if the New York fans were rooting as much for a set of ideals as for the Knicks.

"It was almost like a protest," he said. "You know, I never saw the war as immoral or ignoble—maybe a bad idea, but not an immoral one. We were all aware of the political issues. But when you were in a place like New York, you could feel the anger, the rebellion. I thought it was the end of the nation."

Marin and the Bullets had an altogether different agenda. They didn't necessarily want to overthrow the government. They just wanted to unseat the Knicks.

Bill Bradley (Princeton) and Jack Marin (Duke) were both jump-shooting forwards from comparable towers of ivory erudition. Their similarities as basketball players were most memorably described by George Lois as "two crazy motherfuckers chasing after each other for the whole goddamn night." But when the buzzer sounded, when the dance ended, there was little that Bradley and Marin actually had in common.

Marin, the left-hander, came hard from the political right, and Bradley, the right-hander, leaned to the left. Bradley was the Eddie Haskell of Rhodes scholars. No less feisty, Marin wore his red-hot emotions on his sleeve: his arm was conspicuously marked by a large crimson birthmark from shoulder to elbow that he considered part of his offensive arsenal.

"I used to tell people that one night my shooting was so hot, I set my arm on fire," he said, conceding that he was a bit of a hothead and something of a technical-foul machine. But he claimed that under no circumstances did he ever call Bradley a Communist cocksucker.

"He told you that, right?" Marin said.

"Well, yes, matter of fact, he did," I said.

Bradley offered his side of the story, from a game sometime during the 1970–71 season, as the Bullets' frustration over their inability to beat the Knicks was reaching the boiling point.

Marin was a devotee of Ayn Rand, and I was a liberal. So there were these differences, and then we'd get on the court and there were real battles.

Occasionally we'd talk politics off the court, but not too much, because we were so far apart. So there was one game where he thought I hit his elbow and they didn't call it, and we're running down the floor and you could just see his face light up, and he goes, "You Communist cocksucker!" Thirty years later, we were at some event in Washington when I was a senator and he was with some conservative group. We went out, and I said to him, "Jack, do you remember that night when you called me a Communist?" He looked at me and said, "No, I didn't call you a Communist; I called you a commoner."

That was Marin's version, and he—a Duke-trained lawyer—was sticking to it.

"A guy called me from *GQ* magazine in 2000," he said. "He said he was working on an article about Bradley's run for the presidency, and that he had talked about me and mentioned that because he was a liberal Democrat I had called him a Commie cocksucker. But the real story was that it came out of a golf game I was playing that summer, with Kevin Loughery and a guy from CBS. The CBS guy had a foot-and-a-half putt, missed it, and just came out with this line: 'common cocksucker.' The phrase somehow stuck in my head.

So when we played them the next season and Bradley was hanging all over me—as usual—I turned around and used that phrase. I think I was feeling a bit humorous on the court and it just came out of my mouth."

Since Loughery had no recollection of what was said at the golf outing, the old rivals and ideological opposites had long since agreed to disagree, letting the difference stand as evidence of their competitive enmity. Playing as often as their teams did, six straight years in the playoffs in addition to all those nights they dragged their tired bodies up and down the East Coast during the long and winding regular season, how could it not get personal? "Those games were works of art," Marin said.

Earl Monroe went a step further. "I always felt that our playoff series with the Knicks were the best games I had ever seen, let alone played in," he said. "I think because the Knicks played a lot of great series over the years against the Lakers and the Celtics, people remember them more. But because we were so closely matched up, almost interchangeable, the intensity, the whole aura, led to something that was very special."

Based on those classic individual match-ups—Bradley–Marin, Reed–Unseld, DeBusschere–Gus Johnson, Frazier–Monroe—people for decades have mischaracterized the Knicks and Bullets as mirror images, when the truth was that the rivalry was driven more by contrasts—both existential and ideological. "Everything they were, we were something else," said Loughery, who shared the role of Monroe's backcourt partner with Fred Carter. "They were more of a half-court team. We wanted to run." Added Marin: "They had that championship aura. We were the upstarts. "

At the Garden, Marin would nudge Loughery as the real glitterati, Robert Redford and Paul Newman, strolled the baseline during pregame warm-ups. "It's Butch Cassidy and the Sundance Kid," Marin said. "How are you not impressed?" As the parade of A-list entertainers got longer, the Garden's mystique only grew.

At home, the Bullets had one loyal fan who managed to achieve a degree of celebrity. An acquaintance of Monroe's, Marvin Cooper was a pretty fair Baltimore playground player, a spidery 6'2", but his very best moves were made just outside the lines at the Civic Center, shaking and shimmying in the interests of hexing Bullets opponents. The Knicks had Hoffman, Gould, and Allen behind them. The Bullets had Dancing Harry.

Because the Knicks had championship authentication to go along with intensifying hometown adoration, what the Bullets wished for, the players went at it like brothers battling in their bedroom. "It was like five heavyweight championship fights going on at the same time," said Larry Merchant, the former *New York Post* columnist, borrowing from his HBO boxing lexicon. "My recollection is that most of those nights, the experience almost seemed cathartic."

Unseld and Johnson gave Reed and DeBusschere all they could handle under the boards. Marin relished the dirty dancing with Bradley. Loughery and Carter were able scorers whom Barnett and Frazier had to respect. And of course Monroe was the emerging challenge, launching shots over outstretched fingers from bizarre angles he seemed to invent as some choreographic cross between Dancing Harry and a drunken marionette.

"The thing is," he said at the time, "I don't know what I'm going to do with the ball, and if I don't know, I'm quite sure the guy guarding me doesn't know either." Monroe always loomed as a wild card, a game changer. The Bullets were pugnacious and wanting, but at the same time they were dealing with an opponent more developed and cunning. Merchant said that as the rivalry developed, there was also a sense of New York's manifest destiny, no doubt fueled by what the Mets had done to the Orioles and the Jets to the Colts.

"In a certain way, you always expected that, in the end, the Knicks were supposed to win," he said. By

October 1970, who could blame the Bullets for believing that, too? It was difficult to resist the notion that the Knicks were special, almost chosen, in a way the Bullets were just not.

"You felt it when you were playing them," Marin said. "I remember going to Chicago later in my career, and they were going to run Chet Walker's plays for me. I'm there thinking, 'Am I Chet Walker?' I was a completely different player. They were just doing what they knew without any instinctive feel for the game. But when you played the Knicks, you never had a sense that anyone was ever in the wrong place, much less the wrong role."

Marin admitted that it was never easy to walk onto the Garden floor, where it always seemed to take two baskets for every one New York made. "Some guys in the locker room would say, 'Let's go out and have fun tonight,' " he said. "For me, it was never fun. It was going to be work. Bradley was the most dedicated player I matched up against—well, he and Havlicek. He wasn't all that gifted, but he was always there. His feet literally came down on your feet. I'd have to run him off six picks to get one shot. You'd finish the game with scratch marks all over you."

The subject of those long, grueling nights reminded him of a letter he'd sent to Bradley when the senator had finished his third and last term in Washington, thanking him for his service. Marin wrote: "You were a far dirtier basketball player than you were a politician."

From a distance of decades, the praise for Bradley and the Knicks flowed freely. The nation had survived their uprising, along with their crazed leftist fans. "Now they're all teaching on college campuses or making all kinds of money," he dryly noted. Marin couldn't resist invoking one very rich Old Knick in particular. "Phil Jackson would use the word *establishment* like it was a profanity when he was playing," he said. "But he's turned out to be among the wealthiest people in the sport of the non-owners. I guess the establishment wasn't such a bad thing."

Marin let the thought of Jackson's long, strange trip marinate for a moment—from admitted user of hallucinogenic drugs during the Knicks' glory years to earning $12 million a year by the time he'd won his 11th championship with the Lakers in 2010. "But what do I know?" he said, laughing. "Maybe Phil is giving away a lot of his money these days."

Phil Jackson's return to active playing duty in the fall of 1970 was gradual, with limited minutes and returns. Red Holzman didn't want to push him too hard and risk reinjury, and anyway, roles had been established during the championship run. At 6'8", with his long arms and freakish reach, Jackson was a first-rate disruptor on defense. But Holzman cringed whenever he would dare put the ball on the floor; the coach went so far as to establish a two-dribble limit for Jackson and was constantly on his case about it. While Jackson scrimmaged with the second team against Reed, he was more of a multipurpose frontcourt man than a backup center—which was indisputably the team's crying need with Nate Bowman gone to Buffalo and with Reed's chronically bad left knee.

While the Knicks' principal players remained the same, the end of the bench underwent a forced makeover. Don May and Bill Hosket had also relocated to Buffalo with Eddie Donovan in the expansion draft, while John Warren was lost to the new Cleveland team. The college draft brought new faces but failed to yield serviceable talent. The departure of Donovan seemed to have disrupted the organizational flow. The jobs of GM and coach might have been too much for one man.

Holzman's first-round pick, the Illinois guard Mike Price, was a mistake, considering that a pair of future stars, Calvin Murphy and Nate (Tiny) Archibald, were left on the board. Eddie Mast, a third-round pick from Temple, a free-spirited 6'9" forward, made the team and became fast friends with Jackson. Greg Fillmore, a 7'1" center taken in the eighth round out of little Cheyney University of Pennsylvania, stuck because of his size and the hope that he might be a project. At best, he was a poor man's Nate Bowman.

Jackson officially joined the Minutemen, thrilled to be back in uniform, though he eventually considered the back injury to be one of those opportunistic and even fortunate life detours. Though he had been inactive for the historic season, Jackson's inner coach stirred for the first time, and Holzman occasionally gave him small tasks, such as the breakdown of a scouting report, with which to keep busy when he wasn't taking photographs.

He believes that he owes much to Holzman, who had twice made the grueling journey to Grand Forks, North Dakota—scouting Jackson and then showing up a second time to sign him in his dorm room on the same day that John Lindsay, the mayor of New York, happened to be in town for an event. What were the odds? Jackson had wondered. Listen, Holzman groused, the mayor's trip could not have been as circuitous as his had been.

There was something about the sarcastic Jewish man that Jackson connected to immediately. He didn't try too hard, didn't mince or waste words. "Kind words when they were needed, but mostly a matter-of-fact guy," Jackson said. "It was the middle of the road—not too high, not too low."

Tightening the bond they had formed in Grand Forks, Holzman picked Jackson up at the airport on his first visit to New York on the Friday of Memorial Day weekend 1967. Holzman was at the wheel of a Chevy Impala convertible with his wife, Selma, in the backseat, along with a lamp she had brought along from their home in Cedarhurst. "So we're on the Van Wyck Expressway and some kid leans over the bypass and chucks a stone right down onto the windshield and cracks it," Jackson said. Holzman barely shook his head and kept driving—all the way into Manhattan, double-parking on Eighth Avenue, where the lamp was dropped off for repair. Finally, he turned to Jackson. "In New York, you get tested every day," he said. "It takes a special kind of patience—you think you could live here?"

Jackson suddenly wasn't too sure. He was the son of Charles and Elisabeth Jackson, Assemblies of God ministers of the Pentecostal faith. After marrying, the couple moved around Montana and North Dakota, starting ministries wherever they went. Jackson's fundamentalist childhood was rural and religious to the point that he was allowed only herbal remedies for illness. He wasn't permitted an injection of penicillin until he was 14. He played basketball and baseball and, though he was a strong pitching prospect, he abandoned the sport at 16, already 6'5" and part of a high school basketball team in Williston, North Dakota, that was heralded throughout the state.

At first glance, New York seemed and sounded like a foreign country to him. When he and Holzman sat down with Donovan at the Garden, Jackson mentioned that he had never even seen a live NBA game. "No kidding," Donovan said, looking at Holzman as if to say, "This kid's gonna play here?" Soon Jackson was holding a 16-millimeter film and was told to go ahead, take it back to school, have a look at what the pro game's all about.

First he had his New York weekend, staying in a hotel nearby on Eighth Avenue. He was given some meal money and a player escort, Neil Johnson, who had just finished his rookie season. They went to dinner and hit a pool hall before Johnson wished Jackson well and went on his way, leaving him to explore.

"I had Saturday to myself before leaving on Sunday," Jackson said. "I was wandering around and walked right into thousands and thousands of people marching in favor of the Vietnam War. There were policemen, firemen, sanitation workers, city workers, all over the streets. There were soapbox speakers, literally, in Times Square." Jackson had been under the impression that only liberals and radicals lived in New York. As a budding peacenik, he was disappointed to discover that wasn't the case.

Not sure what to make of the place, he returned to North Dakota the next day, thinking he had seen everything. Then he found a projector, loaded the refrigerator with beer, and summoned his Fighting Sioux teammates. They sat down to watch the game film Donovan and Holzman had chosen for Jackson. It was dated October 18, 1966—the night Willis Reed obliterated Rudy LaRusso and every other Laker who had dared to confront him.

"Nice intro, huh?" Jackson said, recalling that for a few moments he wondered why he had rejected a competitive financial offer from the Minnesota Muskies of the brand-new ABA, which would have kept him much closer to home. But Reed proved advertisement enough.

Jackson reported to training camp the following September and matched his relatively scrawny upper body against the muscular and hardworking Reed. Though it was an unenviable chore, they never scuffled or so much as exchanged a bad word. The raging bull he'd watched in grainy black-and-white was indeed a fierce competitor, but a gentleman of the highest order. Jackson also found himself rooming with fellow rookie Walt Frazier, and that, too, was an education he could never have gotten in lily-white North Dakota. He began making friends, falling in with the antiwar crowd and becoming immersed in the political debate.

It wasn't long before he knew that his decision to sign with the Knicks and come to New York City was going to be the smartest one he would make in his life.

We might have known something bad was brewing when the Orioles won the 1970 World Series over Cincinnati in five games and, a little more than two months later, Jim O'Brien kicked a 32-yard field goal to lift the Colts to a 16–13 victory over the Dallas Cowboys in Super Bowl V. While not directly at the expense of New York, Baltimore was suddenly the reigning champion in baseball and football (where the Mets and Jets had stood the year before), a compelling narrative turnaround that, if nothing else, underscored the fundamental and irresistible appeal of sports.

I actually rooted for both Baltimore teams, being a sworn National League hater, miserable when the American League so much as fell behind in an All-Star Game. And I didn't care for the Cowboys, considering that Dallas in those days still reminded me of

Kennedy's assassination. Naively comfortable on my high horse, I failed to comprehend what Baltimore's athletic vindication was portending for my defending champion Knicks.

The *season after* felt lacking in comparative drama, but how could it not? We seemed to have contracted the malaise known as Who Cares About Anything But the Playoffs? In an expanded league split for the first time into four divisions, the Knicks coasted to the Atlantic title but dropped from 60 wins to 52, losing four times to second-place Philadelphia. They were even beaten twice in Buffalo, where, given major minutes, Don May averaged an eye-opening 20.2 points. The Knicks could have used some of that marksmanship as their bench play declined. Cazzie Russell broke his wrist, missed 25 games, and shot a career-low 42.9 percent. Mike Riordan's numbers uniformly sagged.

The lack of a backup center forced Reed to average a career-high 39.1 minutes—while shooting less than 50 percent for the first time in three years—when his load should have been lightened. In Jackson's opinion, the championship had come at a high cost. "After the torn hip in the '70 series, Willis would never again play at the level he had shown," he said. "The wheels started to fall off."

And yet Frazier's career was still in ascension as he narrowly replaced Reed as the team's scoring leader. DeBusschere was only 30, Bradley 27. Better yet, expansion had removed the gravest threat to a Finals return as Milwaukee shifted to the Western Conference. With Oscar Robertson joining Kareem Abdul-Jabbar and a talented young forward, Bobby Dandridge, the Bucks were now the Lakers' problem, as evidenced by the conference finals. Playing without the injured Elgin Baylor, the Lakers were hammered in five games, their four defeats coming by an average of a whopping 20 points. For a change, Jerry West had no what-ifs with which to torture himself—only a blizzard of Kareem's sky hooks.

Back east, in the first round, the Knicks faced an entertaining but hardly formidable Atlanta Hawks team that featured the estimable jump shooter Lou Hudson and the floppy-haired and droopy-socked rookie Pistol Pete Maravich. The Hawks slipped into the playoffs with a 36–46 record but stunned New York by winning Game 2 in the Garden. Their alarm rung, the Knicks went down to Atlanta, won the next two games, and finished off the Hawks in five. Not their most impressive effort.

On the other hand, Baltimore, their conference finals opponent, had needed seven games to eliminate Philadelphia. The Bullets were banged up and missing Gus Johnson, who was out with an injured left knee. Without Johnson for the last month of the season, the Bullets had staggered to a 42–40 finish. The Knicks again had home-court advantage, not to mention a 21–9 record against the Bullets over the past three seasons.

Following a narrow escape by the Knicks in Game 1 and a blowout in Game 2, the gap was 23–9 and seemed in no danger of shrinking. Reed was struggling with his health again. In addition to his knee, he had sprained a shoulder in the Atlanta series—colliding with Bellamy, who was still getting in his way—but the Merchant hypothesis seemed to be holding. After the Bullets enjoyed consecutive blowouts in Baltimore, the Knicks pulled out Game 5 at the Garden, a game that I—now a Brooklyn College freshman—attended in all my full-throated and foulmouthed glory after an all-night wait for tickets outside the Garden.

Up in the blue seats, we loved abusing the hapless Bullets, not that they could hear us the way they did the courtside denizens. We called Unseld "Younseld" and "Fucking Fat Man." We ridiculed Marin for his birthmark. No aficionados or Woody Allens among us, we couldn't wait for Monroe to misfire—to let loose on him, too.

The Bullets were understandably contemptuous of the whole New York experience by this point. They were tired of the courtside hazing from the likes of Lois and friends and sick to death of reading in the New York papers about Reed's pain and sacrifice. After 94 games, they had their own ailments up and down the roster. Loughery, who ripped off a protective vest he wore after damaging his ribs and suffering a collapsed lung late in the season, was also playing with a painful heel. With knees that already looked held together by pipe cleaners, Monroe twisted an ankle early in the series and initially feared he might have to sit out a game or two.

On top of that, Gus Johnson's absence could not be understated. At 32, he was no longer the 6'6", 235-pound high-flier, the open-court terror who broke backboards with thunderous dunks. But the man known as Honeycomb—"the best all-around player I'd ever seen," Monroe said, with more sentiment than common sense—was the Bullets' veteran rock, their Dave DeBusschere.

After a hard-fought night with Johnson, DeBusschere would go home to Garden City, ease gently into bed, and tell his wife, Geri, how much of a war it had been. He relished the combat, though, residual aches and all. "The strongest individual I ever played against,"

DeBusschere said. "He'd put his hand on your back and you couldn't move. Never a cheap shot, though."

When DeBusschere and the Knicks jogged out to the Civic Center floor for Game 6, there, suddenly, was Johnson—back in uniform, on the layup line, bad knee and all, for the first time in the series. Now Baltimore had its own cause and rallying cry. Johnson gave them 10 points and 19 minutes in Game 6. Inspired, the Bullets toyed with the Knicks, blew them out. Worse, Reed had 3 points and 4 rebounds in 26 minutes. His disturbing lack of productivity put New York on high alert as the series returned to the Garden. Unlike the previous spring, there was little doubt or drama about Reed's availability. But that wasn't the issue.

"Question Is How Long and How Well Knick Star Can Go at Garden Tonight," read the headline above Leonard Koppett's story in the *New York Times*. In other words, how much longer could the Knicks get by with Reed's mere presence?

He was becoming a one-man soap opera, his own medical center, and a fascinating subject for future debate on athletes being pumped with numbing agents. Before the Bullets showdown, Reed received a painkilling shot of Xylocaine in his left knee. At halftime, with the Knicks clinging to a 4-point lead, he took another. But even with Reed playing well, the Knicks could not

shake the Bullets. Marin was outplaying Bradley. Johnson was battling DeBusschere to a standoff. Unseld was
en route to a 17-point, 20-rebound night. Monroe kept
shooting—only 10 for 26 by game's end, but his 26
points doubled Frazier's.

Monroe's jumper put the Bullets ahead 89–88, with
two and a half minutes remaining. He was causing
havoc in the Knicks' defense—near panic in the stands.
When Marin recalled the '71 series, he cited Monroe's
willingness to share as the difference from the previous Knicks series. Bradley that night told reporters:
"At one time you could count on Monroe passing off
only five percent of the time. You can't double-team
him now because he's passing off a lot more." Monroe
himself spoke of a new "gung ho attitude." But then,
Holzman's original scouting report on Earl the Pearl,
while calling him out as a showboat, did indicate that
he always had that cherished court vision.

In what might retrospectively be viewed as an in-
game audition, Monroe killed the Knicks by doing it
their way: hitting the open man. In crunch time, he
twice found Loughery off double teams for jumpers from the key. With the Bullets leading 91–89 and
the Knicks again determined to get the ball out of his
hands by trapping him, Monroe hit Carter for a 20-
footer. Frazier got one basket back. The Knicks dug in

for a stop, but DeBusschere missed at the other end as the clock and season dwindled to 11 seconds. The ball remained in New York's possession. The Knicks called time-out. The Garden fans, along with a live New York television audience, prayed for the familiar bolt of 11th-hour lightning.

The Knicks planned for Frazier to use a high screen from Reed, create off the dribble for himself or the big man rolling to the rim. But Unseld busted the screen and stepped into Frazier's space. "They overplayed me," Frazier said. He had no choice but to surrender the ball, passing to Bradley on the left side.

"He had only one place to go, which was to me, and I had only one place to go, which was toward the baseline," Bradley said. He was briefly open because Marin was screened and out of the play. In the chaos of all the switching, Unseld chased the ball, making a mad dash for Bradley. A more creative player like Frazier might have pump-faked, drawn a foul, or stepped inside Unseld for the shot. But Bradley was more straightforward. He didn't want to risk not getting any shot off. He coiled for the release just as Unseld leaped and stretched his 6'7" frame to its fullest. Unseld got just enough of the shot to keep it from reaching the rim.

In the dying seconds of the Knicks' one-year reign, the ball settled—fittingly, as far as the Bullets were concerned—into the hands of Gus Johnson. The clock ran out. Marin let out a primal scream that resounded through the otherwise quiet, stunned arena. "At that moment, I don't think it mattered how many people were there," he said. "It was all about the guys in orange and white."

The photo of that final scene—with the scoreboard in the backdrop—would become more Baltimore family heirloom than Bullets playoff keepsake. Bradley discovered just how much Abe Pollin relished the victory over Ned Irish's team when he was elected to the Senate by New Jersey voters in 1978—at the age of 34, only a year and a half after retiring from the Knicks. Pollin, a loyal Democrat with contacts in the D.C. area, had helped Bradley launch his campaign. "Now I'm elected, and it's Christmas," he said. "I get a frame from him in a wrapped piece of paper. I open it up. What is it? It's a picture of me with my head down, the Bullets in jubilation, with the score up there [93–91] on the board."

In an accompanying note, Pollin wrote: "If you ever start thinking that you're really hot shit as a senator, just take a look at this."

Calling that game his greatest victory, Loughery hung the framed photo in his basement so he could look at it for the rest of his life. Monroe would say: "After all we'd been through against them, it was a huge hurdle and relief. That was our championship."

Forever the union man and players' advocate, Loughery took special pride in knowing that the Bullets got paid like champs, too. "Before that game, Abe Pollin came into our locker room and made the greatest pregame speech by an owner in the history of sports," he said. "Remember, we're playing in a sold-out Madison Square Garden. It's Game 7. So Abe was getting half the gate. He comes in, looks at us, and says, 'If you guys beat the Knicks tonight, you get my share of the gate.' And then he walks out. We're sitting there, amazed. Playoff money was a big deal in those days—to him and to us."

But the hobbled Bullets never had a chance against Abdul-Jabbar and the well-rested Bucks in the Finals. After finishing off the Knicks on Monday night, they had to fly to Milwaukee the next day to begin the series on Wednesday night. They lost Game 1 by ten points on the way to a four-game sweep, with no margin of defeat closer than eight. Robertson was finally an NBA champion. Abdul-Jabbar won the first of his six rings. "We still wound up with a bigger playoff share, because Abe kept his word," Loughery said. "He gave us the gate from the Garden."

Neither Loughery nor Monroe recalled exactly how much Pollin's munificence amounted to, but Monroe, viewing it as found money, had about $10,000 cash in a paper bag under his car seat as he drove three college friends up to New York to celebrate. Always one to play uptempo, he managed to get pulled over for speeding on the New Jersey Turnpike.

Four black men in a car prompted some extra law enforcement sleuthing. The troopers ordered them out of the car. "They look right under the seat and they find the $10,000," Monroe said. "They obviously think we had robbed a bank or were about to make some kind of drug deal. They actually took us in. It was crazy, me trying to explain to them that this was the money from the gate at the last game at the Garden. They were like, 'Yeah, sure.'"

Eventually Monroe convinced them that the money was related to his pro basketball earnings, and the field trip to New York continued. Much as he considered himself a Philly guy and had enjoyed playing in Baltimore, Monroe said he had long thought the Big Apple was a perfect fit for his nocturnal lifestyle. Like Monroe, New York pulsated with energy and opportunity. "In Baltimore, even TV went off early," he said. "Here, you had early cable. Even if I didn't go out, I could stay up late and there was always something to do."

New York was not only the best place to be with some extra money in his pocket; it was the ideal location to earn even more. Abe Pollin was a good man, a devoted owner; but from the time he had signed his first pro deal, Earl Monroe was underpaid. He was already one of the premier showmen in a theatrical sport where the great ones more often than not would gravitate to a stage worthy of their skills.

Not that Monroe was aware of it at the time, but all he had to do on his drive to New York was take a look in his rearview mirror, where Baltimore had already faded from sight.

12

THE PARABLE OF THE PEARL

When Earl Monroe forced Abe Pollin to trade him to the hated Knicks in 1971—after four seasons as the face of the Bullets franchise—he more than incurred the owner's wrath. He broke his heart. Now, in the fall of 2009, old Abe, 85, was succumbing to a rare neurological disease, progressive supranuclear palsy, and all those unresolved feelings, regret mixed with guilt, were doing to Monroe what he had once done to defenders: in short, making him ill, hobbled, unsure of what to do next.

As he sat in his Harlem apartment, Monroe was dealing with his own medical issues. In addition to ongoing treatment for an enlarged prostate and type 2 diabetes, he had been hospitalized that summer with a severe sinus condition that would, after years of dogging him, finally require surgery. Then there were the vertebrae that needed stabilizing, the hips that had been replaced, the cartilage removed from his knees, and the ligaments sewn back together. He had just about lost count of how many times he'd been under the knife. "I think the next two will be something like my 27th and 28th surgeries," he said.

The weight he felt most heavily, though, had nothing to do with his body. Pollin had invited him to Washington in 1996 to honor him as one of three former Bullets named to the NBA's all-time Top 50 team, and Monroe went with conflicted feelings, more than a few pangs of guilt. There was a dinner, some wine, and a moment, he recalled, when he just had to tell Pollin how he really felt, despite Pollin's old-school tenets, which had once made him too stubborn to accede to Monroe's contractual demand.

"I love you," he said.

Perched in a living room armchair, wearing a T-shirt and shorts, Monroe's legs were still muscular and thin, but a little creaky as the 65-year-old legend rose to move about the room. When the hips started going, in his forties, he would come around the Garden, flash a sheepish smile, and joke that the erosion on both sides of his body was from all the spinning, this way and that, when he was tormenting NBA defenders. It was typical Monroe, inevitably endearing and disarming.

So, yes, despite Monroe's calculated but complicated abandonment of the Bullets, Pollin eventually forgave him, even retired Monroe's number 10 in 2007, showing up in his wheelchair to make Earl the Pearl part of the organizational family forever. In doing that, Pollin also forced Monroe to confront a haunting question for the rest of his life: What if he'd stayed? What if he hadn't let the prospect of more money and the feelings of disrespect convince him to turn his future over to his agent?

In those days, as union general counsel, Larry Fleisher represented not only individual stars but the players collectively. He firmly believed that the union could only be as strong as its best players. But this could also create a fundamental conflict of interest in certain cases that raised the question of agenda: was he acting in behalf of the players or the player? If he steered a star like Monroe to a big market like New York to raise the salary bar, did the financial gain necessarily make it a better move for the player's career? Fleisher had been firing shots over the owners' bow as the union pushed for free agency (which would be won five years later). With Monroe, he took aim at the heart of the matter.

Monroe was in his final contract year and was sick of Pollin telling him, "Listen, kiddo, Baltimore is not Los

Angeles or New York—we simply can't afford the big bucks here." Monroe was a Rookie of the Year, a two-time All Star, an instant sensation who in his second pro game, against the Celtics, attracted the largest cash gate in the Bullets' short history and moved Bill Russell to say, "I don't know how much he's making, but he's worth every penny."

Even by the era's standards, Monroe earned pennies: $20,000 per season as part of a two-year deal he had signed before his college coach, Clarence "Big House" Gaines, could stop him. Monroe was underpaid to the extent that a Winston-Salem friend made a passing remark that he was making a comparable salary teaching school. When Fleisher became his agent about a year before his contract was to expire and convinced him it was time to force a showdown, Pollin antagonized Monroe by pleading poverty to the press. "Abe had said some things early on about what I was asking for that I didn't like," Monroe said. "You know, I was a very cocky and egotistical kind of guy at the time, young and headstrong."

Monroe was not one to suffer persecution—nor the perception of it. Like so many others during the sixties, he had become more socially and politically aware in college. Following President Lyndon Johnson's signing of the Voting Rights Act of 1965, Monroe participated in voter registration drives in Winston-Salem. He attended sit-ins on campus, befriending student activists who wanted, in turn, to know what he, a popular athlete, could do to help.

"Son, you can't do all that stuff—you got to come out here and play basketball," Coach Gaines told him. It was the same refrain Willis Reed had heard from Fred Hobdy at Grambling, except that Monroe's experience growing up in the North made it more difficult to simply look myopically to sports and assume everything would just work itself out.

He was born Vernon Earl Monroe at the Hospital of the University of Pennsylvania in 1944, but his mother, Rose, had migrated north from North Carolina in the mid-thirties, when she was only 14. His parents divorced when he was five and he didn't see his father—a singer and dancer who once worked with Bessie Smith—until young adulthood. On top of that, Monroe lost much of his extended family: ten of his mother's twelve brothers and sisters had met the kind of untimely end—victims of violence and disease—that poverty metes out.

Monroe's family life stabilized when his mother remarried before he reached adolescence. He never lacked for food and clothing, but life in South Philadelphia was fraught with gangs and the inherent collateral damage. When he was eight, Monroe witnessed a fatal knifing, and decades later he would matter-of-factly explain how the killer literally cut the heart out of his victim and threw it into the street.

As a budding athlete, topping six feet by the time he'd reached early adolescence, Monroe was looked after by his cousins, who escorted him down a safer, alternative path. Early on, he played baseball and then soccer until his junior year of high school, developing nimble feet that would serve him well on the cement playgrounds when he took up dribbling with his hands. But he was no instant sensation, calling his early basketball days "trial and error, waiting on the fence to get picked."

Fully grown by the time he was 14, Monroe—at 6'3"—played center at John Bartram High School. By the time he was an upperclassman, he was small for the position and had to maneuver against taller opposition, becoming known for his unorthodox moves and a magnetic dribble, his hand cradling the ball to the extent that many would contend that the chronic palming in the modern game began with him. By senior year he was the talk of Philadelphia, but a novel, perplexing talent. As a frontcourt player, he was considered too small to have any impact in college.

Being black didn't exactly expand his options. A few big schools in the South and Midwest did send letters,

requesting an academic transcript and photo. He dutifully mailed them off. "I'm still waiting to hear back,"
he said.

At Winston-Salem State, where exposure to the
campus protests helped open his eyes to the bigger
picture of America's inequities and outright oppression, he was thrilled when Gaines arranged
for closed-door Sunday-night scrimmages in the
Winston-Salem gym with the NCAA big boys from
Wake Forest. But running the more renowned (white)
players around wasn't enough. He quietly fumed over
how the results had to be kept secret. In his view,
there were worse competitive injustices, like when he
was cut from the Pan American team in 1967, when
the tryouts were conducted by splitting the candi-
dates up into practice groups. Assigned to a squad of
black college players, Monroe scored 22 points in the
last 14 minutes of a scrimmage against a collection of
Armed Forces players, several of whom earned spots
on the roster.

"The whole experience of the time, what it was
like for a black person to live in America, shaped the
way I felt," he said. Those feelings only grew stronger when he joined the NBA and realized how black
players—especially himself—were routinely underpaid. "Basically, like anybody," he says, "I am worried

about making money," he told *Sports Illustrated* during his rookie season. "This is not fun anymore."

As a Bullet, he didn't look for controversy; that wasn't his way. But he had already lived too hardscrabble a life to worry about offending the feelings of people who had never known a day of comparable misery. When asked about the Vietnam War, he didn't sugarcoat his answer. He said he admired Muhammad Ali and doubted openly whether—if drafted himself—he would serve.

"He got a draft dodger reputation," the late Jim Karvellas said during his eighties run as a Knicks radio play-by-play man. Karvellas had been the longtime voice of the Bullets and, like Monroe, had migrated north to call Knicks games in New York. "Things began to get difficult for Earl, and he just said, 'I want to get out of here.'"

At least he thought he did. The truth of the matter—much plainer to him in hindsight—was that Monroe initially wished only for Pollin to pay him more money. He didn't have a good relationship with the Baltimore coach, Gene Shue, a control freak who had never warmed to his style of showmanship and wanted to remake the team. But Monroe loved being the Bullets' premier attraction and considered most of his teammates (and especially Gus Johnson) to be his pals.

The subject elicited a contemplative frown, a pursing of Monroe's lips. "Deep down, I really didn't want to leave, and I'm not sure I would have if it was just me," he said. "But things happened. Larry was an agent. He did what agents do. When he felt that we could and should force a move, I just kind of went along with it."

When Fleisher told Pollin that his client no longer wanted a contract extension, he provided a list of three teams to which Monroe wanted to be dealt: his hometown 76ers, the Lakers, and the Bulls, who in 1966 had filled the vacancy created in Chicago when the Zephyrs moved to Baltimore to become the Bullets.

Pollin was torn. He respected Shue's opinion, but Monroe was his star. The longer he did nothing, the tenser the situation became. Then Monroe and Fleisher walked into his office in early October 1971 and announced that Monroe was essentially going on strike. Pollin appealed to Monroe's sense of commitment to his teammates, if not to him. But while Pollin was on the subject, hadn't he demonstrated his loyalty with the Game 7 bonus the previous spring?

Fleisher wasn't buying, and Monroe wasn't talking, letting the agent speak for him. "Earl's not going to play for you anymore," Fleisher said. "You have to trade him." Just like that, Monroe disappeared from the Civic Center. He didn't inform his teammates, never said good-bye. He left the Bullets bewildered and bothered, at least in the case of Jack Marin, who blasted him in the papers.

"I was frustrated and said some ugly things, but that was because I didn't want him to leave," Marin said. "We had built the team and felt like we were getting closer to the championship." Marin regretted his outburst and eventually realized that Monroe's exit was probably inevitable, given his flash and Pollin's finances.

"Obviously Earl was a talent made for a bigger market," Marin said. "I think Larry Fleisher convinced him of it. We were playing a lot of nights in front of 5,000 to 6,000 people, even as well as we were doing. And Gus Johnson was kind of losing it, with the bad knees and all. But at the time and because of where he wound up, it was a tough pill to swallow."

With Monroe absent and in Fleisher's custody, public resentment mounted against him. Pollin decided to punt. He set the stage for a deal by trading Kevin Loughery and Fred Carter to Philadelphia for Archie Clark, who at least measured up statistically—21.3 points and 5.4 assists the previous season, to Monroe's 21.4 and 4.4. But in making the hasty trade, Pollin wound up with another contractual headache. Clark, too, was campaigning for a new deal, a big raise.

When the Knicks rolled into the Civic Center on October 22, neither Monroe nor Clark showed up to play. Shue was reduced to starting a rookie, Phil Chenier, and a second-year player, Gary Zeller, in the backcourt. The Knicks blew the Bullets out, 110–87. So embarrassed was Pollin that he offered fans attending the game a ticket for another. With his team descending into chaos, he took a phone call from Ned Irish. "I'll give you Dave Stallworth and $100,000 for Earl," Irish said, with all the compassion of a tax collector.

Much as he chafed at the New Yorker's gall, Pollin respected and admired Irish, and anyway he needed the cash. But he also knew he'd be excoriated in the local papers if he accepted Stallworth alone in exchange for Monroe. Without much leverage, he told Irish that he liked the hustling kid on Holzman's bench, Riordan. It was obvious that he was a favorite of the sophisticated New York fans. In Baltimore, he might have upside as a player and a personality.

"Throw Riordan in," Pollin told Irish, "and you've got a deal."

Irish happily surrendered Red Holzman's guy, who happened to have a broken wrist, suffered in a workout. The trade was announced on November 11, stunning the basketball world. Imagine hearing in 1985 that Magic Johnson had been traded to the Celtics—that's how *unimaginable* the dealing of Earl Monroe to the Knicks was in 1971. Even more incongruous was the notion that he and Walt Frazier could share a backcourt. Not only were they impassioned rivals, stars who both wore a perfect 10 on their jerseys, but their efficacy was predicated on control of the ball—no one knew what would happen when they didn't have it in their hands.

The question of whether or not Frazier and Monroe could coexist immediately consumed the sport. Oscar Robertson recalled arguing with teammates, telling them they were crazy to think Monroe wasn't good enough to adapt to the Knicks' style. "A basketball player is a basketball player," he told me. "And Earl Monroe was a great one. There was never any doubt in my mind that he would succeed." He meant Monroe, with Frazier, and vice versa.

In the backseat of a taxi on the day the trade was announced, Phil Jackson—whom Riordan had introduced to "blue-collar New York"—told Bill Bradley he had doubts the experiment would work. Bradley, a fan of Monroe's going back to their summer league shootout in Philadelphia, told him he was nuts.

"Earl will fit right in," Bradley said. "He's a hell of a player."

When Pollin finally agreed to the deal that sent Monroe to New York, Monroe was shocked. He was intrigued by the idea of seeing his act on the Garden stage, if a little concerned about how it would play. Fleisher told him not to worry: his ship had come in, with a new contract that would be worth about $200,000 a season for three years, with an option for a fourth.

Still, Monroe, crazy as it sounded, was conflicted, because what he really wanted was to stay with the Bullets and get paid, too. He called Jerry Krause, who had scouted and befriended him, to vent; Krause was now working for the Bulls in Chicago. "Those bastards don't think I'll give up my game," he told Krause. "They think I'm a loser. Well, fuck them. I'm a winner. I'll give it up. Walt can get the glory, and if they need me in the fourth quarter, I'll be ready."

But Monroe understandably had doubts, and needed a shoulder to lean on, someone to talk him through the dramatic career shift. He went home to Philadelphia to see his longtime confidant Sonny Hill.

Based on the strong bond they had formed through Monroe's participation in the Baker League and in Philadelphia basketball circles in general, he and Hill had kept in touch through college and the Baltimore years. Hill watched his friend play his first game with the Bullets at the Civic Center—October 18, 1967, a 121–98 romp over the Knicks—and often traveled from Philly to Baltimore for the games after that. "We had what I considered to be an inseparable relationship,"

Hill said. "I said, 'We are talking about you leaving Baltimore, your team—can you go up to New York and fit into that style?' And I kept repeating myself—'Can you fit in? Can you fit in?'"

Monroe grew annoyed with the implication that he couldn't. "You have to understand that Earl was the quintessential school-yard player and he was going to go to the team that was the most anti–school yard team in basketball," Hill said. "So I kept asking him, 'Can you be part of that kind of offense? Can you play without the ball?'"

"Sonny," Monroe said, "I can play *basketball*."

"What he was saying was, 'I'm from Philly. I'm from the Baker League,'" Hill said. "'Whatever someone needs me to do on the court, I can do it.'"

Monroe was offended by the skepticism, as if his indivual prowess couldn't shine in an environment more structured than Baltimore's. "You know, Philadelphia's a different animal than New York," Monroe said. "In the playgrounds down there, we pride ourselves on teamwork, on passing the ball, whereas in New York, most of the guys made a move to the basket, one-on-one."

The way Monroe saw it, Philly ball was really more Old Knicks than New York ball was. As Holzman had noted all those years ago in his scouting report,

Monroe knew the game, but like a great jazz artist, he was blessed with the ability to riff. Joe Lapchick once remarked that if a deceased player could rise from the grave, he would think Monroe was playing a different sport.

That said, beyond Bradley and Jackson, other Knicks were skeptical of the deal. Frazier had a view that went beyond Monroe's ability to assimilate. He believed the Knicks, following the disappointment of the previous spring, were in the process of remaking the team. They had already shipped Cazzie Russell out west to Golden State during the off-season for Jerry Lucas, adding a quality big man as protection for Willis Reed's tendinitis-ridden left knee. Frazier dwelled on newspaper speculation that the Knicks were also in the hunt for Houston's talented young post player Elvin Hayes, using him as bait.

"I'm taking that sort of for true," Frazier told reporters. "That's the only way the trade for Monroe makes sense. They don't need both him and me in the backcourt."

Unbeknownst to Frazier, Monroe had put his ego in storage when he packed up and left the Baltimore Civic Center. He sat down at the Garden for a get-acquainted session with his new coach, and when Holzman asked what he needed, Monroe said: "Just one thing. Before anybody asks the question about whether I'm going to start over Barnett, I don't want to. I'll earn my way."

Holzman was surprised. He was prepared to work Monroe in slowly but to make him a starter as soon as he could, having already consulted Dick Barnett, who was on board. "I was 34 years old," Barnett said. "I wasn't going to be playing that much longer. I understood what they were doing."

Monroe's debut that night was a fascinating study in the transition the Knicks were undertaking. For one thing, Golden State was in town with Cazzie, who had left New York generally appreciative of his time there, and grateful for the chance to rebuild his reputation as a big-time scorer, though with some lingering regret that was similar to what Monroe felt over leaving Baltimore. New York had been his first professional home.

"It was strange—me coming back as an opponent, the Minutemen broken up, Earl Monroe and Jerry Lucas in the Knicks uniform," Russell said. "It was a moment of saying, 'Wow, this is really different.' But at the same time, life teaches you to move on."

Russell went forward with a 42-minute, 20-point, 6-rebound, 5-assist performance in a 112–103 Warriors victory that was the Knicks' fourth straight defeat. Appearing for the first time in two weeks, Reed played

23 scoreless minutes, missing all five of his field goal attempts.

Monroe was marginally better, logging 20 minutes and scoring 9 points after receiving what the *New York Times* described as a "thunderous ovation" from the sellout crowd of 19,588. Afterward, he said he wasn't in game condition and would need about two weeks to get in shape. But the real Monroe appeared that season only in occasional flashes. What New York saw that first night was pretty much what it got the rest of the way: 20.6 minutes a game, 11.4 points, 2.2 assists—Earl without his Pearl, fitting in to the point of becoming another foot soldier, a moneyed Minuteman, pressing for minutes off the bench along with the rookie Dean Meminger.

Monroe liked his teammates well enough. "I'll never forget DeBusschere coming up when I walked into the locker room for the first time," Monroe said. "Then Bradley and Reed. And that was good." He found them to be cordial, businesslike. The old line about the Knicks was that when they left the Garden, they hailed 12 different cabs—an exaggeration, but Monroe could see right away that they were not fraternal like the Bullets. And he certainly was not one of them, on or off the court.

"As far as my game," Monroe said, "it went from spectacular to being like a student. It was very hard when the game was at a certain point not to try and take over, because I was so used to doing that. I'd always played at a certain pace and rhythm, managed the game as opposed to just playing it."

More transcendent showman than traditional superstar, Monroe was never as dominant as Oscar or West. But because he was an anti-establishment cult figure in a sport fast becoming a bastion of black expression, his sacrifice was even more painful for devout fans. Those who had watched him or played against him from his earliest playground days didn't recognize the role player he'd become in New York.

"I'd go down to Philly and guys would say, 'Eleven points a game—what's up with that?'" Monroe said. "I got dogged a lot, you know, but I made sure to go down to the Baker League that summer to bust them all up, just so they knew I was still me."

Considered in the context of the modern era, Monroe's sacrifice had a "He did what?" quality that players like LeBron James—secure in his expectation of getting paid, location notwithstanding—would find incomprehensible. Joining forces with Dwyane Wade in Miami was one thing; going to the bench was another. "What Earl did could never happen today," said Kevin Loughery, Monroe's backcourt partner in Baltimore. "Can you imagine an agent or a shoe company allowing a guy like Earl to go to a team where he wouldn't even start?"

Big-market influence remains a persistent story line in the modern NBA, and twenty-first-century players do make sacrifices. Kevin Garnett, Ray Allen, and Paul Pierce happily teamed up to win a 17th title for Boston in 2008, proving to be perfect complementary pieces. James, Wade, and Chris Bosh in the 2010 summer of free-agent insanity at least had the same idea, even if year one ended unhappily. But no NBA star player has ever made so radical a career transformation in his prime as did Monroe.

Though he, too, departed Baltimore in the Archie Clark trade, Loughery conceded that for admirers of the Old Knicks, Monroe over time became the ultimate example of putting team values first.

"It's been one of the great questions: is Earl remembered as an even greater player because he fit in and won a championship in New York, or did his career suffer because he couldn't be what he was in Baltimore?" Loughery said. As the man who coached the revered doctor, Julius Erving, with the New York Nets in the ABA, Loughery reached his own biased conclusion.

"Because of how the league evolved into one that was about entertainment, I think it would have been better for him had he stayed," he said. "I know you wouldn't have seen any seasons where he scored 11 points a game. In Baltimore, he was one of the great showmen, maybe the best. The NBA lost that. Earl lost that."

Monroe wasn't one to hide his misgivings, especially when he knew how much it delighted the Baltimore lifers. "I never thought of myself as a real Knick," he told the *Washington Post* at Pollin's Top 50 dinner. "I always felt as though the Bullets and Baltimore was the way I made my name."

Did he really believe that he'd cheated himself, given up too much individuality for the sake of being part of a cherished collective? Apparently so; when he was enshrined in the Hall of Fame in 1990, he called Pollin and told him he wanted to go in as a Bullet.

"We talked about the Hall of Fame thing many times," Sonny Hill said. "It always came down to: how do you want them to remember you—as a guy who changed, sacrificed, and fit into what the Knicks did, or as Earl the Pearl? He worried that people would see it as being disrespectful to the Knicks. I told him, 'This is not disrespectful to the Knicks. You have your championship ring.'"

Beyond basketball, New York had delivered benefits he always knew Baltimore could not. In New

York, Monroe could chase off-court ambitions, some of which—like the music industry—proved expensive and short-lived. He didn't get discouraged easily. In his mid-sixties, he was still making a go of it, teaming with the dance-pop singer Ciara Corr to launch Reverse Spin Records, specializing in hip-hop and R&B.

There were other creative outlets for Monroe that probably would not have opened to him as a lifelong Bullet. Sitting on a shelf above the fireplace in his Harlem apartment was a Peabody Award for the television documentary *Black Magic*, which he co-produced in 2008 with the filmmaker Dan Klores. The project, tracing the history of blacks in basketball, was thrilling for Monroe because it celebrated so much that the multimillionaire NBA stars knew little or nothing about.

"That's what New York's been about—connections and temptations," Monroe said furtively, in reference to a fast life of risk and reward, highs and lows. In the seventies, an accountant steered him into tax shelters that much later came to the merciless attention of the Internal Revenue Service. Monroe was eventually tagged with more than $3 million in back payments and interest. He and his longtime companion and later his wife, Marita Green-Monroe, plunged into dire financial straits. They had to leave Manhattan for several years, rent in New Jersey, and seek help from their extended basketball family, including the NBA's Retired Players Association, led at the time by Dave Bing, which wrote him a check to stave off the debt collectors.

"There were difficult times," Green-Monroe said, recalling Red Holzman's tender calls, asking what he could do to help. Eddie Donovan's son Sean—a financial broker and consultant who worked with some of his father's old players, including Reed—spent considerable time with Monroe formulating a plan. But it was a painful struggle, days when that $99,000 question— what if he'd stayed on Pollin's team?—loomed much larger. Maybe he would have earned less than he had in New York. But perhaps life would have been simpler, more about the things money *couldn't* buy.

For better or worse, Pollin ran his team like a mom-and-pop shop, long after the NBA outgrew its small-family roots. The young builder grew into a man of uncommon depth after having endured the worst of tragedies, losing two children to congenital heart failure. His wife, Irene, became a psychotherapist specializing in grief counseling. Pollin became committed to charitable organizations that helped feed and educate underprivileged children.

He moved the team, which had relocated from Baltimore to the Maryland suburbs, to the nation's capital. In 1997, at a time when most multimillionaire owners were still asking for municipal handouts, he built the MCI Center (later the Verizon Center), revitalizing a downtrodden neighborhood. The same year, alarmed by the number of gun-related deaths in the district, he changed the team's name to the Wizards.

As the years rolled by, Monroe developed a greater appreciation for the man, understood the impossible situation he had put him in. Pollin had his faults. He was stubborn. He was thrifty. But compared with the hired guns running the Garden in the years after Ned Irish, Pollin was practically a saint.

On the day of his death—November 24, 2009—Pollin was the most tenured and respected NBA owner, the league's paternal conscience. And Monroe still grappled with regrets about running away, off into the arms of a corporate sugar daddy that would later cut him loose without so much as a call.

In 1980, when Sonny Werblin sat down with me for a season-ending chat, Monroe was the last link to the Knicks' championship teams, having just finished his 13th. He was a free agent, however, and Werblin matter-of-factly said that the Knicks would not be re-signing him for the following season, and that the team had "given him enough." The public execution on the back page of the *New York Post*, under my byline, was crushing for Monroe, and another story that was pain-ful for me to write—in effect the career obituary for another icon of my youth.

Monroe read the story and couldn't believe that was how he'd be leaving the game. Maybe he didn't have a whole lot left. But he had been the Knicks' sole attrac-tion after the other core players left, the last link to the glory years. And yet there was no notification, no op-portunity to say good-bye to the fans, and certainly not the hoped-for job offer within the organization.

"I guess for the most part I felt that I should have still been a part of it in some capacity," he said. "Basi-cally because of coming here and having sacrificed to be here, I felt the organization didn't appreciate that. I just felt, if this is the end of my career, there is some-thing I should be doing with this organization. And when it wasn't offered to me, I just went away."

Through the years, many of them luckless for the Knicks, he became convinced that it was a case of ethical payback. The franchise banished Frazier, fired Reed, cut him loose, and what did that say? "The his-tory of what's been here: that should be what every organization is about," he said. "If you don't honor your history, then how can you plot your future? If your history has been clouded, it sends a bad message. You haven't won the championship in almost 40 years;

karma-wise, that may be the reason why. I mean, how long did it take to retire Dick Barnett's number?"

When the Knicks first approached Monroe about raising number 15, he declined, still smarting over his departure from the organization "without signs of humanity or compassion." The second invitation, in 1985, came from Dave DeBusschere, who had returned as general manager. "When your teammate calls, it's different," he said. But by the night of the ceremony, DeBusschere had been fired, leaving Monroe, again, with a bittersweet aftertaste.

Pollin, he knew, never would have treated one of his guys that way. "Deep down, it bothers Earl that his life could have been very different," Marita Green-Monroe said. "How could it not, when all he had to do was look down there and see what Abe was doing for Wes?" Wes Unseld, who might have been his career-long companion, Reed to his Frazier, retired from the Bullets in 1981 and immediately began a long run in the organization as a vice president, general manager, and coach.

Monroe watched other NBA greats carve lucrative administrative careers or get paid the big network bucks. Julius Erving did both, as an executive in Orlando and as a studio analyst. Green-Monroe, a good friend of Erving's ex-wife, Turquoise, knew why

Erving was able to market himself after his glory years: he never had to stop being Dr. J.

For his part, Monroe said his everlasting regret was rooted less in remuneration and more in the sadness that there remained precious little evidence, scant film footage, of Baltimore's Black Jesus. "I was always a history buff, and because of history you're remembered in a certain way, and people down the road won't remember you sacrificed—they'll remember your stats," he said. "People never really get to see what I did on a day-in, day-out basis, the way I was, and what I was capable of doing as an individual."

In the late summer of 1995, I was in Orlando for a story about the NBA's rookie orientation program, chatting up a group of players who were kicking back in the hallway outside the league's hotel office: Kevin Garnett, Antonio McDyess, Joe Smith, and a seven-footer from Kansas, Greg Ostertag, alternately talking trash and feeling each other out for information that might be of benefit when they reported to their first training camp.

Suddenly, from an elevator just down the hall, there came a distinguished figure who could have offered them all pearls of wisdom. Except that, to them, Earl Monroe wasn't famous or even familiar. Monroe passed by without one of them so much as turning his head. I asked if they had recognized the man. No takers. Earl Monroe, anyone? "I heard the name," Ostertag said.

Young people, I thought. At about the same time, Earl and Marita had one in their own home—a teenage daughter, Maya, who would play basketball at Georgia Tech. But when she was just learning the game, her mother wanted her to know about her special gene pool. How could she explain this in plain, simple terms to a child born in 1983? Marita told her, "What Michael Jordan did in the air, your father did on the ground."

But where, in the visual age, was the proof? People—sportswriters especially—talk a virtuous game, espouse team values, but in the end glorify the one-name goliaths, reduce their teammates to *supporting casts* and *Jordanaires*. Maybe Loughery was right: for Monroe, great as Broadway was, it wasn't Baltimore.

The subject would always be a sore one, especially for Green-Monroe, who couldn't help but launch into an occasional diatribe, after which her husband would invariably tell her, "Move on, Marita. Move on." When asked how *he* reconciled his decision, and if he truly did regret becoming a Knick, Monroe smiled and more or less considered it life imitating art, making it up as he went along, of going in whatever direction his creative impulses led.

"One thing about me: I've always been adaptable," he said. "I don't make a big deal about myself. It's what happens, the course of life. Some guys get the better road, some guys don't. You still have to live your life, and that's kind of how I've always taken all of this. Going from Baltimore to New York was the road I was taking. It's like when you think about the most successful guys, whether they know it or not, are out in front, seeing the game before it happens. You see where everybody is, and you see in your head where they are going to be. And that's the way I've tried to live my life: looking ahead. The way I always felt in the end about leaving the Bullets for the Knicks. I knew what it was going to be like, and I wasn't surprised."

He went to New York, found himself an apartment in an old brownstone on a quiet Manhattan street near Central Park West. He bought himself a silver Rolls-Royce (same model as Frazier's), to which he later affixed the black-gloved clenched-fist sticker. Later, when he finally stepped into the Knicks' starting lineup, the Pearl-and-Clyde partnership would be known in some quarters as the Rolls-Royce backcourt.

"The best of all time," Monroe said.

Just not necessarily the best time for him.

13

DECONSTRUCTING CLYDE

Walt Frazier lived in an off-campus trailer at Southern Illinois, with his wife and their baby son, Walt III. He kept to himself. The man who would be Clyde hadn't yet developed an affinity for expensive clothes, fast cars, overhead bedroom mirrors, or after-hours parties. "He was the quietest guy on the team," said Clarence Smith, Frazier's college teammate. "You weren't going to see him at fraternity parties or even in the student union." Incubating beneath Frazier's reserved exterior was someone else entirely, a character—or some would say caricature—known as Clyde. According to Frazier, the trainer Danny Whelan gave him the nickname after seeing Warren Beatty in *Bonnie and Clyde*. During his rookie year, when minutes were hard to come by but the money wasn't, Frazier would occupy himself sartorially. "I wasn't playing well, and in order to pacify myself I'd go buy clothes," he said.

A short man with a long needle, Whelan was unsparing in his ridicule when Frazier walked into the locker room one night with a brown velour hat. "Get a load of Clyde," he cracked. Everyone laughed, but Frazier was, as usual, unruffled. He was sure he looked good. He had never been one to fear standing apart. "I was never afraid of being an individual," he said. "Even if it meant I was going to be ostracized for it."

Clyde was more suited to the constant scrutiny and adulation of big-city sports fans than Walt; he was a mask that alleviated the off-court performance anxiety and allowed Frazier to quiet the part of him that preferred being alone. In the intimidating limelight of Manhattan celebrity, he could be someone he wasn't—even his old teammates from the Midwest didn't recognize him. "We could never figure the whole Clyde thing out," Smith said, noting that when Frazier returned to Southern Illinois for a team or school reunion, he was the same old Walt, pulling vitamins out of his pocket and excusing himself early to go get some sleep. Then he would return to New York and Clyde would take over. The development of the persona and the nickname were one thing. The branding of Clyde was another. Here Frazier needed some help.

"Walt used to come into my office all the time," said the Garden photographer George Kalinsky, fondly recalling a time when the Knicks' administrative offices had open doors for everyone, even reporters. "So he comes in one day and he's wearing a green suit, green vest, green hat, and matching green alligator shoes. I look at the outfit and I say, 'Let's go take a photo.'" Kalinsky posed Frazier outside the Garden, near a lamppost, and loved the result so much that he submitted it to *Newsweek*. "It gets into the magazine and we get about 200 letters from women wanting a copy," he said. Frazier later autographed the photo—"Thanks for making me Clyde"—and sent it to Kalinsky. The Frazier endorsement was all the validation he needed. "I didn't create the nickname," Kalinsky said. "But I felt I created the aura."

The rest of the Clyde legend remains shrouded in ambiguity, largely recounted in impressionistic sound bites that only heighten the historical mystique.

"I think a lot of the Clyde stuff was for the public, but it wasn't who the real person was," said Dick Garrett. "He was a more subdued guy, not a heavy partier. How could he be? He cared more about his body than anything. He would never abuse himself. I think the legend of Clyde started in the media and he just played along."

Whatever the time frame from origin to sensation, Clyde Frazier needed time to cultivate his cool, erase the misperception of himself as detached and indifferent. For that to happen, though, he had to become something special on the court. The trade of Butch Komives to Detroit in the DeBusschere deal opened the door to more minutes. And with the increased time, Frazier drew ever closer to Red Holzman, who would often make him sit next to him on the bench and fill his young guard's head with ongoing observation and, of course, criticism.

Relaxing on the terrace of one of his St. Croix houses, Frazier could laugh about the latter part and throw in a punch line. "There were times Red made me so mad I was tempted to do a Sprewell," he said, referring to the 1997 incident in which the Golden State guard, first name Latrell, attacked and choked his coach, P. J. Carlesimo (which brought him eternal infamy and a trade to the Knicks the following season).

With Holzman giving him more and more freedom, Frazier's game picked up fast and the statistics reflected his progress. From averaging about 21 minutes, 9 points, and 4 assists as a rookie, he was at almost 40 minutes, 20.9 points, and 8.2 assists during the championship season two years later. Like the Old Knicks, Frazier had been a work in progress, unlike the city's other master of suave, Joe Willie Namath.

Namath had hit New York with a massive contract and was immediately considered the savior of an upstart league. Even when Frazier's performance soared, he still had to toil within the Holzman democracy, sharing the ball (and the attention) with a disparate band of emerging media darlings. Namath had no such impediments, given the costumed anonymity of his Jets teammates and most football players. Beyond the dimpled smile, the twinkling blue eyes, and the glorious nickname, Broadway Joe, Namath had the winning personality of a Midtown saloonkeeper. "I used to hang around with Joe and Mickey Mantle a lot," George Lois said. "Mickey was a nasty guy; everybody knew that, especially when he was drinking. But around Joe he'd be different. Joe would say, 'Mick, stay and sign a few autographs,' and, goddammit, Mickey would listen, only for Joe. Frazier was a star, but there was nobody like Joe."

Namath was big enough not only to open his own club, Bachelors III, but to push back when Pete Rozelle ordered him to divest his interest because the club was attracting what the NFL commissioner determined to be the wrong clientele. Instead, Namath called a press conference and tearfully announced he was quitting football. Cooler heads prevailed, but Namath was bigger than ever: James Dean in white football cleats. Even Frazier was impressed. "Joe was such a nice guy, nothing like his image," he said, having run into the quarterback at other East Side haunts. Frazier wore mink, like Namath, but he had a different, less gregarious personality. Even as Clyde, he tended to hang back, coolly observant. But being a Knicks star on a championship team was often all the introduction he needed.

While many of Frazier's teammates were handed ringside tickets for the Fight of the Century, the first of three bouts between Muhammad Ali and Joe Frazier, on March 9, 1971, at the Garden, it was Clyde Frazier who was included in the celebrity sightings in the next day's reports. There he was in the same news columns as Frank Sinatra, Norman Mailer, Ted Kennedy, and Diana Ross. "You name them, they were there," Frazier said, recalling the experience, in part as an affirmation of his own rise to full-blown star. "Sinatra was taking pictures. And then the mink coats—everybody had a mink coat. And that was just the guys." He laughed and added, "And diamonds, too."

He remembered seeing himself on the news the next day, strolling into the Garden in his own full-length mink, not quite sure if he was in the Ali camp along with the majority of the glitterati. As much of a stylist as Ali was, in the mold of Clyde, there was something about the no-nonsense Smokin' Joe that indisputably appealed to Walt's working-class southern roots.

"I was kind of in between, but when Frazier hit him with that left hook in the last round, it kind of hit me: 'Oh, yeah, I guess I'm rooting for Frazier.' But we all knew that we were witnessing something special, man. Nobody left when the fight was over, just standing there. And then when you went outside, there were limousines all around this place, triple-parked. And all the celebrities, every celebrity in the world."

Or so it seemed to the Knicks superstar, who began to feel as if the world were waiting for him every time he stepped out on the Upper East Side and on up into Harlem.

Frazier—as Walt or Clyde—was never much of a drinker. He didn't have a sip in high school and didn't know what to do all those years later when gratis alcohol came his way at famed hangouts like P.J. Clarke's, Jimmy Weston's, and Elaine's. "At first I would say, 'Hey, man, I didn't want a drink,'" he said. "But then a guy I knew told me, 'Don't ever turn one down, because these people will think you're not a good guy.'" Bartenders caught on and kept his alcohol intake next to nothing, though Clyde bent his own rules when it came to entertaining the opposite sex. Divorced not long after he joined the Knicks, Frazier created a new ethos. "Clyde was wine, clothes, song, and a different woman each night," he said. Pressed for a statistical estimate of his scoring totals, he joked that he was nowhere close to Wilt Chamberlain (who, in a 1991 autobiography, claimed to have slept with 20,000 women). One road roommate of Frazier's said the hotel telephone seldom stopped ringing. "Women calling day and night, wanting tickets, wanting a piece of him," the roommate said.

"If they want to see Clyde tonight," he'd say, "they got to pay." He meant for the tickets, his trademark frugality being a habit he was never eager to break.

Few, if any, got too close to Clyde, who was clearly shielding Walt from the superficialities of fame. He understood that self-promotion required only a mastery of commercial invention. Image was everything. Hence, Clyde never had to work too hard for the attention he received, never had to make a spectacle of himself. Walt was always at the controls, behind the curtain, manipulating his wizard of ah's.

A fawning woman might be at his side in a club, and suddenly he would announce he was leaving—with her number in his pocket, of course—to have a bowl of granola and go to sleep. Sometimes it was an opposing player, out on the town on the night before a game at the Garden, who would unwittingly prompt Frazier to call it a night, lest he be more sleep-deprived than the man he might have to guard.

"We didn't have a curfew," Frazier said. "But if I saw someone like Oscar leave at a certain time, that was my cue to get out of there, too."

Once the media were playing ball, all he had to do in order to be Clyde was let people have a glimpse into his material world, allow the occasional photographer access to the bedroom of his East Side high-rise, where the closets were jammed with velour suits and flowing capes and his $5,000 black ranch mink coat. All he had to do was grow the muttonchops, then the beard, and hit the town in his 1965 Rolls. He purchased the car gray but had it painted burgundy and beige before adding the coup de grâce, his gangster whitewalls. "The Clydemobile."

Nobody appreciated Frazier's theatrical pose and natural stage presence more than the emerging director Woody Allen. "He'd come into Elaine's," Allen said of his longtime Second Avenue hangout. "There was this amazing aura about him when he'd step into a room."

Allen was, in effect, the perfect Clyde audience. He only wanted to observe the splendor of the man, not impose on him or so much as chat. When Ira Berkow was co-writing Frazier's book *Rockin' Steady*, in the early seventies, they went out to lunch one day at P.J. Clarke's, settling in at a backroom table on a slow late afternoon. There was one other patron nearby, reading a newspaper but stealing the occasional glance over the top of it. Every time Berkow looked over, the guy would defensively pull the paper up. This went on for a while, Berkow humored by the game of Clyde-and-mouse, until the fellow got up to leave. Only then did he realize it was Woody Allen. As long as he could maintain his distance, Frazier enjoyed the attention, and grew adept at eliciting more of it.

"My first game in New York, he gets knocked down and he's laying there like he's dead," said Butch Beard, who joined the Knicks after the championship years, in 1975. "I rush over there, thinking, Oh my God, he's really hurt." Frazier looked up at his teammate without cracking a smile. "Beard," he said, "how're my fans taking it?" "Fuck you," Beard said. Beard was no NBA star, just an acerbic, tough-minded guard on a variety of teams, including the 1975 champion Golden State Warriors. Frazier had respected Beard after the classic games Southern Illinois had played against Louisville. In New York, Frazier showed Beard around, gave him rides in his Rolls from the team's new downtown gym at Pace College. He got him hooked on yoga. On the road, they were occasional dinner companions, including one night in Chicago when Frazier carried in a bag that he set on the table and left there until the waiter brought over a glass of wine.

"Now he opens the bag, and what comes out but the ingredients for a damn salad," Beard said. "Right there in the restaurant he starts chopping the shit up, and the maître d' actually comes by and watches, asking him all these questions about how he prepares it." Beard shook his head in amazement and thought, "I do that, my ass is definitely out of here."

Frazier was no national media sensation like Magic and Bird would be in the eighties (much less Jordan in the nineties and James now). No NBA player of Frazier's era was. But looking back, people like Kalinsky and Beard marveled at how brilliantly Frazier marketed himself with the help of his New York–based agent, Irwin Weiner. By the early seventies he was in demand all over town, and earned $1,000 per appearance, pocket change compared with his $300,000 salary and $100,000 a year in endorsements and appearances. From the head beneath his wide-brim hats to his canvas-covered toes, Clyde played Cupid in the eventual marriage of pro basketball and the sneaker industry. In 1972, Puma paid Frazier $5,000 (and promised him all the free merchandise he needed) to put his name on a shoe. The Clyde brand was sold only in the New York tristate area, but in the days before basketball players were branded as national pitchmen, Frazier's shoes were hot.

"I did a poster—I had my mink coat and sneakers on," he said. Three decades after his retirement, Puma was still selling the shoe, now internationally, noting on pumashoes.com that Frazier was the first to endorse a casual sneaker that became synonymous with style: "A 1970s basketball icon and renowned ladies' man, he took court style to the streets for the first time. And there was no going back."

Despite the headlines of the time and his proximity to men like Bradley and Barnett, Frazier remained largely apolitical and uninvolved. In the late sixties and early seventies, Frazier didn't win many friends uptown by coming off as uninterested in the movement to empower the black man in America. To some, his dress and lifestyle represented a black male stereotype. As Clyde, he rubbed salt in that perception when he called the Italian bombshell Sophia Loren his ideal woman at a time when black women were picking out their hair, kinky and proud. Black activists also complained when Frazier bought a liquor store in Harlem, arguing that a man of his stature should set a better business example, especially in a community where so many young males were at risk. (He eventually sold the store.)

But as the years wore on, Frazier found himself playing defense in ways he found more irksome. It angered him when sportswriters who had once compared him to Oscar and West accused him of playing hard only during the last five minutes of a game. After the championship years, on a team in decline, he felt singled out, made a scapegoat. Why didn't the press ever go after Bradley or Monroe?

When the Knicks struck first, banishing him to Cleveland in 1977, he found out on a Friday night, his agent, Weiner, waiting for him in the lobby of his apartment building. "Cleveland?" Frazier said. "Come on, man." He was stunned. To make matters worse, the deal had been partly orchestrated by the incoming coach, Willis Reed, who called it "a painful decision to make the team younger." Frazier would come back early that season, get a rousing Garden ovation, lead the Cavs to a victory, and hand Reed his first coaching defeat. But a depressing reality soon set in: he had to return to Cleveland and look for a place to live in a drab and distant suburb, where the Cavs had moved after abandoning the city, though they eventually returned downtown. When a female broker showed him several posh condominiums, Frazier remarked that the closet space in one was scarce, compared with what he had in New York. And how would he get his round bed through the narrow front passageway? The broker responded by directing him to a window with a view of the forest.

"You call that a view?" Frazier said. "I'm used to looking out on the greatest city in the world." When the broker replied that Cleveland was not New York, Frazier snorted, "I'm hip," and moved in with a teammate, Jim Chones.

He tolerated Cleveland until he quit in 1980, returning to New York to resume his life as Clyde. The Frazier name was still magic in the city, and he launched Walt Frazier Enterprises with Weiner and the 76ers great Billy Cunningham. Together they managed the business affairs of some heavyweight players, including Julius Erving and George McGinnis. But Frazier discovered that serving a superstar was nothing like being one. He hated the solicitation, "the glorified babysitting." He began to wonder what the hell he was going to do with the rest of his life.

He soon realized that, being a former player, people didn't quite see him the same way. After a while he didn't care. "I kind of got fed up with all the material things, fed up with New York and that scene, the nightclubs and the cars," he said. "I said, 'Man, I don't want this anymore.' I didn't want to vegetate as Clyde. I was searching for something—I just didn't know what it was."

The year before he retired from basketball, 1979, he had taken his son, Walt III, on a vacation to St. Croix. The boy, then 12, loved to swim, and someone had recommended to him the largest of the Virgin Islands. Coming from most places, the lush St. Croix terrain would have been breathtaking. From Cleveland, Frazier felt the sea breeze on his face and found it intoxicating. He called a real estate broker and within days had purchased a Caribbean-style one-story house with four curved columns that looked like tentacles. The house was on one acre and built into a hill overlooking the water.

Back home, Frazier startled friends with the news. They believed he had acted impulsively, that he would quickly grow tired of the Caribbean commute, of being so far from the Manhattan nightlife. Shouldn't he at least have shopped around? Visited other islands like Barbados or Bermuda? Frazier had an answer for them, his logic, as usual, steeped in financial pragmatism. In St. Croix, a territory of the United States, he wouldn't have to worry about government upheaval and the potential seizure of property.

Initially, St. Croix was just a getaway destination from the New York scene. "I would come and just chill, do nothing," he said. But whenever he gratefully stepped off the prop jet from San Juan or Miami, he felt as if he were exhaling. He began to adjust to the slower pace, the island rhythms. He took a sailing course, got his captain's license, and purchased a boat. He befriended an old island native named Rufus Knight, who became his mentor on the water. One morning, they started out for St. Thomas at 4 A.M. Out at sea, Frazier looked up at the sky to see the first rays of light and thought, "I've found paradise."

Something within him was changing fundamentally. As a man, Walt was growing. Clyde was dying. But unlike Clyde's birth, it was easier to pinpoint the time of his official expiration.

Almost a decade after he had left the game, soon after he began his broadcasting career, which kept him anchored in Manhattan and the mainland for much of the basketball season, Frazier was watching football at his island retreat on Sunday afternoon, September 17, 1989, when the first terrifying winds blew the awnings off his home. The television went dark. The living room windows blew out. He and his lady friend raced for the bathroom, hunkering down for a long, fierce night.

"We sat there, in the dark, hungry and cold, water coming from under the door, wind howling, hearing crashes sounding like freight trains running down the track," he said. Bizarre thoughts rush through your brain in such moments of peril. Frazier recalled how his mother liked to tell him, "You don't know what it's like to not have a roof over your head." He wondered if he was about to find out. The hurricane's full force arrived in the wee hours of September 18. "All we could say was, 'Hold on, house. Hold on,'" he said.

Thank God, he thought, the roof was concrete and apparently hurricane-proof. Little else in the house proved to be of the same durability, but it managed to remain upright all the same.

The next morning, Hugo having left $1 billion in damage to the island, Frazier warily opened the bathroom door, sidestepping the refrigerator that had hurtled from the kitchen. He surveyed his residential wreckage—rooms bathed in water, glass everywhere, furniture gnarled and blown outside. His boat was gone, sunk in the cay. Soon a neighbor would deliver terrible news: Rufus Knight had fallen while scrambling amid the debris and hit his head. Frazier's sailing partner was dead.

Frazier said he felt "like someone stabbed me in the heart," but as he contemplated the dark side of paradise, he also found himself strangely fascinated by the chaos, by forces so far beyond human control that he could only wonder about how he had lived his life in the fast lane, about all the material things he had pursued and collected and what they all were really worth.

The clothes, the cars, the mirrors presenting a reflection of what he—or Clyde, at least—had come to define as success. "I think that was when I started to think about what else I could really do with my life and that there had to be more to it than basketball," he said.

Before that could happen, he had to embrace the realization that he was one lucky man. He had survived nature's onslaught. He was alive. If Clyde wasn't quite dead, Walt at least felt reborn.

Emerging from the tiny St. Croix airport terminal on February 24, 2010, I walked outside and there he was, standing along the curb, arms resting on the driver's-side door of his GMC light truck. Before I took another step in Walt Frazier's direction, it occurred to me how far I had come, literally and figuratively, from our first professional encounter, when I took a deep breath and approached him as a wide-eyed reporter for the *Staten Island Advance*.

"Excuse me, Walt?"

He didn't look up.

"Walt?"

He still didn't look up.

Finally, three words.

"Get lost, *chump*."

Granted, I would experience even worse first impressions of my other idols: Mickey Mantle was stone drunk in the clubhouse after a Yankee Stadium event in 1976. Reggie Jackson met my outstretched hand with an icy glare before turning his back to me and cutting a loud fart. At least Frazier, I later came to realize, had good reason to be grumpy. In his final discontented days as a Knick, he was understandably in no mood to jabber with reporters, much less a greenhorn like me.

We would laugh about the episode years later when I confessed that I'd gone home and contemplated flinging myself out the fifth-floor window of my apartment, clutching my dog-eared copy of *Rockin' Steady*. He told me I shouldn't have been too insulted. In those days, *chump* was a common insult around the team, reserved for friend and foe alike.

This time, Frazier smiled as I approached, extending a hand. A little more than a month from his 65th birthday, he was still remarkably youthful, despite thinning hair and the faintest hint of an expanding midriff. He wore a baseball cap, off-white jeans with painter's pockets, a T-shirt, and a pair of flat canvas sneakers—the Clyde Pumas, of course. By the second day of my stay, I would learn that this was Frazier's island uniform. His current girlfriend, Patricia James, had grown accustomed to asking him on the way out to dinner, "You're not going to change?"

This was no longer the stylish and image-conscious night stalker she had adored while growing up in the north Jersey suburb of Montclair. Frazier of the island was a homebody who had long ago ditched the Rolls and preferred his truck, who couldn't remember the last time he had been out in a club (on this island or Manhattan), who tried to avoid trips to neighboring St. Thomas because it was "too commercial, just like New York."

So who, then, was the nattily dressed legend on the Knicks radio and television broadcasts since the late eighties? He looked like Clyde. He sounded like Clyde. But he was merely a vestige of the past, Leonard Nimoy putting on his Spock ears for a *Star Trek* convention. On St. Croix, where he camped out when his broadcasting duties were finished and to which he escaped whenever he could during the season, the locals knew him more as "Frazier the tree guy." He loved the melodious sound of the extended name; it affirmed what he felt about growth, nature's and his own, from renowned hedonist to home-building horticulturist.

"People in New York who saw me here would probably be disappointed in me," he told me as we eased our way down a shady path and began a tour of his property—which he had transformed from a largely barren single lot to roughly five acres of tropical paradise. He was wrong about that, dead wrong. Old Knicks fans would be fascinated, I told him.

As we walked the grounds, stopping to admire a veranda or a view, he admitted that he often found himself looking around, asking: How did I do all this? Part determination, he said, and part fate. When he ventured outside on the morning after Hugo, he made a startling and miraculous discovery. On the edge of the pool, blown out from the living room, was his wallet—money and credit cards snug in the fold. How could the wallet have not blown away, given the force of the wind? The stroke of luck had provided the means of surviving, the credit cards he needed to stay on and begin the rebuilding process. Not that he wasn't intimidated—there was so much to do—but the oldest of nine Frazier children, the man who would be Clyde, was no resplendent prima donna. Walt had been raised on menial tasks. "As a kid, my job was mopping the floors and taking out the garbage," he said.

On a devastated island, he didn't have a work crew or basic life comforts like electricity or even a bed. For several weeks, he slept in the bathroom to avoid the mosquitoes. Realizing the first thing he needed was windows, he removed the broken glass, measured the spaces, and ordered replacements. He emptied the rooms and the property of debris. He replaced fixtures, scrubbed muck off the walls, and gave them all a fresh coat of paint.

The more he did, the more stimulation he felt, a sense of purpose he hadn't known since his peak playing days. "I began to see there was work for me to do here, work that was going to keep me young," he said. "I was experiencing a metamorphosis, a change for the better."

On the east side of the island, also known as the dry side, he had discovered a well, which on St. Croix spared him the risky dependence on rainwater and the prohibitive costs of purchasing water from private sources. With a well, he could grow to his heart's content. "Called this guy, told him where I lived, and he told me, 'Man, you can't get no water out there,'" Frazier said. "I told him, 'No, come out and see.' He looked at these hills and he said, 'Okay, I'll try right here.' He went 160 feet deep. I paid him $8,000—my best investment. People told me that around here, it was like striking oil."

There were hundreds of plantings—fruit trees and palms and colorful flowers that could match Clyde's most ostentatious outfits. Nurturing them reminded him of running an offense, educating himself about his teammates' needs, knowing what to feed them and when.

He built an intricate system of cisterns that tapped into the well but also utilized rainwater. He hired a gardener to help him, to teach him how to plant and nurture. "Every morning I'd work with him," he said. "He'd pick, I'd shovel." The more the property bloomed, the greener his thumb became and the more determined he was to upgrade and expand. He began buying up the surrounding one-and-a-half-acre lots, most with run-down houses he knew he would want to renovate.

"But I was so naive about most of these things," he said. "I didn't know about boundaries, property lines, zoning, nothing." One time, he cleared land that actually belonged to a neighbor and planted trees—again with fortuitous results. It turned out the neighbor wanted to sell. On the other side of that property he scooped up more land and homes.

He gave each one a name: the Green House, the Pink House, the Pool House, and the Main House, where he and Patricia lived. He redeveloped them with a strong Caribbean flavor, emphasizing decks and terraces, with outdoor kitchens and bathrooms. The furniture was understated: earth tones and bamboo. He still loved mirrors but kept them off the ceilings, confining them to sliding closet doors. "I'm selling you nature, easy living," he said.

He perused home and garden magazines, attended home shows in Miami and New York, scoured outlets and home appliance stores for furniture and fixtures—it became an obsession. When he wasn't working on a house, he was mentally designing additions for the property. His builder, a slow-moving local man named Michael Wynter, grinned slyly when I asked how he and Frazier collaborated. "He comes up with the ideas and I build them," he said. "But he changes his mind a lot."

The project that had Frazier's attention during my visit was one that had begun as a plain wooden deck overlooking a hilly vista. He decided it needed a roof as a cover for rain, and then he expanded the plan to a clubhouse and bar that all his tenants could use. Finally, he added a side room he thought he might rent out, with an accompanying bathroom. Down the road, he said he might build a gym and run basketball clinics for island kids and vacationers staying at the posh Buccaneer Hotel next door.

In the spirit of the island, there was no urgency to any of these plans. About half the houses already had renters, but he seemed in no rush to finish the others.

Most important, Frazier said, was getting a project right. He finessed the details the way he fussed over Clyde's wardrobe and fine-tuned his game, telling me, "I always thought I was the consummate player, that I could do everything." The man was not without humility. He snickered and added, "Except maybe go to my right."

He admitted he was not easy—and occasionally impossible—to work for. In late middle age, if there was one standout regret that Frazier had, it was that he had not spent enough time with his son when he was young, after divorcing his first wife. He was always on the road, playing ball, being Clyde. Just the mention of the separation glazed Frazier's eyes. So when Walt III had finished college, a University of Pennsylvania grad, his father hired him to look after the property while he was in New York. And then fired him when he discovered how much partying and how little work was going on.

Similarly, when Patricia was laid off from her job in broadcast media, Frazier made her property manager—testing her resolve and their relationship. He obsessively scrutinized the work of painters and handymen, distrusting their willingness to cover every spot and their ability to properly wield a squeegee. Walt did windows.

Sitting on a terrace at one of the unfinished homes on a warm, breezy afternoon while Frazier was off watering his trees, I remarked to James how beautiful the property was. She nodded and after a pause of several seconds became teary-eyed. "Until you come here, you don't know what this place means to him," she said.

And there was the rub. Rare was the person who knew Frazier in New York, around the Garden, who had ever set foot on this place he had poured so much of himself into, including much of his earnings as a broadcaster and Old Knicks legend. To them, St. Croix was no more than a rumor, a gleam in their old teammate's eye. He admitted to me that he sometimes wished they could all spend a few days, walk with him up the hill to the one undeveloped tract of his property.

Here was where he was planning to build his dream house, the one he would live in when he was completely done with New York. He would sell off the rest of the property, hopefully rake in five or six million (after an initial investment of $215,000 and an estimated $1.5 million more in additions). He could already envision the open-air living room, alongside a pool, with breathtaking views of Christiansted Harbor on one side and the Caribbean on the other.

Yes, he still loved New York. In fact, months after my visit to St. Croix, Frazier expanded his real estate holdings with a three- apartment investment in Harlem. Attracted by the building's large outdoor spaces that would allow him to exercise his green thumb in the city, as well as the opportunity to reinvest in the community that had once chastised him for his liquor store endeavor, Frazier had decided he would share one of the apartments with Walt III. Father and son had also begun planning another sports-management company that Walt III might carry on when the old man was finally ready to kick completely back and chill in the cool breeze of the island.

When that day might come he couldn't say—possibly never—but the view of Walt Frazier in St. Croix was nonetheless one of a man at peace. If a basketball-savvy tourist did a double take at a nearby table when he was out to dinner or at breakfast, overlooking the grounds of the Buccaneer Hotel, Frazier would smile, sign his name, but never look pained that the attention was for something long ago.

As we walked down the hill, back toward the Main House, Frazier told me he had found the secret to a life beyond the Garden. It was really the same concept that had allowed him to share his prime real estate in the Knicks' backcourt with Earl Monroe. "The main thing is controlling one's ego and being creative in any way you can," he said. He tugged on his baseball cap, pulling it low to shield his eyes from the sun. "Nobody watches me anymore, but that's okay. I get pleasure from what I do. It's what you feel inside." We stopped for a while at the deck and future clubhouse, where the builder Wynter was busy measuring planks while his assistant, operating a backhoe, cleared weeds from a space nearby. Leaning against the rail, Frazier drifted away from our conversation, into a trancelike state. I figured he was scrutinizing the assistant's work, until he pointed to a flock of egrets bobbing for worms in the path of the backhoe.

"It's amazing how they compete with each other, how they jockey for position and then jump out of the way as the shovel comes down," Frazier said. He studied them for several minutes, as if they were neighbors playing a set of tennis. "They're survivors," he said. "They get what they want and then they get out."

Bright lights, big city: Minuteman Mike Riordan battles the Celtics in 1971.

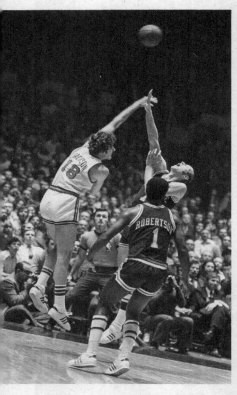

TOP RIGHT: *I know where you live:* Jerry Lucas taking time away from memorizing the phone book.

ABOVE: *Playing hooky:* Phil Jackson's shot wasn't known for its beauty, but New York welcomed his return from back surgery.

RIGHT: *O captain, our captain:* Reed fetches another rebound.

A sense of where he is: Bill Bradley at the free-throw line.

The Willis Reed Show: Willis Reed, Pete Maravich, Woody Allen, and Marv Albert reminiscing.

ABOVE: *Midtown cowboy:* Dustin Hoffman and Red Holzman at the celebration for the Knicks' 1970 championship, at Gracie Mansion.

RIGHT: *The way we won:* Barbra Streisand *(circled)* tries to encourage Holzman and Bradley en route to their second championship in 1973.

The Reel World: A Knicks film session before the 1973 Finals. That's Jerry Lucas at the projector.

The new Old Knicks: Team photo, 1973. Dean Meminger (7) stands behind his man, Earl Monroe (15).

TOP LEFT: *His cross to bear:* Earl "Black Jesus" Monroe, seated in a most unusual position—on the bench.

BOTTOM LEFT: *Changing of the guard:* Dean Meminger helped bring New York a title.

ABOVE: *I am the open man!:* Monroe lets fly while Bill Bradley waits for the pass.

Yes!: Willis Reed hoists Bill Bradley as the buzzer sounds on the last, best moment in Knicks history, the 1973 championship.

14

THE BRAIN DRAIN

Jerry Lucas lost his way. A state champion in high school, a national champion in college, and a gold-medal Olympian, Lucas was a perennial winner who had nevertheless wandered waywardly in pursuit of an NBA title. In Cincinnati, he and Oscar Robertson had toiled in vain to surmount the Celtics, and he soon found himself banished from his home state of Ohio—by Bob Cousy—to a lousy Warriors team. In San Francisco, Lucas broke his hand and went bankrupt when his chain of restaurants, Beef 'N' Shakes, veered sharply into the red. When he filed, to the tune of $822,000, he lost his savings, along with his Cincinnati home. His play with the Warriors suffered.

"The day I was traded to the Knicks, I was absolutely overjoyed, because being in San Francisco was the worst time of my basketball life," Lucas said. But if his two seasons out west were not worth remembering, he couldn't help himself. Every sad detail lay stored in what he himself claims is his "incredibly creative mind."

Wherever Lucas went, he astounded people with his extraordinary mnemonic skills and aptitude with numbers. His was a life of constant counting. During time-outs in the middle of games, he might glance into the stands to determine how many steps were in a particular aisle. On the team bus to the arena, he might lose himself by calculating how many white stripes per mile were painted on the highway. He would be introduced to someone and immediately convert the person's name into numbers that corresponded with the respective place of the letters in the alphabet. He fancied himself an expert magician and card-trick specialist.

When he got to New York, the man who had been Phi Beta Kappa at Ohio State University embarked on a calculated mission to cash in as a real-life Carnac, Johnny Carson's psychic alter ego. While Bill Bradley and Phil Jackson were reading up on Richard Nixon's historic trip to China and the chilling rise of the Khmer Rouge in Cambodia, Lucas was memorizing 50,000 names from the Manhattan telephone book. He ripped out handfuls of pages and studied them on Knicks road trips. His teammates would have thought he'd lost his mind, so he would read in secret to spare himself their worried glances. Given the team's high profile and the large number of Old Knicks fans in the entertainment business, it wasn't long before Lucas's showbiz potential was discovered. He hooked up with the music impresario Don Kirshner, who had played college ball and was often at the Garden.

Presto! With Kirshner behind him, Lucas soon had a 28th-floor office in a Midtown tower and a network television special called *The Jerry Lucas Super Kids Day Magic Jamboree*. He was soon in the celebrity seat next to Carson, Carnac himself, on *The Tonight Show*. He co-wrote *The Memory Book*, which soared to number two on the *New York Times* best-seller list. He earned endorsement deals with Vitalis and United Airlines.

"Let's face it," he reasoned, "New York is the place to be if you have ability." But even better for his mental health than promotional appearances and parlor tricks, Lucas got to mind-meld with the team that he, like so many others, believed was "the most intelligent ever." It was a stroke of fortune that revived his flagging career, in part by returning him to his college position. At 6'8", Lucas had played center on an Ohio State team with John Havlicek and a bullheaded reserve forward named Bobby Knight. But in the NBA, *Sports Illustrated*'s 1961 Sportsman of the Year was considered too small for the pivot and proceeded to become a great rebounding forward, a canny anticipator of the carom, which he credited to hours of studying opposing shooters. In February 1964—when Lucas averaged 17.4 rebounds a game and was third in the league behind Bill Russell and Wilt Chamberlain—he grabbed 40 in one game, a record for a forward.

Critics claimed Lucas cheated by sagging off his man and surrendering easy shots so he could pad his rebounding stats. They claimed he'd lapsed into poor training habits in Cincinnati and was overweight, charges he quieted by dieting in San Francisco and shedding 20 pounds, easing pressure on his knees and back. As a result, the Knicks made out in the deal better than they ever imagined they would. The timing was especially propitious. Holzman acquired Lucas to help at both positions but especially at center, where it was becoming obvious that Reed would never again play at full capacity. When Reed, after 11 games, was declared out for the season due to the tendinitis in his left knee, Lucas was suddenly the starter. Less physical than Reed but a gifted and willing passer off the high post, Lucas was a shooter with as much range as any contemporary three-point specialist.

Growing up in Middletown, Ohio, between Cincinnati and Dayton, the son of a pressman at a local paper mill, Lucas was always the biggest player on his team and as such was typically stationed under the rim. Disinclined to convention, he spent hours every day "shooting from all over." He developed a strange-looking jumper in which his release point was just above his right shoulder, a one-handed push that was only slightly more elegant than Dick Barnett's own contortions. Given the distance most of his shots traveled, his career shooting percentage of 49.9 percent is remarkable.

"But it was when I was with the Knicks and had the opportunity to play center that I was really able to take advantage of it," he said, admitting how much he enjoyed tormenting lumbering seven-footers outside the lane. "Wilt was dumbfounded," said Lucas, yet another enthusiastic abuser of the poor, misunderstood Dipper. "If he did come out, I'd drive around him to the basket or pass off to DeBusschere or Bradley."

Sometime before Chamberlain's death in 1999, Lucas flipped on his television to find him in the chair opposite the interviewer Roy Firestone on ESPN. Firestone asked Chamberlain which player he least enjoyed matching up against. Lucas was sure he'd say Russell, but Chamberlain never would admit that. "Jerry

Lucas," he said. "He took me places I never wanted to go."

On a team of strong, eclectic personalities, Lucas stood out nonetheless. His new teammates wondered about his eccentric personality and were occasionally miffed by his lack of humility. Some were not amused by his memory games and didn't want to be bombarded with interesting but ultimately useless information.

"Lucas was a nutcake," Phil Jackson told me. "He was a gifted guy, but he did that memory thing that drove us all crazy." According to Jackson, least impressed by Lucas was Dave DeBusschere, the ale-loving clock puncher who didn't see the point in alphabetical word games and knowing the number of stairs he was about to climb.

"DeBusschere had no time for Lucas's nonsense," Jackson said. "But they played great together." Opposites in personality, DeBusschere and Lucas were practically interchangeable on the court, with their dark hair and rugged good looks. With Bradley in the mix, the frontline had a throwback appearance, straight out of the fifties, that by today's standards was insanely small and startlingly white. But the bottom line on Lucas—once called by John Wooden "the most unselfish player" he'd ever seen—was that he was a born Old Knick. "Extremely smart basketball player—the game was almost too easy for him," Jackson said. "He taught me how to shoot."

Bradley said Lucas's arrival elevated the team's offensive IQ even higher and provided him with a companion to tap into his own brand of brainy mischief. "A guy would be guarding me and I would come down, the ball would come to me, and I would yell out to Lucas"—here Bradley spewed some guttural nonsense—"and then Lucas would yell something back that sounded the same, and if the guy was a rookie or a young player, he'd be saying, 'What . . . what?'" The gibberish wasn't code for anything, just a way of playing with the opponent's head while Bradley and Lucas improvised the play.

Lucas, laughing uproariously at the mention of his linguistic adventures with the future senator, said he was dazzled and reenergized by the intellectual challenge of playing with his new teammates on the Broadway stage. "People in San Francisco did not know or understand basketball," he said. "There was no real love of the game. In New York, it felt like religion." Lucas thought he'd already been blessed to have played on great high school and college teams. He relished his six years with the Big O in Cincinnati. But there was nothing close, he said, to stepping onto the court with a group that was as exceptionally intuitive as the

Knicks. "On other teams, you'd have guys who would come out of a time-out, look around, and say, 'What are we doing?'" Lucas said. "With the Knicks, that never happened. Red would come in at halftime and ask *us*, 'What should we do in the second half?' I have to say that my time with them was the most fun I ever had, far and away."

At 70, Lucas was still busy promoting himself as Doctor Memory, marketing his Lucas Learning System of retention techniques. He was still wedded to the itinerant life but not very interested in the NBA. "I never look back at the game," he said while driving to the airport after an appearance in Columbus, Ohio, to catch a flight home to California. "It hasn't been important to me for 30 years, because I've had so many other interests. And I really don't think it's as interesting a game as it used to be." From the little he knew of it, what ailed it most, he said, was too much emphasis on jumping and dunking—and not enough on the brain.

Knicks fans could only despair when the Captain went down. Would we ever see him in uniform again? The first title had barely been won *with* Reed; if he was finished, what were the realistic odds of claiming another? To complete the misery, the regular season marked a familiar tormentor's return to prominence, one we had wanted to believe would trouble us no more. Red Auerbach had managed to rebuild the Celtics in two years, mainly by drafting Dave Cowens, the undersize but speedy and hard-nosed center, and the smooth-shooting guard Jo Jo White. With John Havlicek still playing at All-Star capacity, it was hard to believe, much less accept, that the Celtics were already back running their mouths and their vaunted fast break. They won 56 games and took the division by a meaty 8 games over the transmogrifying Knicks.

"Auerbach had always found a way to replace players," said Tommy Heinsohn, the former Celtic forward, who'd replaced Bill Russell as coach after the last championship in 1969. "His philosophy was always quickness and speed, push the ball, attack people. Cowens came my second year, and he was perfect for that style. We developed an offense for him against the bigger centers; he became our point center. Handled the ball a lot and revolutionized the game by the way he was used."

A nauseatingly familiar story line was unfolding: the Celtics were imposing their will, even on the Lakers. Pat Riley had joined the team as a shooting guard the previous season, after three with the San Diego Rockets. He had forged a friendship with Jerry West, who admired the intensity of the former Kentucky Wildcat and had lobbied the Lakers to acquire him. From West,

Riley learned what he would later preach as the dapper and sloganeering coach in Los Angeles, New York, and Miami: there was only one way to evaluate a season—whether or not a trophy sat in your locker room following the last game of the year.

"Jerry epitomized, for me, the most desperate superstar this game has known," Riley told me. "One of the greatest and most caring players ever, and every year he had to endure the torture of losing at the end."

It was enough to drive any man to the brink. West was in a blind rage when he telephoned Riley one day during the summer of 1971. "You won't believe what the fuck is going on," West hollered. "They hired the goddamn Celtics!"

Having fired Joe Mullaney, and needing a third coach in four seasons, owner Jack Kent Cooke had brought in a man steeped in Celtics honor, Bill Sharman, who in turn tapped K. C. Jones to be his assistant. West's horror notwithstanding, Cooke had endured enough humiliation at the hands of the Celtics. If he couldn't beat them, why not hire them? Sharman certainly had the right credentials, beginning with his California roots. Raised in Porterville, California, he starred for USC before teaming with Cousy in the Boston backcourt and winning four titles during the first half of the Russell era. As a coach, Sharman already had an impressive résumé. Besides his title in the defunct ABL with George Steinbrenner's (and Dick Barnett's) Cleveland Pipers, he'd led the San Francisco Warriors to the Finals in 1967. Four years later, he won an ABA title with the Utah Stars.

Sharman hit L.A. preaching green gospel. The Lakers were not going to run their offense through Chamberlain, Baylor, or West anymore; they were just going to run, period. The days of the star system were over. The offensive wealth would have to be spread around. He instituted a new system that included a morning practice on game day, which later became a leaguewide staple called the shootaround. "He gathered the troops and said he would like us to come in the morning before the first game for a practice," Riley said. "We looked at each other and thought, What the hell is he talking about? Wilt was beside himself. He said, 'Here's the deal. You get me once a day, morning or evening. It's up to you which one.'"

Somehow Sharman convinced the big man to give it a try, albeit on his own recreational terms. Chamberlain liked to begin his day early, playing volleyball at Laguna Beach, and took to arriving at the Forum in his tank top and sandals, sand in his hair.

"That's how he walked through the plays," Riley said.

The Lakers began the season by winning six of nine while another drama played out behind the scenes.

During the preseason, Sharman had come to the conclusion that Elgin Baylor was not a good fit for the high-octane offense, given his age and bad knees. He intended to pull Baylor from the starting lineup in favor of the second-year forward Jim McMillian. Once Sharman made clear his intentions, Baylor said he would quit rather than come off the bench.

Sharman had been taught to believe that no one—with the exception of Russell, who practiced when he felt like it, with Auerbach's blessing—was bigger than the team. And since the Lakers stars had never won a championship, they didn't have the right to dictate protocol. "It was," Riley said, "a very bitter time."

McMillian was relaxing at home when word came that Baylor was retiring. He was as stunned and conflicted as he'd been at Madison Square Garden on the night of Game 7, 1970. The Columbia man didn't mind playing behind the certain Hall of Famer. Even being pushed for minutes, Baylor had treated him kindly during his rookie year. "It was a delicate situation," McMillian said. "I mean, how do you sit Elgin Baylor?"

With the benefit of hindsight, the answer was obvious. In the very first game without Baylor, the Lakers beat the Bullets and proceeded to make one of the more bizarre transformations. Upon the departure of an all-time great, they embarked on a 33-game win streak, destroying the mark of 20 that had been set by Milwaukee the previous season.

"We just dismantled teams," West said. "We had a lot of weapons that allowed us to play a different kind of game. It seemed easy, to tell you the truth." While giving Sharman his due for diversifying the attack, West preferred to credit the players more than the Celtics' philosophy. Given his scars, that was too much to ask. "I did the same things I always did but never got credit for," he said.

But Gail Goodrich, who had been reacquired the previous season after spending two years in Phoenix, disagreed. "In many ways we played like the Celtics," he said. "Before that, the Lakers had been pretty much a stagnant team, the offense going through a couple of stars."

The most compelling evidence of the Sharman effect was written in the fine print of the box score. Goodrich raised his scoring average by more than 8 points from the previous season and led the team by a fraction over West, who for the first and only time in his career topped the league in assists. More than any other season, Chamberlain sacrificed personal achievement by averaging 14.8 points, 6 off the previous season and an astonishing 36 off his career high of 50.4 in 1961–62.

Over and over, Sharman stressed the running game, reminding the Lakers of the common misperception that players had to be sprinters to run a formidable fast break. The Celtics' credo—carried on proudly in the eighties by the likes of skilled tortoises such as Larry Bird, Kevin McHale, Cedric Maxwell, and Chris Ford—was their commitment, positioning, and everlasting motion. "With us, we also had the speed, and I guess that's where Showtime in L.A. really started," McMillian said.

Riley would argue that the brand name was still eight years in the making. But for all five titles Magic and Kareem would win in the eighties (four under Riley), he had to admit: "That 1971–72 season was the most glorious ride I've ever had."

To McMillian, the fusion of those Lakers was epitomized in a *Sports Illustrated* photo of Chamberlain starting the break with a long pass, with the other starters—West, Goodrich, and the forward Happy Hairston—all in perfect position. Chamberlain finally was the Lakers' institutional pillar, cast in the image of his longtime Boston rival.

The subject of Russell and the Celtics was never far from Chamberlain's restless mind. Sitting on the bus one day that season, McMillian got an earful on the inequities of the ongoing comparison. "Look here, rookie," Chamberlain said, addressing McMillian as an apprentice even though he was in his sophomore pro season. "I don't know why they're always talking about Russ being the greatest. Look at all the players that played with Russ that are in the Hall of Fame. Look at me—how many? If all you have to do is rebound and block shots, how great do you have to be?"

The definition of greatness for Chamberlain would invariably come down to how he chose to describe it, individually or collectively. In addition to the 33-game streak, the '71–72 Lakers won 69 games, eclipsing the previous record of 68 won by Chamberlain's Philadelphia team in 1967–68. Until Michael Jordan and the Bulls won 72 in 1995–96 in an expanded league littered with lousy teams, Chamberlain could claim to have anchored the two most dominant single-season teams in history. But he also knew legacies were established in the springtime; those 69 wins meant nothing in the playoffs.

In the first round, the Lakers swept Chicago before confronting Kareem and the Bucks, who had pounded them the previous year. Milwaukee had also been the team to end L.A.'s 33-game streak, at the Milwaukee Arena. Chamberlain, of all people, requested a team meeting. He spoke of all the years when he believed that he was a better player than Russell but that Russell won in the end because he'd had the better team. Jim Cleamons, Phil Jackson's longtime assistant in Chicago and L.A., was a rookie guard on that team, soaking up every word. "At one point Wilt looked around the room and said, 'You know what? Kareem is a better player than me, but I know that we're the better team.'"

Coming from the typically bombastic Chamberlain, the admission was a startling concession—to Father Time, if no one else—but his point was well taken. An uneasy alliance of star players, the Lakers had every reason to believe, or at least suspect, that they had finally become a well-oiled machine. They took the penultimate step by strafing the Bucks in six games, reaching the Finals for the eighth time in eleven years. Now came the thorniest part. Never had a team with Jerry West been burdened with such expectations.

"Good as we were that season, the pressure when we got to the Finals was incredible, especially for Jerry," Riley said. "He wanted to be a champion so much. I'm telling you that you could see the desperation in his eyes."

The Knicks, meanwhile, had won 48 games, good enough to account for the NBA's seventh-best record. They were now two years removed from championship glory, and only growing older. The uproar created by the Monroe acquisition had quieted to whispers—fears that both parties might have made a colossal mistake. The bench missed Mike Riordan and Dave Stallworth, while Barnett, 35, was slowed by injuries. The backup center—with Lucas starting—was the one and only Luther Rackley, acquired from Cleveland after Reed went down. Was there any compelling reason to think of the Knicks as serious title contenders? Not really. Yet the playoffs in New York had become a rite of spring that we fervently hoped would consume us for weeks. My friends and I relished spending the few dollars we had on a blue-seat ticket and the occasional night outside the Garden, an urban camping trip in chilly April, to queue up.

The Knicks drew the Bullets in the first round. Though the teams remained rivals, the regular-season meetings were awkward, especially the first one, 11 days after the trade. In street clothes, the injured Riordan stood on the Bullets' side, glumly watching the Knicks warm up. Stallworth got an ovation when he was announced as a starter, but he was dominated by DeBusschere once the game began. No one, however, had a worse time of it than Monroe, who played an embarrassing five second-quarter minutes off the bench, scored two points, and watched the Knicks roll,

125–114. He and the Bullets weren't sure whether to resent or pity each other.

"I didn't know what to say to them and they didn't know what to say to me," he said. "So we hardly said anything."

Archie Clark had replaced Monroe as the primary backcourt scorer, averaging a shade over 25 points on the season, but Gus Johnson was injured and fading, Kevin Loughery and Fred Carter were missed, and the result was a 38–44 regular season that was somehow good enough for a Central Division title and the home-court advantage that came with it. That didn't stop the Knicks from snapping a 2–2 deadlock by pummeling the Bullets in Game 5 at the Civic Center before wrapping up the series at home.

The Celtics, also with home-court advantage, were next in the conference final. After beating Atlanta in the opening round, Heinsohn worried that Cowens and White, in their maiden playoff run, might not be ready for a team as wily as New York. The fears proved well founded when the Knicks rolled into Boston Garden for Game 1 and could do no wrong, blitzing the Celtics early and riding Walt Frazier's 36 points—equaling his championship-night total—to a 116–94 victory.

"Having Lucas at center instead of Reed gave them a whole different look," Havlicek said. He, better than anyone, was familiar with Lucas's shooting range, his unusual skills. "The guy never studied in college the way the rest of us did," Havlicek said. "An hour before a midterm, he'd sit down and read ten, twelve chapters. His brain was different than the rest of us. It was scary how he stored information. When we'd play against him, we'd call out the two play and Jerry would be yelling like a madman, 'Watch the high screen for John.'"

With Lucas countering the youthful energy of Cowens with positioning and experience, the Knicks finished off the Celtics in five games, and suddenly a title without Reed was four victories away. When the Knicks went into the Forum for Game 1, shot 72 percent in the first half, and blew the Lakers out, 114–92, it occurred to us all that we were playing with house money and might actually pull off the unthinkable. Lucas tormented Chamberlain in Game 1 by bombing away from outside for 26 points on 13 of 21 shooting. Bradley made 11 of 12 shots. DeBusschere had 19 points, 18 rebounds, and 6 assists. Frazier had a triple double of 14, 12, and 11. Meanwhile, West's anxiety was painfully obvious: Mr. Clutch missed 12 of his 15 shots.

Chamberlain didn't know what to do about Lucas stationing himself in the exurbs of the offense. "I never saw a team as dumbfounded as they were," Lucas said.

"We were absolutely killing them." But Cleamons insisted that the Lakers shrugged off the walloping because they didn't believe the Knicks would continue that kind of shooting.

"We felt like it was easier to recover from a game like that, because everything they threw up went in," he said. "It happens. I remember the veterans saying, 'Keep doing what we do. Things will turn.'" Sure enough, late in the second quarter of Game 2, fate ran a bone-crunching screen on the Knicks. With Barnett slowed by injury and Monroe still wandering around like a jet-lagged tourist, DeBusschere pulled a muscle in his right side, limiting his minutes and productivity and essentially undoing the team's fragile chemistry. Without three frontcourt players who were outside threats, Chamberlain was able to anchor himself in the lane with impunity and shut down the rim.

"Jackson had to play more, and Phil couldn't throw it in the ocean from the beach," Lucas said, conceding that his shooting tutorials had been largely in vain. Chamberlain had 26 points and 20 rebounds as the Lakers took Game 3 on the road, and the Knicks' last chance to make it a series came two nights later.

On another wild Friday night at the Garden in May, L.A. rallied from a 7-point deficit in the fourth quarter and had a 2-point lead when Frazier tapped in a missed shot with three seconds left. The game went to over-time, then double overtime. Two free throws by West gave the Lakers the lead before Goodrich—scoring in bunches all series long, relentlessly attacking Monroe, who was playing with bone spurs in his foot—grabbed a long rebound off a missed Lucas jumper and went the length of the floor for the game-clinching southpaw runner. Down 3–1, the Knicks were reduced to hoping that a sprained right wrist suffered by Chamberlain might be a factor. He was questionable for Game 5 in L.A., but he took the floor with his wrist heavily taped and still dominated Lucas, who lacked Reed's upper-body strength, with 24 points and 29 rebounds. After the Lakers' 114–100 victory, securing the champion-ship, Chamberlain was handed the MVP trophy.

Who would mock Wilt Chamberlain now? "I know everyone talked about Jerry finally winning a title, but I always thought that series was more of a validation for Wilt," Goodrich said. "Jerry was one of the great-est players ever, but those days people expected the big men and especially Wilt to dominate. He was always under the most pressure because of Russell. When Wilt won a second title and with a second team, I thought that really put a stamp on his career."

Truth be told, West didn't give a damn about the MVP trophy, the accompanying car, the media fuss.

Been there, done that—in a losing cause in 1969. With Riley alongside him, he ran off the floor, feeling an acute sense of relief, stronger even than his jubilation. "I remember saying to myself, Thank God, I'm not going to be a loser all my life, we finally got lucky enough to win," West said. "You know, people say it's not about luck—but that's not true. Ball rolls off a rim, officials make calls. Someone gets hurt. It's a huge element. I felt a number of times that I had the right teammates but the stars just weren't aligned."

He counted Baylor foremost among them, of course. West's lasting regret was not being able to share the moment with his old friend. Even Reed, watching from the sideline, could recall being struck by the merciless irony of the Lakers winning it all months after Baylor had walked. "You felt sorry that he hadn't stuck around," Reed said. "I still wish he had."

But then, who was to say what the inclusion of Baylor would have meant? Would a war of wills with Sharman have affected team chemistry? Would the Lakers have gone on the winning streak and developed their own Celtics-like sense of manifest destiny? Would McMillian have been given the minutes to average almost 19 points as a fluid jump shooter and lane filler, the better frontcourt complement to Chamberlain? There has never been a series and season that wasn't subject to the impossible but irresistible computation of what we might call "the human element." West, for example, could never quite forget how the Lakers were beating the Knicks by 10 points on the night Reed crashed to the court in Game 5, 1970, changing the dynamic of that crucial swing game.

"Through all the years, you remember every turn those games took, every time there was a play you didn't make, every shot that rolled in and out that might have been the difference between winning and losing," he said. "And take it from me: you can drive yourself crazy doing that." Not Lucas, though. He lived by an obscure calculus that only he could solve. "I guarantee you that if Dave hadn't gotten hurt, we could have beaten them four straight," he said. "Guarantee it."

PART IV

Paradise
Regained

15

SECOND COMING

The rage of the sixties had given way to the ruin of the seventies. A war-weary country was looking toward an end in Vietnam, more desperate than triumphant. The airwaves carried word of a political scandal that within two years would derail the second term of Richard M. Nixon. Hope was scuttled, heroes were scarce, and even rock stars who had given voice to youthful rebellion were dying of their own drug-fueled recklessness. The presumed safe haven of sports wasn't spared, either. Eleven Israelis were taken hostage and murdered by Palestinian terrorists at the Summer Olympics in Munich, West Germany. The studio host, Jim McKay, looked red-eyed into the ABC camera on that early September day and uttered the three irrevocable words—"They're all gone"—that would echo forever. Scandalously, the Olympics carried on. Life trudged ever forward. When another NBA season began in October, at least Old Knicks fans had the Garden, our erstwhile Eden and fortress of enchantment, in which to drown our real-world discord and despair.

As they had in 1969–70, the Knicks of 1972–73 started fast, winning 10 of their first 11 with Reed back in the lineup. They were 15–3 when the Milwaukee Bucks pulled into town on Saturday night, November 18, and appeared to be coasting to victory behind Kareem Abdul-Jabbar. In the arena of his rookie discontent, the placid-faced big man was toying with Our Guys, scoring 32 points, hitting 14 of his first 21 shots, making it look as gracefully easy as only he could. The Bucks rolled to an 86–68 lead with 5:50 left in a game for which the Knicks were not at full strength. Jerry Lucas had badly twisted an ankle a week earlier, forcing Willis Reed, who had been coming off the bench, to play more and more on a bum knee. Not that Lucas had the size or strength to deal with Abdul-Jabbar's length in the post: that was more a job for the Captain.

Reed had reentered the game after a rest on the bench at the eight-minute mark, replacing John Gianelli, a mop-haired rookie from the University of the Pacific, as the Knicks regrouped for the obligatory and seemingly futile last run. While a fair number of fans had already headed for the exits, the more sophisticated among them could on some dispassionate level appreciate the grace of Abdul-Jabbar and the all-court wizardry of Oscar Robertson.

So Woody Allen sat with one leg crossed over the other, accompanied by his favorite costar, Diane Keaton. Stan Asofsky and Freddy Klein leaned forward in their baseline seats and baited the refs—while on the other side of the floor George Lois tried to ignore his fairly bored wife. Rosemary Lewandowski-Lois didn't know much about basketball beyond her husband's love for the game, an obsession that had moved her to remark a few weeks into the marriage that he would have to make a choice, "basketball or me." Lois left the room for a few moments and returned with a ball, which he proceeded to dribble. She got the message, learned to work around his passion for YMCA tussles and nights out with the Knicks. As it was, she was attending her very first game, and even Lois had to admit it was a competitive dud. But just when the notion of leaving early in deference to the missus actually crossed his mind, the Knicks began pressing full-court, man-to-man. If they're not giving up, Lois thought, why the hell should I?

Immediately, the press seemed to bother the Bucks, forced them to accelerate their offense. Off a missed jumper, Earl Monroe got out on the fast break, scored on a layup, and cut the deficit to 16. Monroe was a starter now, finally a Knick, at least by the measure of his minutes, with Dick Barnett having turned 36 and more into his graduate studies than basketball. This would be his final full season in uniform.

Monroe's ascension was accompanied by the presence of his Baltimore acolyte Dancing Harry, who began showing up with tickets usually obtained from Monroe. He quickly became a favorite of the Garden crowd and embellished his act with a flowing cape. Harry didn't quite fit the image of the button-down Knicks or management's idea of courtside entertainment, but that was the appeal of Earl the Pearl. He was different from the others. He was spice. On Broadway, he was Cirque du Soleil. With Monroe starting, Lucas, Phil Jackson, and Dean Meminger were the primary reserves on the 1972–73 Knicks. Gianelli received occasional spot duty, as did Henry Bibby, the UCLA guard who would regale Reed, his roommate, with tales of John Wooden and especially the great young Bruins center, Bill Walton.

"The big redhead—can he get it done?" Reed would ask Bibby. "Cap," Bibby said, "the big redhead, he's a motherfucker." Of all the Knicks newcomers, the most intriguing was a man who would log 59 minutes in 13 games, or 59 and 13 more than anyone would

have believed. Harthorne Nathaniel Wingo was a 6'9"
forward with long arms and limited skills beyond running, jumping, and dunking. The small-town North
Carolina native was even less credentialed to be an
NBA player, having kicked around junior college and
the Eastern League, living with an aunt in Harlem,
and working in the Garment District pushing racks of
clothing around Manhattan streets. The barnstorming Harlem Wizards discovered him in a Greenwich
Village pickup game. From there he found his way to
the end of Red Holzman's bench, where, by virtue of
his name alone, Wingo became someone for whom the
crowd would chant when games entered what Marv
Albert liked to call gar-*bage* time.

Another coach might have cleared his bench when
trailing a team as powerful as Milwaukee by 18 with
less than six minutes to play—no point in draining the
hourglasses within Reed's knees. But to Holzman it
was always bad precedent to concede too soon.

"I always felt that you've got no place to go, anyway,"
he said. "You can't go to the movies until after the game
is over. You can't go out to dinner until after the game
is over. So you might as well give it your best shot until
it's over."

Still, against the Bucks, Holzman couldn't have
thought they had a chance. How long could anyone

keep Abdul-Jabbar and his sky hook from the scoring column? "You think about it, we were down 18 and we didn't have the luxury of shooting threes," Frazier said. "To come back, you would have to hold them scoreless, and how were you going to do that when they had Kareem?"

But with the Bucks under intensified defensive pressure and Reed leaning on Abdul-Jabbar, forcing him a step farther from his preferred post-up position, the feel and tempo of the game changed quickly. The lead was down to 11 when Robertson drove against Frazier, thinking one measly basket would put an end to whatever fantasies the Knicks were entertaining. He went up for a jumper near the right baseline. The ball bounded off the rim, right into Abdul-Jabbar's hands for a put-back from close range—a gift of a shot he would probably make nine of ten times. Not this one. Dave DeBusschere's outlet found Bradley, who hit Monroe for a left-baseline jumper, 86–77. Murmurs of hope became spasms of excitement.

Meanwhile, a sense of uneasiness permeated the Milwaukee side. Better than most, Robertson knew how these Knicks had a knack for the momentous occasion, for outright thievery, though his Cousy-in-Cleveland nightmare in 1969 had been more of a shocking left-right combination in the final minute of the game and before his Royals knew what hit them. What was developing now was different, a slow, cinematic build to disaster. When Monroe up-faked his man and maneuvered for a right-side jumper, the Knicks were within seven points, 86–79 with 3:10 remaining. Abdul-Jabbar missed another sky hook, DeBusschere took a handoff from Monroe and buried a long jumper to make it a 5-point game. Bradley found Monroe again for another open right-side look that took the lead down to three. Frazier was fouled, went to the line, and—just as he had in Cleveland three years earlier, in the comeback against the Royals—calmly sank two free throws. Now the Knicks were somehow down by one, 86–85, with 47 seconds left. The Bucks called time. Their coaches—Larry Costello and a young, acerbic assistant named Hubie Brown—put the ball in Robertson's hands to inbound at midcourt with instructions to run off some clock and get the ball to Abdul-Jabbar.

"The fans were making so much noise that you swore the basket and backboard were moving every time we shot," Brown said. "The noise was such that you couldn't hear yourself think in the huddle."

At this point, the Bucks were handed another chance to avoid infamy when Monroe was whistled for tripping the guard (and former UCLA teammate of Abdul-Jabbar's) Lucius Allen before the ball was inbounded—an automatic two-shot foul. But Allen's first attempt hit the back rim and rolled off the front. His second missed, too. Reed rebounded and passed to Frazier, who dribbled upcourt against Allen. "Most coaches in that situation would have called time-out. Not Red," Frazier said. "What was he going to tell me in that situation—get a good shot? They were reeling, man, back on their heels. You didn't want to give them a chance to regroup."

Frazier attacked Allen, spinning left at the free-throw line, creating just enough space to rise for the jumper. But Monroe had drifted out to the left of the lane, clear of Robertson, who had hesitated in following, believing Frazier was going to shoot. In the moment that would symbolically cement their unlikely partner-ship, Frazier followed the blueprint and hit the open man. "Walt had a decent shot, but mine was better," Monroe said. "He knew I would make it." From 16 feet out, Monroe buried the uncontested look of his life for his 21st and 22nd points of the game, 11 of them scored during the incredible 19-point run that had given the Knicks an 87–86 lead with 36 seconds remaining.

Abdul-Jabbar would get two more cracks—the first a makeable sky hook from the baseline, the second a buzzer-challenging turnaround from deep on the other side of the basket. (A brain cramp by Bradley had led to a Knicks 24-second violation and given the Bucks the ball with two seconds remaining.) He missed the first, air-balled the second. The buzzer sounded as Frazier grabbed the ball and carried it like a newborn toward the tunnel. His teammates followed, somewhat stunned themselves. "I don't think we realized what we had done until we got inside," Frazier said. Staying off the floor, the fans cheered madly for several minutes before carrying their exuberance into the street.

George Lois's wife turned to him and said, "That was exciting." He thought, You just watched the greatest fucking comeback ever, and all you can say is, "That was exciting"? But he also knew that it took night after regular-season night to truly appreciate what seemed like only one of 82 meaningless games before the playoffs. Abstractly, Marv Albert agreed that the Knicks' 16th win of that season "epitomized the greatness" of the era perhaps more than any other game. Playoff success and championships won would of course remain history's tried and true barometer of achievement. But scoring the last 19 points and silencing the league's reigning MVP (and ultimately the leading scorer in NBA history) would never be forgotten as a hallmark of the Old Knicks.

"I don't think anything could top that game, not even winning the championship, because that was just something you knew you would never see again," said Woody Allen. Abdul-Jabbar now had more reason to despise the Garden, while Robertson could only console himself with the satisfaction of having predicted, in the first place, that Frazier and Monroe would successfully coexist.

But the real story—or the moral of the story—was how Holzman's coalition of the willing could incorporate even the most flamboyant of scorers while continuing to make sure that the basketball was the team's most cherished star. In twenty-first-century terms, the open man was the franchise or go-to player. Frazier to Monroe for the game winner on November 18, 1972, was not only Monroe's Garden baptism in the home-team uniform; it was affirmation that the team was still collectively capable of greatness. "When that happened, we almost felt invincible," DeBusschere would say years later. "That was when we felt we could do this again."

The Knicks' 57 wins against 25 losses that season would represent the fourth-best record in the league. Out west, the Lakers and Bucks each won 60. In the Knicks' own division, the Celtics put even more distance between the teams than during the previous regular season, crafting a 68–14 record, one win shy of the

Lakers' 1971–72 record. But history had also shown that veteran teams with championship timber could have priorities beyond driving themselves for an extra home game in a seven-game series. Russell's Celtics had powerfully demonstrated the art of lying in the weeds in 1969. The Knicks' first title team had needed the emotional cushion of home-court advantage, but the second one needed to fine-tune, pace, and heal itself. Those 57 wins were achieved while completing the assimilation of Monroe and incorporating Reed back into the frontcourt rotation. Reed, in particular, was a work in progress, averaging career lows in points (11) and dipping under 30 minutes a game (to 27.2) for the first time in his career.

"I was struggling for a lot of that season," he said. "But I started to feel pretty good going into the playoffs." In the blue seats for the first-round opener in the now annual conflagration with the Bullets, someone in my row made that very observation during a third-quarter burst in which the Knicks took over the game. I remember it vividly: Monroe picking up a loose ball off a Bullets turnover, looking up, and, seeing a white uniform streaking ahead, leading him with a perfectly timed pass. Running like a guard—or a 22-year-old rookie—Reed turned it up a gear, beat the Bullet to the ball, cradled it on a bounce, and continued to the rim for a lay-in. Three years after the legendary limp, a year after he'd been shut down for the season, Reed on the run was a rousing sight, in itself enough to make an entire fan base believe.

Phil Chenier heard the question a little too often early in his NBA career, even in the Baltimore-Washington area, where he was starting for the Bullets. There would be stares. There would be whispers. Finally someone would summon the nerve, step forward to ask:

"Are you Clyde?"

"No, sir," he would say. "I am not Walt Frazier."

Chenier didn't really get the whole body-double thing that would shadow him for years. Frazier was bigger, by at least an inch, and outweighed him by 15 pounds. Yes, he, too, had the wide sideburns extending due south, but he didn't move like Clyde, cool and deliberate. He had more pep in his step, like the man he had studied growing up in the Bay Area of California, Jerry West.

But—still—there had to be some resemblance for so many people to have mistaken him for the imperturbable Knick. "Maybe around the eyes, Walt and I were similar," Chenier conceded. His reluctance was understandable. Chenier was a very good pro guard with five consecutive seasons averaging between 19.7 and 21.9

points. But he was not at Frazier's Hall of Fame level, and the comparisons only played to a larger characterization that delighted New Yorkers: namely, casting the Bullets individually and collectively as Knicks Lite.

Chenier was in college at Cal Berkeley when the Knicks came of age. He was riveted by their early series with the Bullets, and especially the backcourt duels between Frazier and Monroe. He was ecstatic when he was drafted by the Bullets in 1971, and chagrined when Monroe left abruptly to join the Knicks, even if the roster upheaval meant instant playing time. After ten years in the NBA, Chenier, like Frazier, went on to a long broadcasting afterlife, with the Bullets-turned-Wizards. With all he had witnessed from backcourt to broadcast booth—from Russell's Celtics to Kobe's Lakers—he still considered the core Old Knicks to be the best team he ever laid eyes on.

"Many personalities, but somehow no egos," he said. Chenier also knew something about the challenges of heterogeneous bonding. Before attending college at Cal, he'd grown up in a modest but diverse Berkeley neighborhood during times of political and social dissent that engulfed the city in the late sixties. As a teenager, he'd witnessed a few things, including his high school gymnasium being taken over by the National Guard after the assassination of Martin Luther King.

"Riots, demonstrations—you name it, we had it," Chenier said. "One day it was about the war, the next day it was about poverty, and the day after that it was about race. For me, basketball was the place you went to get away from it all, where people could actually get along."

How ironic, then, that Chenier, one of the more well-liked NBA lifers, is best remembered in New York for one behavioral misstep, one retaliatory slip. In what may have been the fiercest Knicks-Bullets playoff game of all, bodies flew, whistles blew, and the referees, Earl Strom and Bob Rakel, were abused by both benches and from all sides of the Garden crowd. The players—even the former Minuteman Mike Riordan—were pawing and yapping at one another. Most antagonized was Chenier. Bradley was a master at knocking opponents off stride and getting into their heads. That night, Bradley's elbows seemed to be targeting Chenier whenever they passed in the lane. "That was Bill: every trick in the book," Chenier said. "I was sick of it and made a mental note that I wasn't going to put up with it anymore. So we're in the third quarter, and I go through the lane and he hits me with a forearm. I stop. I'm stupefied. And the next thing I know I'm swinging."

Chenier missed his target, instead hitting the man he was guarding in the back of the neck. Frazier, stumbling in an entanglement of humanity, was somehow whistled for a foul. Chenier went to the line, glancing at his disbelieving look-alike, trying to focus on his free throws while fighting off pangs of guilt. From a distance, he really respected Frazier. Years later, the two broadcasters would pose for a photo with a Garden fan during a Bullets visit, and Frazier would make him laugh by bringing up the tomahawk chop, telling him, "I still don't know how I got the foul." But to Chenier, the most amazing and telling aspect of the incident was that Frazier, who had every right to be furious, did not mouth off or get hit with a technical foul. The man was beyond cool. And then, with the basketball in his hands, he got hot.

"He comes down on the next play and he makes a jumper," Chenier said. "Then he made another shot, then another. I'm thinking, 'Oh, shit, I'm in trouble.' Next time, he pump-fakes, drives around me, uses the left hand, and puts in a reverse. The crowd is going crazy. And let me tell you something: 25 years later, people were still coming up to me and saying, 'I remember when you hit Clyde in the head and he busted your ass after that.'"

Off the top of *his* head, Chenier couldn't pinpoint in which playoff game the punch had occurred, only that it was during his second year in the league—1972–73.

In his 2006 book *The Game Within the Game*, Frazier concurred, pinpointing Game 2 of the conference semifinal. But a check of the clippings revealed that it was actually the following year, spring of '74, in Game 5 of the first round. In that game, Frazier's response indeed was spectacular. He led the Knicks to a one-point victory in overtime with 38 points, making eight of nine fourth-quarter shots. For both men, the memory lapse was understandable, given the passage of time, the blur of six consecutive playoffs series between the teams.

The Bullets began the '73 series with a renewed taste for the rivalry after capturing another Central Division title, this time with a robust 52 wins, 14 more than the previous season. To his credit, Abe Pollin didn't stop competing after the Monroe fiasco, dealing for the talented but enigmatic Elvin Hayes to replace Gus Johnson, who had gone to Phoenix and then to Indiana, of the ABA, for his last season. Chenier grew up fast, averaging 19.7 points. But the most pleasant surprise—again, to Pollin's credit—was the emergence of Riordan, who thrived at the Bullets' faster pace, averaging 18.1 points and leading the team in minutes played.

After the Knicks won the opener, they were engaged in a tight second game at the Garden before pulling away behind Frazier and Monroe, who combined for 61 points. Frazier added 13 assists and 9 rebounds, barely missing a triple double. With Reed in decline, Frazier, at 28 and the height of his prime and fame, was the team's most potent two-way player. Making life easier—especially in the absence of a consistent low-post threat—was Monroe, the kind of bailout option the Knicks had never had.

"That team was so smart, they knew how wise it was to utilize Earl's one-on-one skills," Chenier said. "He was always there for them in the last seven or eight seconds of the shot clock if they needed him." The Milwaukee comeback was a stunning demonstration of what Monroe brought to the Knicks. But for him, the Bullets series was even more gratifying, coming as it did a year after he had contributed so little. He tormented his old team with waves of tantalizing dribble drives and midrange jumpers. The Knicks brushed off the Bullets in five games but had no time to celebrate. The Celtics were next. They headed to Boston, where Red Auerbach was already blowing smoke about the restoration of royalty, the rightful return of his team to the top of the Eastern Conference—and beyond.

Tommy Heinsohn never believed in the prevailing notion of Willis Reed as the Knicks' heart, soul, and

1970 savior. While he was certain that leprechauns resided in the bowels of Boston Garden, he didn't quite get the Reed mystique in Madison Square Garden. Heinsohn rated Walt Frazier as one of the great guards in NBA history, thought Bill Bradley was nonpareil running the baseline, and appreciated Dave DeBusschere's rugged determination. But in Heinsohn's opinion, explained with a Celtic's smug assurance that made the Old Knick fan in me want to lash him with my digital recorder, Reed was no more than "a hardnosed player, a plugger who fit that team, but someone you could take advantage of."

There was more, unsolicited: "I mean, Russell could outplay him at the end of his career because he was a defensive player who could take away his offense. And we always felt Cowens could beat him down the floor with his speed. If you tried to put Willis up there with Russ, Wilt, and Kareem, come on, give me a break. They put him in the Hall of Fame because of the whole New York thing. Willis came on board when I was playing, and we would absolutely kill them. So they put together a team around him—a very unusual team—that was kind of made to beat *us*."

Born in Union, New Jersey, Heinsohn was a New York metropolitan-area native—like Auerbach and Cousy—and actually a charmer if you didn't let blood rites or partisanship get in the way. But by 1973 Heinsohn was as loathsome a sight to New Yorkers as Auerbach had been, looming over the court at 6'7", arms folded, head bent so that his shaggy hair shaded his eyes, and wearing a perpetual frown and a loud sports jacket.

Paul Silas, on the other hand, spent only four of his twelve NBA seasons in Boston, and while he came to enormously appreciate what the franchise achieved and represented, he didn't parrot every party line. "We came in about the same time, and Willis was the most amazing basketball player I'd ever seen," Silas said. "To be such a tough guy, to rebound and score the way he did against bigger men, and then have that feathery touch from outside—there was something special about Willis that you couldn't explain but you could feel." Like many old-time enforcers, Silas relished the days when not every altercation in a physically grinding sport turned into an overnight referendum on myriad social (and racial) issues, with every fracas shown countless times, from every conceivable angle, on ESPN. Because Silas worked as an assistant coach in New York and New Jersey before being hired as LeBron James's first pro coach in Cleveland, I'd heard many an old war story from him. One of his favorites concerned a turbulent night in Atlanta when he got into it with Phil Jackson, and Reed rushed over to stand up for his guy. Fists were soon flying. Nate Bowman somehow wound up in the stands with his head in a railing, long before Ron Artest was a glimmer in his parents' eyes. "It was just chaos, everybody fighting," Silas said. "But Willis was in the center of it all—and nobody wanted to go after him."

As much as anyone, Silas put the *power* in *power forward*. On a good day, his offensive range was about five feet, but when Silas was generously sent to the Celtics by Phoenix for the 1972–73 season, Dave Cowens had the perfect complementary frontcourt partner. His 13.3 points and 13 rebounds a game elevated the Celtics from very good to special. Everyone expected a brutally competitive series as the Celtics pushed to regain their standing while the aging Knicks were making what felt like a last stand, if only because Reed was playing on borrowed time. "It was amazing what he put himself through that season," said Henry Bibby, who, as Reed's roommate, had the closest look. "He would rub this ointment on his body to loosen up his joints, just spread it all over himself like it was sunblock, except it made your skin feel like it was on fire. He'd even rub it on his feet—I swear it ate the skin right off. You could see the white on his toes."

Reed wasn't the only key player in the series to cope with infirmity. After the teams each won a game at home, Monroe bruised a hip in Game 3 while diving for a loose ball and departed in the third quarter. Chasing Bradley in the same game, Havlicek smacked into a granite screen set by DeBusschere, suffered a separation of his right shoulder, and barely played in the fourth quarter after compiling 29 points, 9 rebounds, and 6 assists. When the Knicks pulled out a 98–91 victory, the series returned to New York, where neither player could suit up. When Havlicek walked onto the floor in street clothes, the Garden fans cheered, many of them standing. "They showed me respect, and that told you a lot about the intelligence of that crowd," he said. But Game 4 would not be remembered for mutual admiration. For three quarters, behind Cowens and Jo Jo White, the Celtics dominated the Knicks, leading 76–60 with ten minutes left. But Don Chaney, their backcourt defensive specialist, fouled out at the 8:51 mark after keeping Frazier, who had 17 points, reasonably contained.

"They started blowing the whistles against us and it got out of hand in the fourth quarter," Heinsohn said. Time, naturally, had made the performance of the referees—Jake O'Donnell and Jack Madden—even more abusive and dishonorable in Heinsohn's memory. He recalled "something like 19 straight calls going against us," which of course was an exaggeration. A check of the box score showed the Knicks shooting 15 more free throws over the course of the game (not exactly the worst home-court playoff hosing in the history of the league). Most significantly, Chaney's exit freed Frazier, who attacked Jo Jo White, who was also in foul trouble and whose offense was too important for the Celtics to lose.

On his way to a playoff career high of 37 points, Frazier scored 15 in the quarter, and his jumper with 17 seconds remaining pushed the Knicks into overtime—though not before they dodged an end-of-regulation bullet: Don Nelson took an inbounds pass with the game tied and called for time-out in the backcourt, violating a rule implemented that season meant to force the offensive team to advance the ball and not bail itself out by calling for time. "I'm standing at the other end of the court and Madden blows his whistle," O'Donnell said. "He runs down to me and says, 'Did you see him call time?' I said, 'Jack, it's your call.' He gives the ball back to the Knicks, and Heinsohn is ready to pop a vein."

The glut of whistle blowing took its toll on the Knicks as well. Reed fouled out. After 38 minutes in Monroe's stead, so did Dean Meminger. On the floor for the Knicks at the start of the second overtime were Frazier, DeBusschere, Jackson, Bibby, and John Gianelli.

Gianelli may have been the freest of Old Knicks spirits, a beach lover who yearned for the West Coast life, who would build a cabin with his wife in the mountains between Yosemite and Tahoe and play several years in Italy after seven-plus NBA seasons. In Milan, his team won the 1982 championship when Gianelli hit teammate Mike D'Antoni for a title-winning shot. The future Knicks coach sank the jumper, and the two U.S.-born stars, or *stranieri* (foreigners), were carried off the floor. Gianelli was skinny as a rail, but Red Holzman played the hunch that his length would be more effective against Cowens's bullish rushes to the rim than what Jerry Lucas had shown. Gianelli wound up playing 16 minutes in total, hitting all four of his shots and drawing Cowens's sixth foul.

"He's my roommate," Frazier bragged afterward. "I guess something must have rubbed off on him." DeBusschere broke a tie with a long jumper, Jackson stole the ball and drove for a layup, and the Knicks pulled away, 117–110.

"People forget about that game, but it was one of the all-time best," said George Lois, whose game face made it into the next morning's *New York Times*, along with his younger son, Luke's. Played on Easter Sunday, the game exhausted everyone. Looking older than his 32 years, DeBusschere sat on a table in the trainer's room after playing 51 minutes and said, "I couldn't have gone another." Frazier logged 57 of a possible 58 minutes. Silas, who grabbed 23 rebounds, was wrapped in cold towels, unable to make it into the shower. But no one needed to chill more than Heinsohn, who left the floor in a red-faced rage, screaming at Madden and O'Donnell through the tunnel, all the way to their locker room. When Madden left the following season to ref ABA games, Heinsohn was convinced that it was because there was so much consternation in the league office over the Game 4 calls.

"Just our luck, we go down to Carolina to play the Cougars in an exhibition game and Jack's doing the game," he told me. "He fouls Cowens out in about six minutes and he throws my ass out as soon as I open my mouth." For all of Heinsohn's fury, the Celtics weren't done after Game 4. Back in Boston, Silas saved the series in Game 5 with his 20th rebound, following a missed jumper by White with the Celtics trailing by one and seven seconds left. Reed, guarding Cowens, was screaming, "Block out, block out!" But Silas slipped by Lucas, grabbed the ball, and was fouled by DeBusschere.

"He makes the free throws and we lose," Reed said. "Everybody says, 'Don't worry about it, we're going home.' What happens? We get beat on a Friday night, we don't play worth a damn, and now we've got to go back to Boston on Sunday." But not before they were bitterly reminded by Ned Irish at practice the next day that the Celtics had never lost the seventh game of a playoff series on their home floor. "You could have won it last night; now look what you've got to do," Irish fumed, mixing F-bombs and other choice words into his diatribe. "You blew it."

Irish stormed out, convinced that his team had cost him the lucrative finals gate. Either that or he was a master reverse psychologist. As an analytical man, Bradley long ago rendered a verdict on Irish's speech as more motivational than hysterical. "If you needed incentive, he provided it, and, you know, it had the desired effect." But the Irish speech was just another chapter in the legend of the Old Knicks, destined as they were to make that other Garden their own piece of Eden.

16

CHANGING OF THE GUARDS

The new guy looked sad, alone, and Dean Meminger, an NBA player for all of one month, felt kind
of sorry for him. This was back on November 11, 1971,
Earl Monroe's first night in uniform with the Knicks,
when he found himself sheepishly encouraging Walt
Frazier and Dick Barnett as they discarded their sweats
and walked onto the floor, leaving him behind.

Monroe had signed his new contract just that afternoon, then pushed open the door to the Knicks locker
room, not knowing what to expect. Bill Bradley got up
to greet him, then Dave DeBusschere. Monroe relaxed
and dressed quietly, pulling his number 33 jersey from
his shoulders and tucking it into his home white shorts.
The hardest part, out on the Garden floor in a game
against the Golden State Warriors, was still to come.

Strange, Meminger thought. Hadn't it been only weeks since he had watched the Knicks go at Monroe and his Bullets as if it were Game 7? It wasn't—"Just a damn exhibition," Meminger said, cackling at the memory and the intensity of the Knicks-Bullets rivalry. Yet there Monroe stood, alongside Meminger, blurred at the edge of his periphery like a white-and-orange hallucination. Earl the Pearl, he thought, a Knick, trying to pretend he knew how to act under these bizarre circumstances, beginning his new life as a celebrated scrub.

If Meminger was uncomfortable just watching Monroe, imagine how the Pearl felt as the starters strolled toward midcourt for the opening tip, leaving him to figure out where to sit.

Meminger sat down near the end of the bench and fixed his gaze on Monroe, keeping it there until the Pearl raised his head. Eye contact made, Meminger nodded, his message unspoken but clear.

Right here, next to me. It's cool.

The seeds of a lifelong relationship were sown in the seconds it took for a relieved Monroe to fold himself among the row of Minutemen.

"The other guys were courteous, but they weren't going to hang with him, because he was a Bullet and they had their own things going," Meminger would tell me when I asked about the origin of the friendship. "But I was new myself, looking for someone to have dinner with on the road. We became friends right away, hung out more than any of the others. I saw what he went through that first year, people asking, 'What happened to you?' He'd just shrug. He knew he'd have to make adjustments, but 11 points a game—not *that* kind of adjustment. He wasn't Jesus in the community anymore. It was damaging, and Earl suffered, and that's not something I read in a book."

Friends and teammates called him Petey—his full name was Dean Peter Meminger—but fans would remember him as Dean the Dream. That was the nickname he was given by his coach at Marquette, Al McGuire, who recruited the stoop-shouldered guard out of Rice High School on West 124th Street in Harlem. After a race for his services that included UCLA's John Wooden, Meminger wound up in a courtside Garden seat the night Walt Frazier and Southern Illinois beat McGuire's team and his star guard, George Thompson, from Brooklyn's Erasmus Hall High. "I went to see George," Meminger said. "I'd never even heard of Walt Frazier."

At six feet tall, Meminger was no high-flying dunker, no graceful showstopper: his jump shot often launched with the trajectory of a bullet train. But with a pedigree of a respected Division I program and a first step famously described by McGuire as "quicker than 11:15 Mass at a seaside resort," Meminger was the 16th player taken in the 1971 NBA draft.

"I was more of a structure guy," he said, explaining why he signed with the Knicks instead of the ABA's Indiana Pacers. He was proud of the street-savvy mentorship he'd received from McGuire (to say nothing of the mean streets of Harlem) and grew eager to take his game downtown to the Garden.

He drew heat from his old Harlem pals for moving to an apartment in Peter Cooper Village, but it did little to dull the pride most of the neighborhood felt toward Meminger. He was a graduate of Urban League programs who had gotten out of Harlem before the inherent temptations turned him into another school-yard city legend, dribbling here and there and fast-tracked to nowhere, trapped in the Rucker League prison of what-if. In other words, Meminger had made it downtown, where the real games were played.

He knew that what happened at the Rucker ultimately meant nothing, even if the guys on the streets would tell you about it forever. "If I got 35 in the Rucker and someone dropped 50 on me up there, I didn't care," he said. "You have to understand, even in college, it wasn't my day job. Someone up there might be after you, but you weren't going to worry about what happened on a stage for could-have-beens. I'm not saying it to put them down, because there were some really talented guys. But they never got to play on Broadway; what happened in the park meant a lot more to them than it meant to me."

In 1972–73, Meminger averaged 18.2 minutes a game, a few more than he had as a rookie. Holzman was not normally one to rely on inexperienced players, but he loved Meminger's New York sass, his capacity for making things happen with his quick hands and his knack for being around the ball. He was a hell-bent defender, a royal pain in the ass—Holzman's kind of player.

Undersized as he was, Meminger had long arms and legs that extended like tentacles from a torso that was shaped like a loaf of bread, with his head sitting on top. He had an innate sense of timing and managed to take his share of rebounds from much taller men. Knowing that most everyone he guarded was bigger than him, he developed the exquisite habit of banging his head against their chests, knowing it wasn't a foul as long as he kept moving his feet.

Meminger once frustrated Pete Maravich to the point that the exasperated Pistol cleared space for himself with a well-timed elbow in the mouth. "Wound up in the dentist's chair at 1 A.M., having a tooth put back in place," Meminger said. "But you know what? I went right back after the next guy. I always knew how to play defense. I knew my role."

A student of defense, he knew how to take advantage of the rules allowing him to Velcro a hand to an opponent's right hip, forcing the dribbler left with his right hand held low. "That hand has to come up to shoot, and I will not let you bring those hands together," Meminger said.

In the 1973 conference finals against Boston, straight-up man-to-man defense was not so much the problem, because the Celtics, with their trademark motion offense, forced teams to constantly switch to avoid leaving jump shooters open. Dave Cowens and Paul Silas were especially ruthless screen setters, and Jo Jo White, who peeled off many of them, was an explosive pull-up shooter. While John Havlicek was planning to play in Game 7, he couldn't possibly have recovered so quickly from the slight shoulder separation he had suffered earlier in the series. The Knicks knew that White would have to be the focus of Boston's perimeter offense and that they would have to do a lot of talking on defense. This very subject came up at a film session in Boston the night before the game as the Knicks watched White break them down in Game 6. Meminger complained that his teammates weren't communicating with him, calling out the picks fast enough.

"Don't bitch about the screen—just get through it," Holzman barked.

("Pure Red," Phil Jackson told me when I asked what he remembered about that session. "Don't worry about what someone else is doing, only about what you're supposed to do.")

Old Knicks didn't complain, at least not about one another. Referees, of course, were another matter. None too appreciative of the Game 6 calls, Holzman had cornered John Nucatola, the league's supervisor of referees, under the stands before Game 7 and "bawled the shit out of him, called him every name in the book." Nucatola, knowing emotions were running high on both sides, turned off his hearing aid and didn't hear a thing. Good, Holzman joked later. Nucatola might have kicked his hostile ass right into North Station.

Holzman had other, in some ways more stifling, concerns about Boston's home court. For starters, barefoot players risked having their careers mangled by clumsy, stressed-out sportswriters loitering in the tiny visitors' locker room, not much bigger than a Manhattan walk-in closet.

Somehow the league let Red Auerbach and the Celtics get away with providing conditions that were barely suitable for even the stray rats that occasionally scurried across the bowels of the arena. At the Garden, the visiting team dressed in a dimly lit, poorly ventilated, and often overheated little room that featured hooks on the wall for clothing instead of dressing stalls. The wooden benches for the players to sit on were splintered. There were peeling walls with frayed and presumably dead electrical wires connected to nothing. This room—locker room number 7—once inspired Brendan Malone, then a Detroit assistant coach, to quip: "There are guys doing 25 years who would refuse to come in here." But the effects of the room weren't always funny. In February 1991, Bernard King of the Washington Bullets had to be rushed to the hospital after suffering a severe allergic reaction to mold spores.

For years, this was all part of Auerbach's master psychological blueprint: make the opponents uncomfortable. Get under their skin, inside their head, using every ploy imaginable. When hotel alarms mysteriously went off in the middle of the night—I experienced that phenomenon myself while staying in a new Marriott at Copley Square with the Lakers in the eighties—sleep-deprived opponents could only suspect that Auerbach's leprechauns were everywhere, including the hotel maintenance office. On game day, it didn't matter if Auerbach had been involved or not, as long as the visiting team showed up to Boston Garden expecting the worst.

When the Knicks arrived late morning on the Sunday of Game 7, the door to their decrepit digs wasn't even open. There was no one around who seemed to have a key. They stood outside waiting, while the Celtics strolled in, one by one, at the other end of the dingy corridor. Meminger and Monroe were especially annoyed, anxious to get inside, plop down on the bench, and maybe take a pregame snooze, sitting up.

"Earl and I hung out all night before that game—but I won't give you the gory details," Meminger told me. The two friends were destined over the next couple of years to be regular contributors to the Holzman punctuality fund.

The hip that Monroe had bruised in Game 3 was feeling better, allowing him to line up for the center jump, matched up with White. Though he was in uniform, Havlicek didn't start, and Don Nelson took his place. "My shooting arm, I couldn't lift it," Havlicek said. "When I got in, I tried to do whatever I could, but it wasn't much." The book on Havlicek was that he always drove right because he didn't have much of a left hand. With his right arm hanging limp for much of the 23 minutes he gamely contributed, he had no choice but to go left and hope for the best. Not much good came of it, four points, forcing the Celtics to run their offense through White and Cowens, as Holzman had suspected they would.

To deal with Cowens, whose quickness made him a difficult cover for Reed and his deteriorating knees, Holzman made a pregame defensive adjustment, shifting Dave DeBusschere onto him. The move allowed Reed to match up with Paul Silas, who seldom did much on offense except crash the boards. Despite lacking the slide-step quickness to fight through the screens, Monroe guarded White because Holzman preferred Walt Frazier to guard the Celtics' primary ball handler, Don Chaney, a poor outside shooter whom Frazier could all but ignore in order to stalk passing lanes.

White had an effective, if not dominant, start. He scored six first-quarter points and drew two fouls on Monroe as the Celtics took a 22–19 lead. At the outset of the second quarter, Holzman inserted Meminger along with Jerry Lucas and Phil Jackson. In the huddle, Meminger was already jacked up. "We got these motherfuckers," he gushed while his teammates eyed him suspiciously. "And Jo Jo is mine."

To watch this game on the only surviving video—a grainy black-and-white scout film, spliced to eliminate dead balls and inbounds passes—would make any romanticist of the glory days, any critic of the modern game, pause to reconsider. Play was frantic and sloppy, with both teams shooting poorly—the Celtics under 40 percent. But there is no mistaking whose entrance changed the feel and flow. Meminger began the quarter inauspiciously, shooting an air-ball jumper from the key area, but from there he no doubt became the alarm Heinsohn never heard the night before as he counted Celtics titles and passed into a deep sleep.

With the score tied at 24, Meminger drew a charge on White, and at the other end he nailed a 17-footer from the left wing. On the Knicks' next possession, he pushed the ball and scored on a drive. He poked it away from White and scored on a layup. He ran a two-man break with Bill Bradley and dropped in another deuce. He hustled back on defense and contested a missed jumper by White, then raced to the other end to find an opening under the glass in time to rebound a missed jumper by Bradley. Boston fouled him in exasperation.

The Knicks outscored the Celtics by eight in the second quarter and took a five-point lead into halftime. Holzman was sold. "We're going with you. Keep working," he told Meminger before the start of the third quarter.

"At that point, even I said, 'What the heck is this?'" Meminger recalled, referring to his surprise that Holzman had tabbed him to start the third quarter, ahead of Monroe. But when he thought about the strategy from the distance of decades, it made perfect sense. "I think Red knew we couldn't let Jo Jo go off. What'd he get—18, 19?" Actually, I told Meminger, White scored 21 that day, 10 field goals made with 21 shots taken, but only 1 free throw in 2 attempts before fouling out with a minute to play. He nodded and noted that White needed to have done more damage with Havlicek hurting. "See, he needed to have a big game and he didn't," Meminger said. "And Red knew if we got down to them in the second half in Boston, it was over."

Meminger injected into the Knicks a dose of the Celtics' own medicine, a panacea of gritty defense and transition offense. Once his playground instincts were harnessed by McGuire's fundamental teachings, Meminger always believed he could have switched uniforms, fit either team. "I played the kind of basketball Boston was known for, did the tough things a lot of other guys didn't want to do," he said.

Frazier, still the Knicks' best player on the floor, was on the way to a 25-point, 10-rebound, 7-assist gem.

But Meminger continued to impose himself, making plays at both ends. He found Reed with a nifty pass for a layup as the Knicks' lead grew to double figures. He snuck inside the trees and grabbed an offensive board off a missed jumper, which eventually led, after some classic ball movement, to a sweeping hook by Jackson. Meminger harassed White into another turnover. The lead reached 15 after three.

"You tired?" Holzman asked.

"I'm good," Meminger said, noticing Holzman glancing uneasily at Monroe, who remained on the bench, never to reappear, as Meminger played the last 36 minutes. As he walked out for the start of the fourth quarter, Meminger did not look back at Monroe, did not so much as shoot him a glance out of the corner of his eye. From the moment they had made eye contact before Monroe's first game as a Knick the previous season, Meminger felt that a bond had been established. He knew Monroe was cool with this, putting aside his own ego while Holzman rode the hot player.

But what about everyone else? Imagine the media firestorm that a three-quarters benching of a superstar, a Top 50 all-timer, for a second-year sub would have set off in a Game 7 of today. Obviously the contemporary superstar carries more clout, means more to his team in an expanded and watered-down NBA. So balanced were the Old Knicks that one starter subtracted from the lineup for a role player did not fundamentally alter their MO.

"Earl wasn't really benched," Bill Bradley reasoned. "We *won*! It was a normal substitution, Dean for Earl—gave him a blow—but then Dean took off. We were a team; it wasn't a matter of who got the credit." Echoing Bradley, calling Game 7 "Dean's game," Willis Reed added: "That was no knock, because Dean was a good player, a quick, aggressive guy, and we needed somebody to put the clamps on Jo Jo."

Largely forgotten is how much more Meminger contributed to the win than defense. His numbers (13 points, 6 rebounds, 3 assists) fail to convey the impact he had on the game, how his fearlessness in spite of the pressure and the location ignited the Knicks.

Naturally, the Celtics' version of what happened was something else entirely.

"I don't remember Dean Meminger beating us, and I don't think he quote-unquote *stopped* Jo Jo," Tommy Heinsohn said. "What I do remember is that we didn't have trouble with them during the regular season and then Havlicek got hurt. We won 68, but the team that won 68 didn't play them in the playoffs."

How, then, had the Celtics managed to win Games 5 and 6? Reed, plagued as he'd been by injuries, didn't want to hear any excuses. "Hey, we went up there and did it, when no one thought we would, even after our owner cursed us out and called us losers," he said.

No one concurred more than Holzman, grinning ear to ear in the triumphant locker room, punching the air with a primal glee. That day, interviewed on television, he called the victory "the most satisfying I've ever been associated with." Bradley recalled watching Holzman celebrate in a manner he almost never did—letting everyone know just how good it felt—and realizing how much it meant for him to beat the Celtics, beat Auerbach, in a seventh game at their own famed arena.

"The rivalry with Auerbach was obviously something Holzman felt deeply," Bradley said. For so many years, Auerbach—that preening trash talker—would light up his victory cigars as if to intentionally goad Holzman, or to shame him. It was true that the Knicks had won the previous year's series, finishing in Boston, but this was a deciding game against a Celtics team that, by virtue of their regular-season record, believed they were the better team—the best in the league. And here they were, unceremoniously dismissed before a crowd of their stunned, subdued faithful.

However tempted he may have been, Holzman would never have blown smoke in a vanquished opponent's face. But on April 29, 1973, he indulged himself as much as he ever had or would again.

"This was their year, 68 wins, and we got 'em," Holzman told a reporter. "We got 'em in *their* year."

The morning after, in Leonard Koppett's *New York Times* story on Game 7, there was only brief mention of Monroe's absence over the last three quarters. Wrote Koppett: "Actually, the team started moving in the second quarter with Dean Meminger, Lucas and Phil Jackson in action. Meminger played the rest of the game, instead of Earl Monroe."

An accompanying sidebar by Thomas Rogers told of how Meminger had been encouraged by Holzman to shoot his jumper after passing up open looks during the first six games. That was it. There was no explanation from Holzman on why he sat Monroe, no quotes addressing the decision from either player. Nor had the camera fixated on Monroe during the national broadcast, homing in on the action, not the ego, which Monroe insisted was not even bruised.

"One of the things about me I don't think people really understood was that I always enjoyed my team and having my teammates do well," he said. In college,

Monroe would get his 40 as fast as he could, then fake an injury so Big House Gaines would take him out and his teammates would get theirs. "Dean was my friend—I was happy for him," he said, affirming what Meminger had felt all along.

No doubt the team's equanimity made Holzman's decision feel more benign. Everyone sacrificed in one way or another. With Reed back, Lucas had accepted a lesser role (though Reed expected to be replaced in certain situations). Bradley and even DeBusschere sat during the stretch of some games while Jackson locked down a scoring forward. And while the team absorbed and dealt with personal issues, external forces also ensured that the Monroe benching caused not a ripple of disgruntlement.

There is no question that the story would have been more flammable in the antagonistic, invasive sports culture that athletes operate in now. At the height of his sensitivity, Monroe would have been grilled by quote-hungry reporters demanding to know if he felt *disrespected* by his coach. He would have gone home to watch countless close-ups of his face from the bench while Meminger played. Friends and family and no doubt his agent would have texted their concerns by the time he was out of the shower, all aggravating the fragile human divide between graciousness and victimization.

"You know what?" Meminger said. "Earl and I never really talked about it. We didn't have to. And our relationship just kept getting stronger."

Exhibit A, Meminger said, was his daughter, Maisha, who was married during the summer of 2009 in the Washington area. He was especially proud that Monroe had made the trip down from New York, despite his ongoing sinus and vertebrae issues. "Earl is my daughter's godfather," Meminger said. He also could admit that in a less formal but more painfully realistic way, Monroe and his wife, Marita, were like godparents to him as well.

Like many NBA players, Meminger did his share of partying during the decadent seventies, when he was young, single, and earning six figures. Around town, people were eager to have him into their homes, their back rooms, where he got high and eventually hooked. He was one of the unlucky ones, discovering too late that he was genetically predisposed to addiction.

Substance abuse no doubt contributed to the abrupt end of Meminger's six-year career (which found him back in New York after two seasons in Atlanta). After he retired, he came around the Garden on many game nights and mingled with reporters in the press lounge. Meminger was bright, conversant on a wide range of social issues. He was well liked, universally respected for what he had done on that Sunday afternoon in Boston. Yet there was also discomfort when Meminger became demonstrably animated, and a little too loud, while talking about a new fascination—applied kinesiology. Knicks insiders worried over his well-being.

He tried to stay in the game as a coach, first in an early women's professional league, then with the Albany Patroons of the Continental Basketball Association. He rode his players too hard, was fired, and asked his replacement, who happened to be Phil Jackson, for a tryout in the backcourt. Jackson indulged his former teammate, let him give it a shot, but he could see he was after a fix more than he was craving competition.

When Meminger returned to the city and to old familiar haunts uptown, his cocaine abuse spiraled out of control. He left New York for a while for treatment at the Hazelden facility in Minnesota. He even found work as a substance-abuse counselor. But there was always another relapse as he drifted from one false start to another, trying to escape what he described as an ache of emptiness.

"I did a lot of self-medicating," he said. "I went to places I really didn't want to go." For several years he lost touch with his children, who were launching their own successful careers—Maisha, a Johns Hop-

kins graduate, as a social worker, and a son, Dean
Meminger Jr., as a reporter for the cable news station
NY1.

During an extended run of sobriety into 2003,
Monroe recommended Meminger for a coaching position at a small college, Manhattanville, in a northern
suburb of New York, where Marita Green-Monroe
worked in the office of development. Meminger landed
the job but didn't stay long. "I felt Dean needed that
shot," Monroe said. "He did okay, but it just didn't
work out for him."

There were other acts of kindness, responses to his
cries for help. "There were times when Marita really
tried to look after Dean," Monroe said.

He had tried to date Sandra Johnson, a model
turned social worker, when he was still earning NBA
money, but she resisted, wary of his lifestyle. Years into
a friendship, romance finally blossomed when Meminger convinced Johnson, or she convinced herself, that
he could beat the drugs. They married after the turn
of the century. With her support, Meminger managed
to stay clean. But even happiness brought trauma, then
tragedy. In 2002, Johnson was diagnosed with cancer
and underwent surgery to have a tumor removed.
Months later, Meminger took her to Lenox Hill Hospital one night when she complained of stomach pain.

A perforated ulcer had caused her organs to become infected. On the operating table, she suffered a heart attack.

Meminger called Monroe, who rushed over to cry and pray with him. Though Johnson survived, the cancer would take her life within a few more years, leaving Meminger emotionally adrift once more.

Asked in his apartment during the summer of 2009 if he believed his old friend and roommate would ever have clear sailing, Monroe shrugged and crossed his fingers. Monroe and others who cared about his well-being knew better than to speak with assurance. "Dean seems to be doing okay," he said. "I saw him dance at his daughter's wedding. I hadn't seen him dance in years." But months after the wedding, Meminger, at 62, was rescued from a fire, unconscious near his bed in a single-room-occupancy building in the Bronx. Newspaper reports said several crack pipes were found on the scene.

Meminger recovered, tried again to move on, with the Monroes standing by him. Throughout his own physical and financial struggles, Monroe never could bring himself to cut Meminger from his life. Meminger was a good man, he believed, the most loyal of friends. As Meminger moved on from the Bronx fire episode and resumed working basketball clinics, drawing on his lifetime connection to the basketball community of Greater New York, he could be sure that Monroe would be there if he needed him.

"I think Dean's always known he could count on me but also that I'd tell him what I thought about things, even when it was painful," Monroe said. The truth could hurt, but it was the only way forward, just as it was for Monroe after Game 7 in Boston, when he had to admit to himself that Meminger, at least on that Sunday afternoon, was the better man for the job.

Dwelling on the past, Monroe liked to say, was for those who were powerless to do anything about the future. "As soon as the Boston series was over, I actually started thinking about Gail Goodrich," he said. "I'd heard it a lot after the '72 Finals—you know, how Gail ate me up. It didn't matter to me that I was hurt. Great players make no excuses. Now that we were back, there was no time to think about what happened in Boston."

A mob of fans greeted the Knicks as they returned from Boston, filling the arrival area at LaGuardia Airport and briefly (mistakenly) engulfing the Kansas City Royals baseball team, which had arrived at a nearby gate simultaneously. The Knicks had only one night at home, jetting to Los Angeles the next day after their request to delay the start of the Finals from Tuesday to Wednesday—so they could have an extra day to recover from the Boston pressure cooker—was denied.

The Lakers were finishing practice when the Knicks' bus arrived at the Forum for a light practice late on Monday after they touched down in L.A. As they walked onto the floor, Meminger heard a familiar voice.

"Hey, Dream, over here." It was Wilt Chamberlain, ambling off the floor, barefoot, the biggest man in the gym summoning the smallest.

"Little fella, I'm going to tell you something, these motherfuckers wouldn't even be here if it wasn't for you," he said.

Meminger snickered. "What else do you want to tell me?"

Chamberlain loved Meminger's brashness. Playing along, he turned back to the court and pointed at the lane, painted Lakers purple.

"See that area?" he said. "You'll be fine if you keep your little ass out of it."

Meminger didn't flinch. By this point, he pretty much embodied the contentious mind-set of his team-mates, who had heard that the Lakers—after disposing of Golden State in five games in the Western finals—

were not so keen on renewing their one-sided series with the Celtics a year after they had handled the Knicks with relative ease.

"I'm coming for you, too," Meminger told Chamberlain.

The games of the 1973 NBA Finals are never presented as classics on ESPN or the Madison Square Garden Network. There is no special moment to romanticize, or signature performance to immortalize. "I always say a lot of people don't even remember that we won a second championship," Willis Reed said.

Other than being the reverse of the Finals the year before—when the Knicks lost four straight after winning Game 1—the series proved unremarkable indeed. This time, the Lakers got the jump, 115–112, behind Gail Goodrich's 30 points (to Monroe's 18) and Jim McMillian's 27.

Worse, in Game 2, Monroe tweaked his already sore hip when he collided with Bill Bridges, the Lakers' power forward, in the third quarter. But once again, his roommate rode to the rescue. Meminger clamped down on Goodrich, who finished with 14 points, and the Knicks claimed a 99–95 victory behind Bill Bradley's 26. The series was squared heading back to New York for Games 3 and 4.

As always, or so it seemed, there was a key player hurt. Jerry West, weeks shy of his 35th birthday, was suffering from tender hamstrings in both legs. "That's part of the game," he said, consistent as ever in eschewing the alibi. "I seem to remember that when we beat the Knicks in the Finals, they had a couple of fellows who were hurting or out."

After scoring 32 points in Game 2, West managed only 16 in Game 3. Monroe finally outplayed Goodrich, outscoring him 21–14 while adding 6 assists. Phil Jackson had his Meminger moment, replacing a foul-plagued DeBusschere in the third quarter and staying on for 21 of the last 24 minutes, scoring 8 points, grabbing 9 rebounds, and being a nuisance on defense.

But it was Reed, sensing the crowning completion of his long road back, who led the Knicks with 22 points and contributions that typically were undetectable in the box score. With the Lakers down a basket, inside a minute to play, he mustered every ounce of strength after a typically grueling night and denied Chamberlain a low-post position, forcing Keith Erickson to launch a jumper in vain with the shot clock running down. Reed claimed his 10th rebound and the Knicks held serve at home, 87–83.

In Game 4, they were coasting by 13 after three quarters but lost Walt Frazier to fouls in the fourth and were clinging to a 4-point lead with less than a minute to play when Bradley missed a 15-footer. Chamberlain and Reed went for the rebound and deflected the ball right to DeBusschere, who scored on the put-back, was fouled by Chamberlain, and made the free throw. De-Busschere's 33 points and 14 rebounds gave the Knicks a 3–1 series lead going back west.

One win away, with West hobbling and Chamberlain looking all of his nearly 37 years in what would be his final season: what could possibly go wrong? But after failing to close out the Celtics early, the Knicks were wary, determined to put the Lakers out of their misery. They built a 14-point lead with about eight minutes to play in Game 5.

DeBusschere, scoreless in the game, went barreling in for a layup, landing awkwardly and in pain. His ankle badly sprained, he was done for the night and possibly the series. Sensing an 11th-hour stay from the governor of fate, the Lakers went on a tear, cut the lead to 4. But in a series that lacked consistent play by the principal stars, in which DeBusschere could score 33 points one night and 2 the next, in which Monroe could follow up his 21-point Game 3 by shooting 1 for 11 in Game 4, here came the Pearl to go all Baltimore Bullet on the Lakers in the last 2:15. He scored 8 of his 23 points in the final stretch of the 102–93 clincher.

Meminger sat on the bench watching his friend erupt after all he'd been through and thought: "This is one cool mother."

As Frazier dribbled out the final seconds, Bradley jumped into Reed's arms. Jerry Lucas looked up at the clock alongside Holzman in front of the bench with fists raised in the air. In a fast-emptying Forum, the Knicks charged off the floor, into a locker room that Marv Albert would remember as eerily empty and composed, compared with 1970. It was about 1 A.M. back in New York, most editions of the newspapers long gone to bed.

The championship was claimed 3,000 miles west and was celebrated while the City That Supposedly Never Sleeps was dozing in the middle of the night. In the years before the Finals had a fixed prime-time tip-off, regardless of location, three of the five games were played at the Forum beginning at 10:30 New York time, leaving only diehards and college students like me—thrilled to have an excuse to blow off morning classes—bleary-eyed but boisterous in front of our television screens.

Word came that Reed was again named series MVP, though it was commonly understood that the award was symbolic—given to the Captain because no Knick had risen above the rest. The composite box score told a story of true teamwork—Bradley leading in scoring with 18.6 points a game, Frazier following at 16.6, then Reed at 16.4, Monroe at 16.0, and DeBusschere at 15.6. Amazing balance for the most democratic of championship teams.

"That night, I said in the locker room that the three happiest people in there were Earl, Jerry Lucas, and me," Reed said. "Because those guys had won their first title, and I had come back after they'd gotten all the way to the Finals without me. If we didn't win it with me, what did that say?" With the trophy in hand, it said the weight of Reed's leadership—along with the bulk so effective in keeping Chamberlain from the rim—was the difference between second best and a validating second title.

The imagery of 1970 could never be surpassed, but one memorable snapshot was taken in the locker room, with a bare-chested Reed flanked on his left by Jackson and Bradley and on his right by Frazier and Lucas, all of them holding up raised index fingers. The photo was incomplete, of course, without DeBusschere, who was having his ankle treated, and without the two guards who usually showed up last and now were the first to slip out.

"When the buzzer sounded, I went up to Dean and said, 'It's over, man, let's go get something to eat,'"

Monroe said. "I was never one to go all crazy. I'd rather be subdued, reflect on what we'd done. We ate, got into bed, and watched TV."

After a while Meminger turned to Monroe in the other bed, studied him carefully just as he had that first night on the bench. Yes, his friend was not the emotive type, not the easiest man to read, but Meminger hoped Monroe could appreciate what he had achieved, what he had been part of. He hoped Monroe finally felt like a New York Knick.

"You good, Earl?"

"Yeah, man," Monroe said softly. "I'm good."

Bonded as more than champions, they turned out the light on the championship season and—in a sense— the best time ever to be a professional basketball player in New York City.

17

AFTERGLOW

T here was no mighty fall. No collision or bloodletting or even a noticeable limp. "I'm running down the court and I feel this little snap in my right knee," said Willis Reed of his last injury as a pro. "The *good* one."

It was November 2, 1973, early in the season following the second championship. Once again, the Knicks were playing the Lakers in Los Angeles under cover of the New York late night back home. The ghost of the retired Wilt Chamberlain haunted the court at the Forum while the Knicks dismantled the home team, led by Walt Frazier's 44 points.

"So many things happened in my life, and somehow the Lakers were always involved," Reed said with a smile both rueful and sardonic.

He sat out the last 33 minutes of that game and all of the next 7 with a strained joint capsule behind the knee-cap. Nothing serious, the doctors said. Sure enough, two weeks later, Reed returned to play 35 minutes and scored 22 points against Kareem Abdul-Jabbar and the Bucks, while favoring that knee for what it still gave him. But the pain and swelling persisted, and Reed finally flew to one Dr. Don O'Donoghue, the orthopedist who had treated the bad knee two years earlier.

The good knee, it turned out, was not that good. Reed had torn some cartilage and would miss at least two months. He initially thought he would be just fine. "I'll have the surgery, and I'm thinking I'll be back for the playoffs," he said.

But while rehabbing with a trainer in Long Island, he began to ponder a life after basketball. "I'm starting to ask, 'What are you doing it for?'" he told me. "One thing I knew I wanted to do was go on some hunts, and I was going to need two legs to walk on for that."

Still, recalling how the Knicks had gotten their playoff act together the previous spring, Reed fought off the notion of quitting right there. The hunter in him also fancied one last championship chase. So he put in the work, tried to come back, suited up for a handful of games at the end of an acceptable 49–33 regular season. But when the playoffs came around in the spring of

1974, Reed knew he couldn't compete anywhere close to the level to which he was accustomed. "Wasn't ready, couldn't play," he said. Reed being Reed, he dressed for the games anyway, contributing 12 minutes a game as a backup to John Gianelli, now finishing his second season. Reed averaged about a paltry 5 points and 2 rebounds.

In the first round, the Knicks met their old rivals the Bullets, now playing in a sterile arena in the Maryland suburbs and renamed the Capital Bullets. Phil Chenier was their leading scorer now, followed by Elvin Hayes and Mike Riordan. Dave Stallworth was hanging on as a seldom-used sub (and would, in fact, return to the Knicks for a seven-game cameo the following season).

Neither team was a serious contender anymore, but out of habit they battled ferociously, pushing to a seventh game at Madison Square Garden on April 12, a Friday night. For the fifth time in their six-year playoff continuum, the Knicks took the series, winning Game 7, 91–81, before 19,694 fans. Earl Monroe further tormented his former team with 30 points, but everyone agreed the difference in the game was Gianelli.

Playing 41 minutes, he scored 12 points and hauled down 15 rebounds, but it was his big D on the Big E, Hayes, that most affected the outcome. With his long arms, Gianelli harassed Hayes into a 5-for-15, 12-point shooting night, 16 points below his average for the series. Afterward, the praise for Gianelli flowed like champagne.

"What a job he did on Hayes," crowed Dick Mc-Guire. "The kid was the whole show." Hayes raved about Gianelli, crediting him for his bad night and predicting he would be a handful for Dave Cowens in the next round against Boston. Gianelli wasn't crazy about being fussed over. Nor was he thrilled to be presumed as the replacement for Reed.

What made him even more uncomfortable was that Reed's dressing stall was next to his own. Reed played five measly minutes that night, scored one basket, and pulled down a rebound. In the celebratory locker room, he talked about giving Gianelli advice and encouragement and how much he had improved. "When he puts on a couple of pounds and gains some strength, he's going to be a terror," he said.

They were all getting a little ahead of themselves. Gianelli would never really replace Reed, would never become a star and, in fact, would last only two more seasons in New York. Worse, not only was it all but officially over for Reed, but the victory over the Bullets had merely postponed the departures of two other frontcourt linchpins, Dave DeBusschere and Jerry

Lucas, who had announced their pending retirements before the playoffs.

Lucas's back had been barking all season, and he had decided to devote himself fully to his educational memory business. DeBusschere had tired of the pounding, night in, night out, and the travel he was never enamored of to begin with. At 33, he believed he could still play, but he already had a lucrative parachute—an offer to run the ABA Nets, who played a short drive from his Long Island home.

"Dave felt he had given everything, and after they won the second title he started thinking about stopping," Geri DeBusschere said. "But he was torn because he loved the guys so much, especially Bill, so as long as they were together and had a chance to win, he felt he owed it to them to play."

But DeBusschere saw the deterioration in Reed, and he knew better than to believe that Gianelli could replace him for the long haul. After the Game 7 victory, he cautioned everyone to keep things in perspective. "Don't get me wrong, I'm happy as hell," he said. "But this is one game. You can't go celebrate tonight knowing that the Boston Celtics are around the corner."

More than the others, DeBusschere seemed to understand that his team was probably experiencing its last triumphant hour. The lasting symbolism of that night was the juxtaposition of the two centers, Reed and Gianelli, representing the team's glorious past and its at-best-uncertain future. Beyond the euphoria of another Game 7 survival, the era of the Old Knicks was about to signal its ultimate decline.

In their diminished state, it was beyond expectation and probably belief to think the Knicks had earned anything more than a proper burial at Boston Garden. They did manage to win Game 3 of the series—in Boston—but returned for Game 5 down 3–1, clinging to life. On April 24, a Wednesday night, they hung with the Celtics for three quarters, but John Havlicek, fully recovered from the shoulder injury of the previous year, riddled them for 33 points, completing the transfer of power that had begun with the drafting of Dave Cowens and Jo Jo White. Much as it pained New Yorkers to admit it, Red Auerbach had every right to huff and puff.

Having made what would be his farewell appearance in a two-minute cameo in Game 4, Reed sat out the entire fifth game, his only DNP in that postseason. Lucas logged 14 minutes, missing his only two shots. DeBusschere labored through 16 minutes with a painful rib injury, scoring 2 points and grabbing 3 rebounds. Five years after the Knicks were defeated in

Bill Russell's farewell title run, they lost 105–94, and dressed quietly in the same dingy room where Emmette Bryant had assured Reed that the Knicks were on the cusp of winning it all.

"We knew that was it," Frazier said. "We'd had our run. I remember thinking, If it had to end, then at least we went out to a great team." Indeed, having seized conference supremacy from the squad that had taken it from them, the Celtics proceeded to claim another NBA championship—the franchise's 12th—by winning a seventh game in Milwaukee, another notch on the belt of the NBA's lone dynasty, pre–Magic and Kareem.

"Honestly, in comparison to the Celtics, we were almost nothing," George Lois said. "But we had our taste, a nice little run, two great championships."

Marv Albert always believed that if Reed had been healthy, a run of four straight titles would have been possible. But the record is what it is, and a perception exists outside New York that the phenomenon was overstated, based more on location than on merit. My friend Marty Beiser, a former editor at *GQ* magazine and Free Press, grew up in Philadelphia. He liked to crack, "So many books, so few titles."

Havlicek told me that the Old Knicks' literary indulgences were also a subject of discussion in Boston.

"I know some of our guys saw all the books being written about the Knicks and thought, If our team had been in New York, instead of 100 books it would have been 500," Havlicek said. "I also know up in Boston, after the Knicks won in '70, people said, 'How can they make such a big fuss about one championship?'"

Bostonians would argue that while New Yorkers thought of the Old Knicks era as a religious experience, it was more the opium of the Big Apple masses, two drops in the bucket compared with the 11 titles won by the Celtics in the 13 years prior to 1970. But partisanship misses the larger point of what the Old Knicks represented to their fans and to many neutral basketball connoisseurs: the game distilled to near perfection. "We weren't the team with the best players or the leading scorers," Reed said. "But to have played with a group like that, well, that maybe happens once in a lifetime."

To his credit, Havlicek more or less agreed with Reed. He understood and accepted the cultural differences between Boston, a hockey town, and New York, a basketball mecca. He preferred not to play to provincial passions, mimic Auerbachian bluster. In fact, when the Boston Garden crowd twice stood and cheered for the retiring DeBusschere in the fourth quarter of his final game—just the way New Yorkers had saluted him the previous spring when he had to sit out Game 4 with his separated shoulder—Havlicek was moved by the show of graciousness to the man who would become his Florida snowbird neighbor and close friend. "Let's face it," he said, "those Knicks were really good, and anyone who thinks they were overrated should look at the number of Hall of Famers."

Counting Holzman and Phil Jackson as coaches, the Old Knicks happened to have eight. But even then, any good adman with a baseline seat for the half decade of high drama could tell you that evaluating the impact of the Old Knicks by conventional measures was missing the point. Reed's pathos, George Lois maintained, may have diminished the achievements, but it also enhanced the team's Broadway legend.

"Listen, the fans from that time, we know how good the Celtics were, and we know who we were, too," he said. "The Knicks get a lot of credit, undeserved and unwanted, for changing the game. They didn't change the game. But they did bring a romance to it, the pure love of an unusual team that basketball hadn't seen before. And those years when they were such a treat to watch—it was really '68 to '74—you didn't have to think too much about Richard fucking Nixon."

In fact, the televised Watergate hearings began one week after the 1973 championship season, and Nixon's resignation came three months after the Old Knicks' last stand in Boston. One era ended in disgrace, the other with unquestioned honor.

My father was never much of a sports fan beyond a hankering for a good boxing match. He grew up on Manhattan's Lower East Side in a time when boxing was as big league as it got in America's teeming ethnic strongholds. When I was young, he would regale me with stories of his cousin, a lightweight named Danny Bartfield, who won 41 of 46 bouts between 1940 and 1948, several of them in the old Madison Square Garden.

As a family man, Gilbert Araton—whose parents immigrated from the Galicia region of Eastern Europe, formerly part of Poland and now Ukraine—was an outer-borough guy, commuting to the general post office on Eighth Avenue between 31st and 33rd streets. He worked days in the mailroom when I broke in as a beat reporter across the street in 1978, at the new Garden, on the Knicks night shift.

After he'd finished work and before I began, we would occasionally meet for a late-afternoon meal. Then he would ride the subway home to Brooklyn, to which my parents had returned after what he considered an eight-year exile to bagel-challenged Staten Island. I would hustle inside the Garden press entrance on 33rd Street, next door to the old Charley O's restaurant, to cover games my father would seldom watch but would persistently archive in the bottom drawer of his bedroom bureau.

A man whose own immigrant father was functionally illiterate, my father was stunned and delighted to discover the family name in his beloved tabloids, first the *New York Post* and later the *Daily News*. From the beginning, he faithfully cut out my Knicks dispatches, filing them haphazardly in that bottom drawer. It didn't matter what I had written—game story, sidebar, notebook. They were all crammed in faithfully. When I left the *Post* for the *Daily News* in 1983 and the editors ran a flattering promotion introducing their new basketball reporter who'd been lured away from their blood rival downtown, he cut out the same blurb that ran for several days.

The plan, he said, was to make a scrapbook, but when he'd catch me sitting cross-legged on the carpet during a visit, searching for a clip I easily could have gotten from the newspaper morgue, he'd say, "Take what you need."

"If you want me to take them, why are you saving them?" I'd say, pretending to be clueless.

He would grin, shrug, and continue clipping—right up to the day the telephone rang in my Brooklyn

Heights apartment on the Sunday of Memorial Day weekend 1990. It was my younger sister, Randi, calling with the terrible news that he'd suffered a heart attack at my parents' apartment on the outskirts of Canarsie and had been rushed to the hospital.

The trip across Brooklyn was not too far, but by the time I navigated the holiday traffic to the Brookdale Hospital Medical Center on Linden Boulevard, on the edge of the Brownsville neighborhood, where we'd lived until I was ten, my father was gone, dead at 67. I had turned 38 earlier that month, and my firstborn son, the child who assured my father the family name would live on, was only seven months old.

It was late in the evening by the time we returned to my parents' apartment on East 78th Street off Flatlands Avenue. Wrapped in the Sunday comics, the *Daily News* rested in its customary position, on the edge of the living room coffee table. In those early hours of mourning, when mind and body seem to be acting independently, some part of me couldn't leave my father's ritual unexamined. So one last time the story I had written—a baseball column about a father and son—was cut from the paper and carried into the bedroom. But when I tried to place it onto the pile, I couldn't. The drawer was packed so tight I could barely open it.

"Did he stop cutting out my stories?" I asked my mother.

She looked at me and laughed.

"Check the bottom drawer in the other bedroom," she said.

There I found the clip annex, and that was the moment when it finally hit me—as hard as I'd ever been hit—that my father was gone. I sat there and cried and promised myself that I would make something of his collection, a scrapbook for his grandson.

Here were the boldface headlines, the *Post* exclusives, including "Willis to Sonny (Werblin): In or Out," that had launched my career and helped in getting Reed fired. Here were the screaming "Knicks in Turmoil" standbys that took a morsel or two of in-house controversy and ratcheted it up to outright mutiny.

Perusing those stories, deciding which ones to save, I realized there was much more there than a dozen years of tabloid indulgences, more than a narrative of Old Knicks afterlife, but instead a whole trove of Old Knicks afterglow: the chronicled ceremonies of jerseys retired, appointments of various players to organizational positions, successes and failures and inevitable firings. Above all, my father's collection reflected not only profound shifts in the methodology of covering mainstream sports but the general coarsening of a culture.

In the years between 1973 and 1978, professional sports underwent their most impactful changes since the breaking of color lines. Players were empowered by the courts to market themselves as independent contractors. With union director Larry Fleisher behind him, pro basketball's labor champion was Oscar Robertson, then of the Milwaukee Bucks. As president of the players' union, he attached his name to a lawsuit seeking to block an NBA-ABA merger in 1970 and to change the system that bound a player to a single NBA team in perpetuity. As a result, the merger was blocked until 1976, when the suit was settled and a form of free agency was adopted, though too late for Robertson—who, like the trio of Knicks frontcourt men, retired in 1974.

Along with richer, more empowered players came agents promoting agendas that sounded antithetical or even heretical to the core team-sport principles. This revolutionary change was more complicated in the NBA, whose stars were increasingly African American and were often subjected to harsher judgments when they took advantage of their newfound leverage. In racially charged Boston, for instance, Havlicek and Larry

Bird could play hardball with Auerbach and remain beloved Celtics, in part because they were white. When Paul Silas and Cedric Maxwell took a stand, they were derided as greedy and shipped out of town.

In New York, the nascent labor conflict was intensified by a man named George Steinbrenner. Months after promising to stick to building ships—to, in effect, leave his freshly purchased Yankees to his baseball people—Steinbrenner's first season of authoritarian decrees began as the Knicks made their second championship run. Three years later, the Australian press lord Rupert Murdoch got his hands on the *New York Post* and soon after—merely by the force of their personalities and their desire to shake up the establishment of their respective industries—had consummated the perfect marriage of industry titans and intemperate tactics: Steinbrenner was the perfect tool for what Murdoch's people deemed to be back-page news.

Steinbrenner himself contrived a business model in which winning was less a collective pursuit and more a contractual demand. Payback for failure—especially for the most well compensated—became a bold-faced flogging on the back page of the *Post*. In turn, this forced the other papers, especially the *Daily News*, to amplify their negative coverage. Steinbrenner established these new terms of administrative engagement with his Billy Martin–Reggie Jackson teams and his tirades of the late seventies. When Sonny Werblin took over as president of the Garden in 1978, he enthusiastically played by the new rules in targeting Reed, the Knicks' most beloved player, in a heartless exercising of executive power. When Werblin fired Reed and returned Holzman to the bench after my *Post* story gave him an opening, Old Knicks values seemed as obsolete as the quaint idea that the new Knicks would always prepare and police themselves in the evolving age of enhanced reward and risk.

Upon returning, Holzman barely recognized the working environment he'd left in 1977, or at least the one in which he had achieved his greatest successes. In the world he was used to, reporters were part of the extended family. They could walk into the Knicks' Garden administrative offices, kibitz with the secretaries, prowl the hallways like trusted staff members. "It was small, intimate, like family," said Gwynne Bloomfield, who began working for the Knicks on December 18, 1969, answering telephones with the directive to never give out a player's number. On her first day, a man called asking for the number of "the butcher." She frantically searched the Rolodex before giving up and asking one of her colleagues if they knew who this butcher was. It took a few seconds before they realized she was talking about DeBusschere. Embarrassed, she returned to the caller, apologizing for the delay and for being unable to furnish a player's number. "But this is Bill Bradley," the caller said. Bloomfield didn't know who Bradley was, either.

"Somehow they didn't fire me," she said. She worked 12 years for the Knicks, had a front-row seat for home games next to the wife of *New York Post* columnist Milton Gross, and eventually had a guest list that was the envy of many when she married and became Mrs. Gwynne Bloomfield-Pike. As the years passed, she never missed an Old Knicks reunion. She loved all the players like brothers, and all the coaches, too, with the exception of Holzman. To her, he was a kind of father, whistling Rodgers and Hammerstein's "Oh, What a Beautiful Morning" when he strolled into the office.

"I always said that team ruined it for all of us who covered them," said Ira Berkow. "Because they were so bright and so interesting that everything else after that couldn't come close."

Sportswriters in the twenty-first century—long gone from the team planes and hotels, reduced in many cases to asking questions at sterile press conferences televised on the Madison Square Garden Network or with public relations people eavesdropping on the most benign chatter—would be shocked by the access their predecessors once had. Leonard Lewin, who was still at the *Post* when I got there, was a close friend and co-author of Holzman. When the Knicks held a victory party after winning the title in 1970, Lewin got up to speak on behalf of the writers, who were feted and fitted for championship rings.

"You have to understand how different it all was in the fifties and sixties," said Phil Pepe, a colleague of mine after I left the *Post* for the *Daily News* in 1983. "When I started with *World-Telegram & Sun*, we would never have traveled with a pro basketball team." With newspapers unwilling to pay the road freight, the Knicks picked up the expenses to ensure daily coverage.

Pepe, who became a *News* columnist, never wore his ring or profited from it, either. "Removed the diamond, made a pendant for my wife, and then got divorced," he said. His son took the devalued ring; Pepe kept the memories. "We hung with Red a lot, him and Frankie Blauschild," Pepe said. "We'd go out to dinner on the road all the time."

The tradition continued when Holzman returned, but only sparingly. With the exception of the *Times*' Sam Goldaper, the beat reporters were younger, edgier, professional acquaintances who needed to be kept at a safe distance. In the arena of circumspection, nobody was tougher than Holzman. When I would occasionally call late at night with a deadline looming, I would beg Selma's forgiveness and then wait for Red to come to the phone. "Boy, are you in big fucking trouble," he'd say, knowing I had to be desperate, at wit's end, to be putting my story in his hands.

But the Garden became a strange, bewildering place for Holzman in the nearly four seasons of his second coming. He inherited some young talent from Reed, but it was undisciplined to the point of being uncoachable. When point guard Micheal Ray Richardson, Reed's prized draft pick in 1978, lost his playing time under Holzman because he couldn't keep a healthy percentage of his passes out of the stands, the rookie fumed until he could no longer contain himself.

"This old man, he don't want me," Richardson, an endearing but troubled kid, told me (with a severe stutter) one night in the locker room after a road game. "I'm calling my agent to get me out of here. Write that."

When I asked him if he was sure, he went off again on Holzman, who happened to be standing a few feet away, out of our sight line, pretending he wasn't listening. Turning to rush my scoop into the paper, I noticed the coach and trod by carefully. Holzman leaned into me as I passed: "That poor schmuck thinks you're gonna help him." When the story led the back page the next day, Richardson went to Werblin's office and tearfully told the Garden boss that he wanted to stay.

Sowing my tabloid oats, I took to playfully attributing sensitive material to a loquacious and quasi-fictitious character named "One Knick." Many players said things they didn't want their names attached to, but Holzman, unaccustomed to the muckraking, became convinced that One Knick was just one Knick: he suspected it was Mike Glenn, an unthreatening but chatty shooting guard. While the team and traveling party sat on a bus one day, Glenn was outside with the coach, vigorously denying that he was Deep Throat.

The anonymous nitpicking intensified during a miserable 1981–82 season, undercut by rampant womanizing and drug use during the height of the NBA's cocaine era. On the way down, Richardson uttered his famous line "The ship be sinking." And when Nat Gottlieb of the Newark *Star-Ledger* asked how low it could go, Richardson marvelously reasoned, "Sky's the limit."

Through it all, Holzman coached and comported himself as he always had. He never confronted reporters, as he had John Nucatola before Game 7 in Boston. Never got too high or too low, responding to our declarations of doom by reminding us that he was going home to have a scotch and dinner with Selma. By early spring of '82 he knew that Werblin was going to make another coaching change. In Boston (where else?) for his final game, I asked him if he wished to comment on his players' effort that season.

"Maybe I'll say something soon," he said. He looked away, then back with a trademark sly grin that told me I should have known better. "Probably not."

Still taking advice from Howard Cosell, Werblin replaced Holzman with the rising coaching star (and unabashed know-it-all) Hubie Brown, while also bringing home Dave DeBusschere to direct the organization. While not quite persona non grata, DeBusschere had not been the most welcome Old Knicks legend during his time with the Nets and a subsequent stint as ABA commissioner. In fact, the Knicks waited seven years to retire DeBusschere's number 22, loath to honor him while he was working for a local competitor.

His professional marriage to the combustible but always entertaining Brown was of the shotgun variety, as Werblin, in trying to replicate his magic with Joe Namath's Jets, was more enamored of marquee names and less interested in allowing the president of basketball operations to select his own coach and create a unified partnership. Though the Knicks had some modest success after DeBusschere landed the high-scoring Brooklynite Bernard King—they went seven games in the second round of the 1984 playoffs with Larry Bird and the Celtics—Brown was never a DeBusschere ally, complaining about his work ethic to every reporter who would keep his name out of the paper.

The relationship still might have worked out had King not torn up his knee months before DeBusschere's most memorable coup—which, granted, was attributable to the cooperative Ping-Pong ball that brought Patrick Ewing to New York via the inaugural NBA draft lottery in 1985. Brown proceeded to alienate his prize rookie by playing Bill Cartwright at center and Ewing at power forward, making him defend quicker opponents much too far from the basket and stressing his tender knees. When the team collapsed under an avalanche of injuries, DeBusschere was fired, and Brown tumbled down soon after. The franchise moved into a period of continuous ownership and administrative transition.

Not the type to whine to reporters, DeBusschere would express his frustrations to confidants—the broadcaster John Andariese, his old pal Bradley, and his wife. "Dave never really enjoyed his time in the front office because it was run by a corporation and he always felt hampered," Geri DeBusschere said. He would hash out a deal with another team and have to run it through an unresponsive chain of command. He would fume. The deal would die. And then Brown would blame DeBusschere for being inactive and lazy.

DeBusschere grew wary of the media responsibilities, calling one reporter back when a story was developing and saying, "Just tell the other guys what I told you." When the ax fell, he was relieved to exit the basketball stage, once and for all. He would be fine, he said. Two things DeBusschere never lacked: employment suitors and drinking buddies.

But the organizational infighting didn't end with DeBusschere and Brown. Werblin's celebrity matchmaking established a haunting precedent. Front-office conflict became a way of Garden life: Al Bianchi versus Rick Pitino, Ernie Grunfeld versus Jeff Van Gundy, Isiah Thomas versus anyone perceived to be in his way, even after he was replaced by Donnie Walsh (thanks to Thomas's strangely symbiotic relationship with the congenitally contentious Garden strongman James Dolan). While the intramural contests played out endlessly on the back pages, the team struggled for traction and the years without a third championship turned into decades.

Even when the Knicks were a conference power and NBA finalist in 1994 and 1999, the Garden was a Midtown shark tank. In 1995, after captivating the city, Pat Riley made an inside move for more power in personnel matters. Dave Checketts, who had hired Riley and restored competitive order to the franchise, resisted the coup. Riley responded by faxing in his resignation and signing a sweeter deal giving him total control of basketball operations with the Miami Heat.

Checketts, a devout Mormon from Utah who was recommended to the Knicks by David Stern, was a brilliant front man for the organization, a quick study of the New York fan. "Everywhere you went around town, you could still feel a love for those championship teams," Checketts said. "They were the standard for everything we did. And though we started having success pretty soon after Pat came in, I didn't want to distance ourselves from that. I wanted to embrace it. The bar was set really high, but that's what I wanted our goal to be."

Checketts brought Holzman back into the fold, made him part of the organizational process. Holzman would sit in on draft meetings and admit he didn't know who the hell the others were talking about. But that wasn't the point, as far as Checketts was concerned. He wanted Holzman around for the legacy he represented, for who he was.

When the Knicks flew to Houston for the first two games of the 1994 Finals, they threw a big party between games at a ranch outside the city with a rodeo theme, called it the Knicks Lone Star Hoedown. It was there that I experienced one of the great moments of my sports journalism life: the sight of Holzman and Spike Lee, two famously hardnosed Brooklynites, chatting away in tall cowboy hats.

About ten days later, back in Houston for Game 6, the Knicks led the series 3–2 and were trailing the Rockets 86–84, with the ball in the final seconds. The star-crossed Ewing—obscured in college and in the pros by Michael Jordan, who that season had taken leave of the Bulls—set a high screen for John Starks, the streaky shooting guard. Starks was freed momentarily on the left wing, behind the three-point line. But Hakeem Olajuwon switched off Ewing, in pursuit of Starks—just the way Wes Unseld had chased Bill Bradley at the conclusion of Game 7, 1971. It was the same area of the floor and the same result. Olajuwon deflected Starks's jumper, the Rockets went on to win Game 7, and Holzman never saw his beloved Knicks get that close to a championship again.

Days after he died in November 1998, in the funeral chapel on Queens Boulevard, not far from the old training site, Lost Battalion Hall, Checketts eulogized

Holzman in a quavering voice, calling him the "patriarch of the Knicks . . . a great coach who forced his will on a group of players." As he spoke those words, he nodded to those players, who would carry their old coach in his coffin, to the hearse, on the way to his eternal rest.

In the spring of 2003, in the 30th year of the Knicks' championship drought, a celebration of better times was planned for June 6 at the NBA Store on Fifth Avenue, open to a limited number of fans. It was to be the first reunion of the championship cast since the death of Holzman, and the guys eagerly anticipated standing tall for the man who had given them the confidence and license to, in effect, coach themselves.

But three weeks before the gathering, on May 14, news arrived that was both shocking and devastating: DeBusschere, 62, had suffered a heart attack during a workday on a lower Manhattan street and died at New York University Hospital.

"If you told me cancer, I'd say okay," Geri DeBusschere said. "But the heart? I mean, he was so strong." Her husband had had no diagnosed history of heart disease, though maybe there were clues that went unheeded, going all the way back to the night of the first championship in 1970. On the way home DeBusschere had thought he was having a heart attack and had Geri rush him to the hospital. Palpitations, he was told; too much excitement, a few too many drinks.

"Then the year before he died, we were in Florida and Dave was playing golf with Billy Cunningham," she said. "Billy said, 'Dave didn't look too good; he didn't finish.' And then he told someone else he felt shortness of breath." Athletes are commended for soldiering on in spite of the pain, and nobody was better at dismissing his own discomforts than DeBusschere. When Bill Bradley eulogized him at his funeral, he said: "If I had $100 for every night Dave played hurt, I could buy a nice car."

If not for Bradley, DeBusschere would have been mourned without fanfare. Several times, he had told his wife that if anything were to happen to him, "I don't want anything, no big deal, just bury me with the family."

"What are you going to do?" Bradley asked Geri DeBusschere on the phone, calling as soon as he'd heard that his old roommate—who had proudly watched from the gallery when Bradley was sworn in to the Senate—was gone. His voice was choked with emotion. She could tell he'd been crying.

"Dave doesn't want anything," she said. "I'll just get a cemetery plot."

"Oh, no, Geri, you can't do that," Bradley said. "Too many people loved Dave."

He talked her into a public funeral and then took it upon himself to make all the arrangements. On May 19, 2003, mourners filled the pews of the St. Joseph Roman Catholic Church in Garden City. They included DeBusschere's core teammates, though Earl Monroe said he had gone as friend and foe, as Old Knick and Baltimore Bullet. Someone, he said, had to represent Gus Johnson, who had died 16 years earlier of brain cancer in Akron, Ohio. "Dave respected Gus so much; he always told me that," Monroe told me that day outside the church. "He always respected the opponents."

The feelings were mutual. John Havlicek—whose shoulder was separated in the '73 series by a DeBusschere screen—was among the speakers and pallbearers. His son had called with the news, to spare him the shock of hearing it from a television talking head. "I was devastated," he said. "Dave had become like a brother." Dave Cowens was another Celtic who came to pay his respects, along with Dave Bing of the Pistons, Cunningham of the 76ers, Oscar Robertson of the Royals and Bucks—every franchise from the Eastern Conference of 1970, present and accounted for.

Too distraught to speak at the funeral, Reed asked Bradley to represent the team. Bradley spoke lovingly and irreverently of his six-year roommate. DeBusschere may have been an incorrigible snorer, he said, but there was no more loyal friend or less pretentious man once he was awake, no one prouder to be an Old Knick.

"Championship teams share a moment that few other people know," Bradley said. "The overwhelming emotion derives from more than pride. Your devotion to your teammates, the depth of your sense of belonging, is something like blood kinship, but without the complications. Rarely can words express it. In the nonverbal world of basketball, it's like grace and beauty and ease, and it spills into all areas of your life."

If only legislative bodies could be so committed to the cause, Bradley mused. But Harry Reid—his friend in the Senate from Nevada who would become majority leader—was so moved when he read Bradley's eulogy that he placed it into the *Congressional Record* and sent Bradley a copy of the document. Bradley hung it on a wall in his office, never second-guessing himself for refusing to honor DeBusschere's request.

"I felt that whatever Dave would say about the funeral—'I don't want it'—that it was a matter of people being given the chance to pay their respects," he said. "I thought he deserved that and the family deserved it, too."

Even with the media coverage, it was difficult to rationalize and accept the loss of Dave DeBusschere. As time passed, some would even forget he was gone. "It's hard for me, you know?" Geri DeBusschere said in early summer 2009. "It's an unusual name, so people make the connection when they meet me and you'd be amazed by how many say, 'Oh, what's he doing now?'"

Her voice seized, tears flowed. Six years had passed, four grandchildren born to her three children, starting with Peter DeBusschere's first of two. When Peter's wife, Kristin, an Upper East Side physician, got pregnant several months after his father's death, the baby was born a full week after the due date in a bittersweet twist of fate.

Little David was born on November 22. "Dave's uniform number," Geri DeBusschere said, her face brightening even as tears still flowed. "We felt like he was sending us a message that everything was okay."

A couple of months after my interview with Geri DeBusschere, Bradley called and said that she wanted to speak with me again. I had heard through the Knicks' grapevine that she had suddenly turned ill and had undergone surgery, and I didn't wish to impose. "No, she wants to get on with her life," Bradley said. "She has a funny story to tell you."

So I called, and she talked about how DeBusschere, during the 1970 playoff run, had gone out with Reed to a shooting range on Long Island and returned with a deep and ugly-looking gash, still bleeding. DeBusschere's gun had kicked back and taken a chunk of his forehead. "Dave didn't want to go to the hospital because he was embarrassed," she said. "He kept saying, 'What the hell am I going to tell everyone?' Finally, we got the bleeding to stop and I said, 'Tell them Michelle cracked you with her bottle.' So that's what he did—the big, tough Dave DeBusschere assaulted by his 18-month-old daughter."

It was a sweet story from a courageous woman, who weeks after her husband's death had gone to the NBA Store for the '73 team's reunion and received the biggest ovation of all. Sadly, Geri DeBusschere would not get the chance for a repeat performance when the Old Knicks gathered for the 40th anniversary of the 1970 title, as she succumbed to liver cancer weeks after we last spoke. Months later, Dick McGuire died of a brain aneurysm, casting yet another pall over the franchise and leaving the extended family that remained to wonder if the Garden would, in our remaining years, ever be Eden again.

18

THEN, NOW, AND FOREVER

Making the courtside rounds in Orlando before the
Lakers took on the Magic in Game 3 of the 2009
NBA Finals, Spike Lee became engaged in a feisty
discussion with Mark Jackson. The ABC analyst from
St. Albans, Queens, got under the skin of the director
from Fort Greene, Brooklyn, by making the sacrile-
gious claim that the Knicks' teams of the late eighties,
featuring Patrick Ewing at center and Jackson himself
playing the point, would have handled the Old Knicks,
their titles notwithstanding.

Jackson argued that each succeeding generation is
athletically enhanced and therefore superior to the previous one—somewhat out of character for a guy who
compiled 10,334 career assists primarily with guile and
vision (and who in 2011 would become the head coach

of Golden State). Ally and supporter of the modern superstar, Lee nonetheless countered by saying that the Old Knicks' level of collective excellence in most cases far exceeded that of contemporary teams and would compensate for an inability to play on a high wire. Then Lee excused himself, walked across the court, and bumped right into Cazzie Russell.

For Lee, the chance encounter felt like an act of providence, akin to a hilarious scene in Woody Allen's *Annie Hall*, where Allen's character, Alvy, complains to Diane Keaton's Annie, while standing in a Manhattan movie line, about a Columbia professor pontificating on the work of the Canadian media theorist Marshall McLuhan—whom Allen proceeds to pull out of thin air to question how the professor ever got to teach at Columbia in the first place.

Lights, camera, satisfaction! Lee caught Jackson's attention, while pointing to Russell, who yelled out, "Mark, you better stop smoking whatever it is you're smoking."

Months later, back at the Garden for the 40th reunion of the 1970 team, Russell could laugh off the slander. "No one will ever know, right?" he said. "But I will say this: we had a pretty decent center, didn't we? We had a couple of great guards and a power forward who wasn't backing down from nobody." Old wounds being better left unopened, Russell didn't get into the other forward position, which, of course, would have been Bradley starting ahead of him.

Granted, it is difficult, especially for young people, to watch NBA footage predating the Jordan era and not be amused by the tight shorts, with far less use of the three-point line or no line at all, fewer blow-by dribbles and ESPN-worthy highlights. The rare video preserved from the seventies can look as ancient as Egypt.

Conversely, the old-timers watch the predictable exhibitions and shake their heads at the bastardized product that seems to mimic a video game—so many mad dashes to the rim and low-percentage shots. "I once asked Oscar, 'What do you think of the modern player?' and he said, 'Other than the fact that he can't dribble, shoot, or pass, he's okay,'" said Bill Bradley, who didn't agree with the Big O and believed the talent of twenty-first-century players to be jaw-dropping, in many cases.

"But the point is that the game changes, so the criteria you used before to determine who's good, or best, can't be used," he said. "If we were playing by the rules of the sixties and seventies, when we played with our feet and with finesse, well, that's very different than the rules of today, where's there's not a premium put on movement, where the game is played with upper-body strength, there's a lot more intentional contact, and the three-point rule changes the flow. I've had people who were major Knicks fans tell me that they've stopped watching the games, partly because the game changed."

Vintage political Bradley: liberal Democrat straddling the pragmatic center. But his generational rival John Havlicek shifted from his right-side leanings (driving to the basket, that is) for a more radical assertion. "I certainly think we could compete, and, given the same latitude—wraparound dribbles, three or four steps to the rim—we would be even better," he said. "For every dunk they'd get on us, we'd probably get two backdoor layups on them."

Still a respected and unbiased analyst of the modern game as an octogenarian, Jack Ramsay said it was also wrong to assume that players of 40 years ago would be grossly outclassed athletically in an open-court game with—for argument's sake—Steve Nash and the Suns. After all, he said, there was something called the ABA, the renegade NBA rival, which had its share of flamboyant sky walkers and three-point bombers. It wasn't as if the more grounded players of the Old Knicks' era never had to face players who were more athletic.

"I have no doubt that teams like the Knicks of the seventies, my Portland team, the old Celtics, would adapt and still be very good," Ramsay said. "I always hear things—like Bill Russell would be overpowered today by bigger, stronger guys—and I always say: absolute nonsense."

I've always believed the best NBA decade to be the eighties—as epitomized by Magic Johnson and Larry Bird. These were big men with little-man skills, heralding a new-age athlete still equipped with old-school fundamentals and imbued with team-first values. Asked during an ESPN Classic taping to choose my greatest team of all time, I picked the 1984–85 Lakers—still with a potent Kareem Abdul-Jabbar, the young veterans Magic and James Worthy, and the likes of Bob McAdoo, Jamaal Wilkes, and Michael Cooper off the bench.

But I also try not to gush too much about one decade or era, because they all come with qualitative extremes. During a college panel discussion in Boston in 2006, a reporter from a local newspaper rambled on about how amazing the eighties were while blasting the contemporary players as essentially uncommitted and clueless. Much as I agreed that the Bird-Magic rivalry was the best NBA story line ever, I had to point out that the eighties had its share of very bad basketball, and we watched more than enough of it in New York.

As much as the NBA's reputation sank after embarrassing losses by the American national team in the 2002 World Championship and 2004 Olympics, Phil Jackson told me that his Shaq-and-Kobe Lakers team that won three straight titles starting in 2000 reached a point where it was as cohesive as any team he'd ever coached, including Jordan's Bulls, or played on, including the Old Knicks. "The first year was a test pattern," he said. "But the middle years they swamped teams for about 150 games, went 15–1 in the playoffs. They really knew how to play together."

I would also maintain that the Spurs, my favorite team of the early twenty-first century, would have been recognizable and formidable in any NBA decade. Yes, league officials cringed whenever they made a run to the Finals, because it augured a television ratings nosedive for the lack of a sexy, shoe-company-hyped superstar. The numbers were irrefutable, but they reflected more on our celebrity-driven culture of superficiality and a sport dumbed down for teenage consumption than on the brilliant San Antonio team foolishly typecast as a collection of boring South Texas hicks.

Had that team been transported to Madison Square Garden or assembled in New York, it would no doubt have been characterized very differently. In the nation's media capital, Tim Duncan would have been cast as the second coming of the Captain, celebrated for his quiet leadership, his fundamental purity. The Spurs would have been a proud reflection of the great melting pot, with their rich blend of international stars: Duncan of the U.S. Virgin Islands, Manu Ginóbili of Argentina, and Tony Parker of France. With their beautiful pick-and-roll passing game, they would have been hailed for reinventing basketball as an art form, just as the Old Knicks had been.

Like Red Holzman, Gregg Popovich effectively deployed players who, when judged individually, were unimposing, especially by the measure of modern metrics. Bruce Bowen was an earthbound career journeyman, a scratch-and-claw midsize defender with the ability to knock down an open three. After David Robinson retired, the Spurs used a rotation of ordinary role players at power forward or center, depending on how you preferred to define Duncan. But as a unit, they were brilliant at maximizing their strengths, spreading the floor, running their half-court offense through the multi-skilled and exceedingly unselfish Duncan. In other words, the team's whole was significantly greater than the sum of its parts.

According to Mike Riordan, that was precisely how the Old Knicks would have imposed themselves on the best teams, regardless of when they played. "You see all the double-teaming they do now?" he said. "We would have welcomed that, because we were a great—not good, but great—passing and jump-shooting team."

Months after the Phil Jackson–coached Lakers won the '09 title by defeating Orlando, Riordan used the Magic to make his case that the '70 Knicks would have matched up favorably against an elite modern-day squad. "The Magic are a light-it-up team, without great size except for their presence in the middle, kind of like we were," he said.

Asked if he thought Willis Reed could contain the chiseled man-child Dwight Howard, Riordan said, "Are you kidding me? Willis stood in there against Wilt Chamberlain! He was a lot better than people give him credit for. He was strong enough to play center, but he had the skills of a forward. You think Dwight Howard would like having to go out and defend against that lefty jumper?"

With good reason, Riordan also liked his guys' chances in the backcourt, with Hall of Famer Walt Frazier matched up against Jameer Nelson and Dick Barnett against Courtney Lee. At forward, he was certain that Dave DeBusschere, while surrendering a few inches, would kick the jump-shooting derriere of the one-dimensional Rashard Lewis, while Bradley would hold his own against the streaky Frenchman Mickael Pietrus.

Riordan's point was well taken: for all the assumption that the athlete of old would be in over his head, the Magic would hardly have been a physically intimidating opponent for the Old Knicks. "How many games did they win against the Lakers, one?" Riordan said. Yes, one, though had the rookie Lee converted a lob to the rim at the end of regulation in Game 2, the series would have gone longer. "Okay, maybe they get one against us, too," Riordan said.

In the aftermath of those '09 Finals, one coronation indisputably affirmed Old Knicks eminence—Phil Jackson's tenth coaching title, breaking a deadlock with Red Auerbach. One of the purest joys for Jackson was in establishing the new mark (which he improved on a year later against the Celtics), one not likely to be broken in his or perhaps anyone else's lifetime.

"He is the reason why I am a coach, obviously," Jackson said of Holzman, who always told him to not make the game more complicated than it was. "It's not rocket science, Phil," Holzman would say. "It's see the ball on defense, hit the open man on offense." But while Jackson's X's and O's strategy, his celebrated use of the triangle offense, came from another old lifer, Tex

Winter, his best coaching trait was in knowing how to handle people. Zen philosophy stripped away, Jackson was much like Holzman: he allowed his players to succeed through self-discovery.

Never was this more evident than after Game 3 of the 1994 Eastern Conference semifinals, when the Bulls—having found a way to flourish without the baseball wannabe Michael Jordan, winning a stunning 55 regular-season games—found themselves in a deadlocked battle for survival, already down 2–0 in the series, at home against Patrick Ewing and the Knicks with 1.8 seconds left.

Jackson called a play for Toni Kukoc, the Croatian star, whom Jerry Krause, the GM, had pursued faithfully, even as his team was in the midst of winning three consecutive titles, rankling Jordan and his wingman, Scottie Pippen.

Ninety-nine times out of 100, the ball would have gone to Jordan, but he wasn't around, and Pippen was furious that Jackson would dare nominate Kukoc, an NBA rookie, over him. Pippen sat down during the time-out and refused to get up. Kukoc, the better shooter, proceeded to drain the game-winning jumper from straight out.

In the locker room, the players were stunned by what had occurred. Given Pippen's standing, it was a pivotal moment for Jackson, not all that different from the one Holzman had faced when Russell took his racial-profiling anger out on white teammates and Reed. Holding back deliberately, Jackson watched Bill Cartwright, the respected veteran center, stand up to tearfully confront Pippen. "Scottie, how could you?" he said.

Chastened by a colleague, not his coach, Pippen apologized. Jackson never had to say a word to exert his authority, much less berate Pippen in the way the media would in the aftermath of the Sitting Bull episode. His teams policed themselves and as a result were stronger for it.

"A lot of people thought the 1.8-second denial would define Scottie's career, but it was a learning moment in his life," Jackson said on the eve of Pippen's 2010 induction into the Naismith Hall of Fame. "He came back as the leader of teams for another decade."

Jordan's return helped, of course, but so did Jackson's willingness to loosen up on the reins and allow Cartwright to make it easier for Pippen to express his remorse, just as Holzman had done through Reed. Pippen's reputation as one of the great multipurpose players in NBA history actually grew when Jordan returned for the Bulls' second three-peat, extending Jackson's ring collection to a second hand.

When Jackson closed in on a share of the record in Los Angeles, Auerbach, who would die in 2006, conceded that he was a clever guy, a good coach, but would also occasionally tweak him for working with teams that were "ready-made for him," for never building a championship team from the ground up, as Auerbach had in Boston.

Auerbach seemed to forget that the teams he coached in Boston were disproportionately dependent on Bill Russell. Jackson was never a GM, never responsible for compiling talent. And while all of his championship rosters included the best player in the game—Jordan in Chicago, Shaquille O'Neal and later Kobe Bryant in L.A.—none of them had so much as sniffed a title before Jackson began filling their heads with the tenets of togetherness gleaned from Lost Battalion Hall.

The notion that Jackson had been handed much of anything was also a misappropriation of the facts. Rare was the modern head coach who put up with the bush league life—as Jackson had—for the chance to hone his skills. More than a decade after he retired as a player, when nobody would even give him an assistant's job in the NBA because of his iconoclast image, Jackson spent summers coaching in Puerto Rico, as had Holzman. It would be good for him, Holzman had advised, because the environment was rabid and the language barrier would force him to find alternative ways to communicate.

During the height of the Bird-Magic era, when Pat Riley fell into the plum Lakers position, Jackson was in Albany, New York, on a career treadmill in the CBA, or Cockroach League, as he called it. Commuting from his home in Woodstock, more than an hour away, he won the title his first year, 1984, and promptly wrote a two-page letter to the GM, pleading for a raise to $30,000 and a per diem hike to $25. He drove the team's van on road trips of less than 200 miles, checked the team into cheap hotels, and did everything for the players short of squeezing toothpaste onto their brushes.

"It's a more organic experience," he told me one night in early 1987 when our paths crossed in Pensacola during his fourth year on the job. I was there doing a feature for the *Daily News* on the comeback of a former Knicks center, Marvin Webster, with the Pensacola team. After the game, Jackson and I hit a roadside seafood shack that fit his meager budget and then a downtown bar. With a houseful of children, he said he was nearing the end of his coaching rope; he couldn't afford to hang on much longer. He didn't think anyone in the NBA would hire him and was formulating plans for law school.

But all those years ago when Holzman was keeping a scout's eye on him in North Dakota, so was Krause of the Baltimore Bullets. A maverick of sorts in his own right, Krause had tried to get Jackson a job on the staff of the Bulls' head coach, Stan Albeck, in 1985. Jackson showed up in jeans and sandals, with his hair unkempt and a scruffy beard. Albeck, no bohemian, was not impressed.

Two years later, with Albeck gone and a sudden vacancy on Doug Collins's staff, Krause again called Jackson in for an interview, along with Butch Beard. Knowing both had played for Holzman and that Beard had served as his Knicks assistant, Krause called his old scouting companion at home in Cedarhurst. "They're both your guys—want to tell me what you think?" Krause said.

Holzman wasn't about to talk up one at the expense of the other. He loved both. As with his players, he wanted Krause to come to his own conclusion. "You'll figure it out," he told him.

Partial to Jackson, Krause told him to wear a suit and cut his hair. Jackson complied, impressed Collins, and got the job. As the 1988–89 regular season was winding down, one in which the Bulls would go 47–35, Krause, believing the team wasn't playing to its full potential, went to the owner, Jerry Reinsdorf, and asked about replacing Collins with Jackson. That spring, Jordan hit one of his most famous shots—a buzzer beater over Cleveland's Craig Ehlo to eliminate the Cavs in a decisive Game 5. "You still want to make that change?" Reinsdorf asked Krause.

Krause told him he did; he believed Collins was too emotional, too stressed out, and the more cerebral Jackson was the logical guy to go the distance. After the Bulls lost to the Pistons in the conference finals, Jackson was hired and immediately installed Winter's triangle, predicated on movement and passing, to diversify the attack (at least until the shot clock wound down and Jordan took over). Within two years, with Pippen growing into the role of second star and anchoring a fierce unit of agile and team-oriented defenders, the Bulls were champions.

The league's second-greatest dynasty after the Bill Russell Celtics would ignite an unprecedented growth period in revenue and global expansion of its product with six titles in eight years. Chicagoans—especially Krause and Reinsdorf—would forever believe the run would have been eight straight had Jordan not walked out for a year and a half following a frenzy of 1993 headlines on gambling excesses and the murder of his father, James.

As with many great things, competing agendas brought the Bulls dynasty to a disagreeable end, with

Jackson, Jordan, and Pippen united against Krause, who was forever reminded (especially by Jordan) that he had taken over the GM job after Jordan was drafted and who alienated His Airness by saying, "Organizations win championships." The team disbanded in 1998 and Jackson eventually moved on to the Lakers, where he continued adding rings to his collection—one that ironically had begun with him out of uniform in 1970.

Jackson said he prefers not to compare the teams he has coached with the Old Knicks; he doesn't see the point. Comparing great teams across different eras is like comparing Angelina Jolie to Rita Hayworth. But Bill Bradley, for whom Jackson once nearly quit coaching in order to work on his friend's presidential campaign, played along with a Bulls–versus–Old Knicks matchup. He began by reminding me that while the Bulls had Jordan, routinely referred to as the best player in history, his team, at least the 1973 version, countered with five players (Reed, Frazier, DeBusschere, Monroe, and Lucas) from the NBA's all-time Top 50 team selected in the league's 50th anniversary year, 1996. Only Jordan and Pippen made it from the Bulls.

"First off, Willis versus Bill Cartwright: give that one to Willis," Bradley said. "Then Horace Grant versus DeBusschere, give it to DeBusschere; Frazier versus B. J. Armstrong, give it to Frazier. Earl versus Jordan: that's Jordan, but Earl's also going to do some things with the ball, make him work on defense."

Even more than Jordan-Monroe, he conceded that the small forward position was the most problematic. "Now I get Pippen," he said. And here, he agreed, was the ultimate embodiment of the generational stereotype and divide, Pippen representing the evolutionary nightmare—6'8", long-armed, terrifyingly elastic and athletic.

"You really can't make that comparison, can you?" Bradley said. "So when it gets to that one, what am I going to do? I'm going to cry: *'Help!'*"

And yet if Bradley could count on anything during his years in professional basketball, it was on defense—as with all great teams, help was on the way, all part of a preordained rotation.

In early June 1999, I was asked by my editor at the *Times* to do a column attempting to explain how the Knicks, in a matter of weeks, had gone from dysfunctional embarrassment to potential champion. During a lockout-shortened, 50-game regular season, Dave Checketts fired his GM, Ernie Grunfeld, and was chasing the idle Phil Jackson as a coaching replacement for

Jeff Van Gundy. Suddenly the team pulled together; sneaked into the playoffs as the conference's eighth seed; and in succession knocked off Pat Riley's Miami Heat, the Atlanta Hawks, and the Larry Bird–coached Indiana Pacers on the way to San Antonio for Game 1 of the league Finals.

With the aging Patrick Ewing injured and unable to play, these had become the Knicks of the likable Van Gundy and the smooth-shooting Allan Houston. But the team took its personality more from Latrell Sprewell—notorious for his intimate relationship with the neck of his former coach, P. J. Carlesimo—and the preening Larry Johnson, among other renegades not exactly destined for a Senate run, much less sainthood. Starving for a title, the city was nonetheless turned on by the surge of an embattled underdog.

I decided to check in with Dave DeBusschere to see what he thought of the possibility that this motley crew might tread on the Old Knicks' sacred championship ground. (Instead, San Antonio won the series in five games, behind Tim Duncan and David Robinson.) DeBusschere laughed and said that a couple of his children had actually called to make the same point.

"What are you talking about?" he told them. "We won our second title 25 years ago." (It was 26, but who aside from the long-suffering fans was counting?) Then

DeBusschere paused as if he wanted to say more but wasn't sure he should.

"Off the record?" he said.

Whenever DeBusschere was about to say something sarcastic, he had the habit of contorting the lower part of his mouth so that the words would tumble out the side. After I agreed to keep whatever he wanted to add out of the paper, I could picture him as he said, "These assholes could never have what we had in New York."

I didn't think him arrogant or unfair. He was merely stating in locker room vernacular what he had every right to believe. DeBusschere's teams were the city's first true basketball love, consummated in the years before the romance of sport became complicated by money and the constructed divide between athlete and fan.

But which fans? And for how long? During a bleak decade from the turn of the century, those runs to the Finals in 1994 and 1999 under Pat Riley and then Van Gundy had become the *good old days* to legions of younger Knicks fans. Remember when John Starks threw down that thunderous left-handed dunk in Michael Jordan's airspace during the '93 playoffs? When Ewing stood on the Garden press table, soaking in the love after Game 7 of the conference final against

Indiana? When the lane parted for Ewing in Game 7 against the Pacers in '94 and he back-rimmed his layup to end the brief but compelling Riley era?

Those were the playoff epics that Peter DeBusschere—born in 1971, too late to remember his father in uniform, save a couple of wheezing contests that passed for legends' games during all-star weekends—remembered fondly. "Those were my teams, Ewing and Charles Oakley," he said. "There were some amazing games at the Garden."

He would go with his father and brother, mostly on Sunday afternoons, holiday games on Christmas, not so much at night because "Dad didn't like waiting around after work." But playoff nights were invariably worth it. "I remember sitting there with him in the front row for Starks's dunk," he said. And for Larry Johnson's 4-point play that brought the Knicks back from the dead in Game 3 of the '99 conference finals in front of a crimson-faced coach, Larry Bird, on the Indiana bench.

These, too, were magical Garden nights, the appeal of those wild and more than a little crazy Knicks teams unmistakable. But, no, they didn't win it all, and if they had, they would have been sentenced to an eternity of comparisons reveling in their inferiority. The comparative performance of the seventies and the nineties

Knicks amounted to the difference between the oration of a Clinton and a Bush.

Old Knicks fans could appreciate the lunch-pail intensity of the nineties teams, but would always mourn the loss of the artistry. "To watch DeBusschere and those guys play was beautiful, the intelligence and teamwork," the screenwriter Bill Goldman said. "I'll never have days like that again." His despair was echoed by George Lois, who, while unable to kick the season-ticket habit, occasionally wanted to flash a crucifix, like Oscar Robertson, when he watched one side of the floor clear out, and the hypothetical star—call him Otis Elevator—pretend he was playing in a school yard by himself. "Some of it is fucking unwatchable," Lois said.

But to others, the game's seismic shift toward entertainment was not so objectionable. Woody Allen was one Old Knicks fan with a New Age agenda. "I absolutely think New York could have the same love affair with the Knicks because other cities have done so—Chicago, L.A.," he said. "You could see the Garden light up even for those small things, when Sprewell came, for instance. What they would need are one or two great members of the cast, not a group of faceless people who just grind it out. LeBron James or Dwyane Wade—that would have captivated the city right away."

Alas, Allen never held out great hope that either would come, despite a two-season write-off by a new Knicks regime headed by Donnie Walsh to free up enough money under the salary cap to pursue James. Following LeBron's rebuff, there was such panic at the Garden that the embattled owner, James Dolan, sent Isiah Thomas, loathed by fans and media alike after a disastrous tenure as team president and coach, to Ohio to flash his championship rings and dimpled smile. That didn't work, either, as James was bent on teaming with Wade and Chris Bosh in Miami, forming a superteam, at least on paper, reminiscent of the West-Chamberlain-Baylor Lakers.

"My theory is that the Knicks have a curse on them, like Boston's curse of the Bambino, and it started when they traded Walt Frazier to Cleveland," Woody Allen decided. His fatalism was a running joke during his long film career, most comically highlighted by Alvy's admission to Annie that he essentially broke humankind down into two categories: the horrible—which he described as people with blindness and deformity—and the miserable, which in effect was everyone else.

By Allen's measure, the Knicks emerged from the summer of 2010 as merely miserable. If the James-Wade-Bosh model represented a trend, New York had to sign at least one premier free agent to eventually attract another. Hence, most NBA critics applauded them for handing a nearly $100 million and uninsurable contract to the all-star power forward Amar'e Stoudemire, who had sustained serious eye and knee injuries while in Phoenix. But despite the Suns' concerns about Stoudemire's prognosis for extended good health, he didn't miss a game in the 2009–10 season and had long regained his explosiveness. Upon signing with New York, he boldly declared, "The Knicks are back."

The addition of Stoudemire enabled the Knicks to trade David Lee, who played the same position and instantly became trade bait to keep the payroll flexible under the salary cap, presumably for the next free-agent star trying to strong-arm his way to a bigger market. Technically, these moves made sense, though many fans and organizational insiders were saddened by Lee's departure.

As the last pick of the first round in 2005, he was Thomas's signature achievement—however modest. Lee was a rebounding vacuum, an earnest if not ultra-blessed specimen who improved his game every year to the point where he was the franchise's best and most popular player during some very bleak years. Mario Cuomo, for one, argued that Lee was the only reason to watch a Knicks game during that period and was never anyone's problem, and therefore deserved to be part of the solution. "He played center for you, he gave up his body, and now he has to go?" Cuomo said. "Why? To bet on some superstar to be your savior? How many times have we seen that before?"

Cuomo's point was that there was much more to love about Lee than his improved jumper or his nose for the ball. He was one of those players committed to a cause higher than the padding of his stats, who seemed to say and do the right thing. Days after Lee was traded to Golden State, in fact, he attended the funeral of a longtime and beloved NBA and Garden security official, Scott Jaffer, who had battled cancer for three years without saying a word. Stunned by the news, worried that the Knicks would not be represented, Lee flew to New York from his home in St. Louis, drove an hour north of the city, and took a seat in the back of the funeral home, where Jaffer's wife noticed him during her eulogy.

After writing a column about Lee's last act of hustle for the Knicks—and noting that he had also been the only current Knick to attend Dick McGuire's funeral—I received a Facebook message from Arthur Pincus, a former *Times* editor, who wrote that the piece had reminded him of another funeral, many years earlier, when the father of Sam Goldaper, the paper's Knicks beat reporter, had died. "One player from the

Knicks came out to pay his respects," Pincus wrote. "You would not be surprised to know that it was Willis Reed. And he sat in the back with his head sticking out of the crowd, just like David Lee's."

Old Knicks—Reed and Bradley, in particular—had taken notice of the throwback qualities in Lee, and had made a point of telling him as much on the night of their 40th anniversary title celebration—when only Lee had left the locker room at halftime to watch the ceremony. "I enjoy watching him play because he's what I call a 100 percenter," Reed said. "David may not be having a good night, but it won't be because he's not putting out, and those are the guys the fans can relate to, the guys that bring teams together."

These were attributes that were impossible to quantify but easy to recognize. But to Stoudemire's credit, he adjusted beautifully to his new environment, surprising even Mike D'Antoni, his former coach in Phoenix, who had moved to the Knicks in 2008, with leadership skills he had not shown out west. Younger teammates such as Danilo Gallinari, Raymond Felton, and Wilson Chandler formed an immediate bond with Stoudemire, and a rookie shooting guard from Stanford, Landry Fields, drafted in the second round, earned a starting position. Early on, Fields even drew some premature and exaggerated comparisons to John

Havlicek and Bradley with his instincts and willingness to move without the ball.

D'Antoni's entertaining up-tempo, motion offense had helped restore elegance to the NBA product with the high-scoring Suns in Phoenix, and the Knicks executed it well enough for much of the 2010–11 season to support Stoudemire's declaration. They were back, at least in the playoff mix following a seven-year absence. Everyone agreed they needed to make another move or two to make a deep run, but there was considerable debate—even within the organization—on how to best complement Stoudemire and nurture the promising dynamic they had established.

Three days before the February trade deadline, they reeled in one of the bigger names and sexier talents. Carmelo Anthony arrived from Denver after a months-long game of chicken with the Nuggets' management over Anthony's ability to opt out of his contract in the summer of 2011. On cue, New York revved up as if the Stoudemire-Anthony tandem were the second coming of Magic Johnson's Los Angeles alliance with Kareem Abdul-Jabbar.

Walsh, a Bronx native, was 70 when he made the deal—or at least was forced into it by Dolan—that also brought the respected but aging point guard, 34-year-old Chauncey Billups. In return, the Knicks were forced to surrender four young rotation players (Gallinari, Chandler, Felton, and a young Russian center, Timofey Mozgov) plus multiple draft picks. Walsh wanted Anthony, but not at that price. He had planned to wait until the final hours before the trade deadline in an attempt to force the Nuggets to negotiate on the Knicks' terms. But given a looming labor crisis that would diminish the value of the long-term contract, Dolan had good reason to fear that *Anthony* would go to New Jersey if the Knicks didn't agree to what was tantamount to gutting their roster.

The notion that the Nets and their new Russian owner, Mikhail Prokhorov, would land a marquee name like Anthony to bring to downtown Brooklyn upon the completion of their new arena made Dolan queasy. On top of that, he was planning a major ticket price increase for the 2011–12 season to help fund the Garden's ongoing renovation. He knew the acquisition of Anthony, a charismatic player born in Brooklyn and married to a gorgeous TV celebrity named La La Vasquez, would provide cover.

Those who had been around the longest, fans for life of the Old Knicks, were furious when the invoices arrived in the mail. The increases averaged 49 percent across the arena but the price of courtside seats skyrocketed—in some cases from an already painful

$330 to as much as a staggering $900 per game. Fifty-nine-year-old Lewis Dorf of South Orange, New Jersey, had been going to Knicks games since the mid-sixties, when he was a teenage ball boy assigned to the visitors bench. He was 15 when he struck up a friendship with Willis Reed and invited him over for dinner at his parents' Stuyvesant Town apartment. Naturally, Reed showed up. After that, there was no way Dorf could ever kick his Knicks fix, and he wound up sitting directly behind Woody Allen, even coaxing a few lines of actual conversation from the reticent director.

But Dorf, the owner of a small business, was hardly in Allen's league when it came to disposable income. For him and others, the price increases were a potentially fatal low blow, forcing the most faithful of fans to find and beg a rich benefactor to lay out the cash with the hope of buying back a few games. "A normal person cannot afford almost $2,000 to go to a basketball game 44 times a year," Dorf said, voicing the fury of those who had continued digging deep during the darkest of Knicks decades, praying for a miracle.

The Knicks proceeded to lose 9 of 10 games, with Anthony struggling mightily to mesh with Stoudemire. The Knicks looked and played like the team of strangers they were, further hamstrung by a shallow roster of players who seemed incapable of stepping up to meet the most routine of defensive challenges. Meanwhile, Denver, with its superstar-less roster deepened by the new band of "Knuggets," went on a tear that only magnified New York's misery.

There was no arguing that Anthony—at 6'8", with 230 pounds of finesse and power—showed extraordinary skills as a natural-born scorer, and was lethal at just about any spot on the offensive end of the floor. Anthony was no defensive stopper, that was for sure, but he was certainly more intimidating with the ball at the end of a close game than, for comparison's sake, LeBron James. As a sample demonstration, he won a game for the Knicks in Memphis with a last-second jumper, then did it again in Indianapolis as the team went on a tear—albeit against downtrodden opponents—over the final two weeks of the regular season.

Hopes were raised that the Knicks were peaking for the playoffs, but what worried the old-timers like George Lois and Freddy Klein was that, overnight, Anthony became the essence of what they loathed: a gifted player who demanded the ball on the wing and often reduced his teammates to four statues spread across the hardwood. In other words, what fell into the category of what Lois called "fucking unwatchable." Still, the city was on high basketball alert when the Knicks drew the Celtics in the opening round, the first postseason meeting of the two old rivals in 21 years. The ghosts of playoffs past—Havlicek and Heinsohn to Bradley and Barnett—seemed to hover over the series in the days leading in. The Celtics were three playoff springs removed from their 17th championship, with the same core of Kevin Garnett, Paul Pierce, Ray Allen, and Rajon Rondo. But a February alteration of their roster and an injury to Shaquille O'Neal had left them shallow at center and slumping at the end of the regular season. Despite finishing 14 games ahead of the Knicks, there was a sense that the Celtics might be vulnerable. Peter Vecsey, the *Post*'s impertinent NBA columnist, talked himself into picking the Knicks to win the series in six games, despite the Celtics' 4–0 regular-season sweep.

In Game 1, powered by a dominating 28-point performance by Stoudemire, they had the Celtics all but beaten, leading by 3 with 37.8 seconds left. But the Celtics—aided by a questionable offensive foul call against Anthony—proceeded to run two inbounds plays that were brilliantly choreographed by their coach, Doc Rivers, and beautifully executed by five players thinking as one. When Allen's 3-point shot from the left wing nestled in the bottom of the net, the Celtics had a 2-point lead with 11.6 seconds left. Out of time-outs, the Knicks rushed the ball past midcourt, where Anthony dribbled into a fast-approaching double-team about 25 feet out to the right of the key. A few feet away, the guard Toney Douglas—an erratic but fearless second-year player who had accounted for the 3-point lead with a long jumper moments earlier— was waving his arms, wide open.

Anthony might have passed to Douglas. Or, down by just 2, he might have driven the ball to the basket to score, gotten fouled, or opened a passing lane to Stoudemire. Wearing Dean Meminger's old number 7 (Anthony had been given permission by Earl Monroe to un-retire number 15, which had also been Dick McGuire's, but chose not to), Anthony pulled back for an off-balance 3 that clanged short. Game over. His maiden Knicks playoff voyage earned him a well-deserved roasting on the back pages of the New York tabloids.

Much to their credit, the Knicks flirted with victory again in Game 2, despite Billups's being out with a strained knee suffered in the final minute of Game 1 and with Stoudemire stuck on the bench in the second half with severe back spasms. Left to his born calling—dominating the ball without having to answer to anyone—Anthony drew resounding praise for a 42-point, 17-rebound, 6-assist masterpiece. At least until he found himself in an end-game situation almost identical to the one that befuddled him in Game 1.

After Garnett gave the Celtics a one-point lead with a jump hook in the lane over Jared Jeffries with 13.3 seconds left, D'Antoni called his last time-out. Without Stoudemire and Billups, his options were limited. But by running the play through Anthony, knowing the Celtics were guaranteed to double-team, D'Antoni succeeded only in turning his best and arguably only legitimate option into an observer once he made the prescribed pass to the low post—to Jeffries, one of the worst offensive players in the league. Smelling blood, the long-limbed Garnett hustled over, and Jeffries, all thumbs, tried to pass to a cutting forward, Bill Walker—who had taken 11 shots and missed them all. Garnett deflected the pass and dived on the loose ball as if it were his wallet, a sequence that would not be readily apparent in a box score but was an unmistakable sign of true championship character.

Anthony, conversely, sometimes came across as a genial diva, not particularly bothered or burdened by much of anything in his wonderful celebrity life. After Game 2, he seemed more relieved to have made "the right play" with the pass to Jeffries than upset by its outcome and another crushing defeat. He uttered a word to describe the night—"fun"—that would never have left the mouth of a Jordan, a Bryant, a Reed, or a Frazier under such circumstances.

When the series returned to New York, the big story was whether Stoudemire would be able to play. An hour and a half before game time, he strolled to the court, wearing a soft brace on his back, to shoot jumpers, mostly flat-footed. Naturally, Willis and the Old Knicks were invoked, as they typically are whenever an injured athlete had to answer the bell in some significant degree of pain. Reed was the industry standard, almost to the point of cliché. But by the middle of Game 3, it was clear that Stoudemire's admirable determination would not be defined as an act of heroism. Anthony and what was left of the Knicks—a virtual cast from the West Fourth Street playground—proved to be no match for the Celtics. The games at Madison Square Garden became a throwback clinic of fundamental excellence that might have elicited smoke rings of eternal satisfaction from Red Auerbach's grave.

The point guard Rondo in particular toyed with the Knicks, penetrating their defense at will, finding the shooters Pierce, Allen, and Garnett, who roamed the perimeter and met the kind of limited resistance generally seen in all-star games. After winning the first two games by 5 measly points, the Celtics wrapped things up with a 17-point blowout and a 12-point victory in which they led by 23, extending the Knicks' winless playoff streak to a full decade and their championship-less vacuum to a confounding 38 years.

Afterward, the Celtics were kind to the Knicks, both Rivers and Pierce going out of their way to forecast longer playoff runs to come. So, too, did Anthony, in the wake of his seventh first-round play-off exit in eight NBA seasons. "This is the first step of something great," he assured Knicks fans. But how many steps would be required for a squad lacking in so many areas to become cohesive, much less a con-tender? Old Knicks fans remained skeptical. They had seen their share of saviors—Spencer Haywood, Bob McAdoo, Bernard King, even Patrick Ewing—come and go, and still the Knicks remained on the treadmill.

Frustrated by ownership, Walsh soon after an-nounced that he would not return as the Knicks' president in 2011–12. No matter who headed the front office, there would always be deep corporate pockets—Dolan's being the latest—to provide purchasing power. And while the prospect of a hard salary cap in loom-ing labor negotiations sent shivers through the build-ing, the Knicks went into the summer of 2011 with the belief they would eventually have salary-cap flex-ibility to land a third star—perhaps one of the emerg-ing young guards who seemed to be taking over the sport—to compete with the Miami triumvirate that came up small in the Finals against Dallas.

The party line was that the Knicks would be challenging for a title soon enough, but Bill Bradley, keeping an eye on his old team from a distance, was skeptical of the methodology of the eternal star quest. Granted, times had dramatically changed from the early seventies, when there was no free agency and no possibility of microwaving a contender by writing a few large checks. But Bradley argued that championship chemistry was not a commodity that was available on the open market.

"There's always the illusion that one more player actually will make it all work," he said.

But hadn't that been the case with the acquisition of DeBusschere? Hadn't one player put the Old Knicks over the top?

"In a sense, yes," Bradley said. But he added that the foundation of success was already in place, it was years in the making, and from the moment DeBusschere arrived he fit into the puzzle as if he had been there all along.

Willis Reed could well remember the growing pains of his early Knicks days, when he wondered if the losing would ever end. Looking back, he believed the tough times were necessary to build the team's character and became an important part of its legacy and special relationship with New York. Yes, things had changed a whole lot since then, and the younger fan, living in a world of iPad pleasures and immediate gratification, was conditioned to the free-agent madness. But if character and commitment were the most unifying threads across the decades, then identifying those who in the end mattered most was nothing you could declare during a one-hour special on ESPN. The most important traits were demonstrated over time, with actions or sacrifices that were plainly transferrable into everyday life.

Almost four decades after Zero Mostel stood up at Leone's and wished for a day when a man like Willis Reed could become the so-called Leader of the Free World, a tall, slender African American known to have hoisted a few jump shots in his time did step onto a Chicago stage late on a November night in 2008 as the president-elect of the United States. Barack Obama knew his basketball, and his Old Knicks. In the spring of 2009, when he attended a Washington Nationals game to see sensational rookie Stephen Strasburg pitch against his hometown White Sox, Obama was introduced to my former *Times* colleague Ira Berkow. "You're the guy who wrote the book with Clyde,"

Obama told the startled scribe, a native Chicagoan. "I bought that book when I was twelve."

Like Frazier, Obama often struck people as aloof but was also blessed with a classy, eye-catching style. Like Reed, he hailed from modest but proud beginnings. Like Bradley, he was an intellectual with liberal leanings, but liberals considered him more of a centrist. Like DeBusschere, he had blue-collar values, eschewing the moneyed track after Harvard Law School to work as a community organizer. Like the Old Knicks, Barack Obama was a proud mixing of black and white, and rose to prominence at the end of a turbulent decade, making a powerful statement to all Americans—including the many millions who opposed, feared, or loathed him—about what was possible in their country.

"There's a big difference between someone who is president of the United States and somebody who wins the championship," said Bradley. "But I do think that was one of the things the Obama campaign elicited in people—I mean, his selling of the word *hope* was really one of the geniuses of his effort because that did and still does make you feel that there are possibilities that didn't exist and now exist—though he was dealt an extremely difficult hand with the economy, two wars, and unfinished business at home with health care, education, pensions, energy, and the environment.

"But during the campaign he convinced people that they couldn't imagine having a better person there and those were like the feelings that were created in New York around the Knicks, especially when we won that first championship—and there was that moment when people felt like, *we did it*! The collective did it. Well, Obama won the election but we—meaning the people—did it together, with him and for him. The Knicks won but we—the people, the fans—did it, too. And I think what in our best moments we reveal is a kind of ideal and a realization of that ideal, whether it's brotherhood, cooperation, excellence, teamwork, joy, self-fulfillment, however you want to say it, probably a little bit of all of those, that's what we represented. And the fans really did feel they were a part of it, because we engaged them at a very deep level. And that kind of engagement, I think, has for so many people lasted a lifetime."

EPILOGUE

Weeks after LeBron James made the most grandiose show of free agency of any professional athlete in history, turning a simple declarative sentence ("I'm going to take my talents to South Beach and join the Miami Heat") into his all-about-me hour on ESPN, the sport presented its softer, adult-driven side when the Naismith Memorial Hall of Fame held its 2010 inductions in Springfield, Massachusetts. Among the honorees were Scottie Pippen, a six-time champion, and Karl Malone, who never did win a ring but was considered the prototype power forward of his time and arguably of all time.

Malone grew up in Summerfield, Louisiana, a tiny, unincorporated town of about 250, with a red light and a grocery store at its crossroads, about a ten-mile drive on Highway 2 from Bernice in the heart of what was—back in the late sixties and early seventies—Willis Reed country.

In the late seventies, Reed had seen Malone play in high school when Bernice—with its star Benny Anders, soon to team up with Hakeem Olajuwon at the University of Houston—met and defeated its Summerfield rival. Malone never forgot the night Reed stepped into the gym.

It meant something in those parts—especially to the black folks—that Reed had stayed home to play college ball, and black and white alike swelled with pride when their guy went on to become the star center for the professional team in New York City. Two decades later, Malone would follow Reed's lead, though in the post-integration years he earned a scholarship to what had once been all-white Louisiana Tech in nearby Ruston on the way to becoming a famous—and much wealthier—NBA star.

Teaming with the point guard John Stockton for the Utah Jazz for 18 of his 19 NBA seasons, Malone became a rare leveraged black man in Mormon-dominated Salt Lake City. The Mountain West suited him more than Los Angeles or New York. Like Reed, the Mailman, as he was known, preferred the woods to the city, a hot truck to a fast car. Malone was certainly no choirboy, dogged through his NBA years by unflattering tales of out-of-wedlock children. For better or worse, he was also an outspoken force of nature against a tide of sound-bite sophistry.

In the fall of 1992, Malone handed me a national scoop after the Summer Olympics in Barcelona by asserting that Magic Johnson's intention to return to the NBA while HIV-positive was not necessarily good for the game if it meant that players would shy away from contact with him. Dribbling against the swell of support for Magic, Malone (much to my relief, as I had written his quotes down instead of taping him) did not make any attempt to deny what he'd said or claim that the quotes had been presented out of context.

An unconventional man, Malone had one last surprise in him on the night of his induction. It had already been announced that Pippen, not surprisingly, had chosen Michael Jordan, who joined the Hall the previous year, as his presenter. Most people assumed Malone would want Stockton, who was also inducted in 2009 (along with their longtime Jazz coach, Jerry Sloan) and had assisted Malone countless times on the Mailman's way to becoming the league's all-time second-leading scorer behind Kareem Abdul-Jabbar.

Reed, in fact, watching from his den in Grambling, wondered why the Hall hadn't waited on Stockton and

Sloan an extra year—Malone, having opted to play a 19th season with the Lakers, would not be eligible until then—and inducted all three of them together.

When the Naismith people pressed Malone to name his presenter, he hesitated; yes, Stockton or Sloan or both would have made perfect sense. But the more Malone sorted through his feelings—recalled how much another Hall of Famer had impacted his life—the more the decision came to him as naturally as a rebound. It was less about basketball than it was about roots, about home, about honoring one's past. Malone never forgot how Willis Reed had taken the time to attend the funeral of his mother, Shirley, in 2003.

And so, on a fishing trip to Alaska, Malone acted on the impulse and made a telephone call beginning with the familiar area code 318.

"Mr. Willis?" he said when the line picked up.

"This is not Mr. Willis; this is Willis Reed."

"I know who this is, and what I need to know is, will you present me at the Hall of Fame?"

"*Me?*" Reed said. "You don't want *me*."

"Of course I want you. You were the first basketball player I knew."

"Well, okay, but you'll change your mind before then."

Not a chance, Malone told him. With his cell phone signal wavering, he laughed and said, "I'm just like you: once I decide something, I'm not changing my mind."

On the night of August 13, 2010, the two hardheaded outdoorsmen of north-central Louisiana climbed a stage together, with Reed taking his assigned place slightly behind Malone and to his right. They looked out into the most credentialed congregation of basketball talent since the NBA had brought together 47 of the players voted to the league's all-time Top 50 team in October 1996, at the '97 All-Star Game in Cleveland. (Pete Maravich had died, while Shaquille O'Neal and Jerry West were unable to attend.)

In Springfield, every member of the freshly inducted '92 Dream Team was present, including Michael Jordan, Magic Johnson, and Larry Bird. Ditto the 1960 gold-medal Olympic team starring West, Oscar Robertson, Jerry Lucas, Walt Bellamy, and even Bob Boozer, still a Knick when Reed had first arrived in New York, the big brother who showed him where to get a haircut, and a good steak, when he and Emmette Bryant moved into a Midtown hotel.

Abdul-Jabbar was in town as a presenter for the longtime Lakers owner Dr. Jerry Buss. Earl Monroe and Wes Unseld did likewise for the posthumously inducted Gus Johnson. For Reed, it felt like a high school reunion, except that, Monroe and Lucas aside, his most intimate old friends were missing. He couldn't help but wish that Clyde and Bradley, Barnett and DeBusschere, Action Jackson and his coaching mentor, Red Holzman, could have all been there, together once more.

For those wondering why Reed was even up on the stage, Malone explained how humbled he was to have his boyhood hero as his presenter. You see, little Karl was just weeks shy of his seventh birthday on May 8, 1970, when Reed walked out of the Madison Square Garden tunnel, into a storybook, and won the first of two championship rings he never bothered to wear. ("I don't wear rings. I'm an outdoorsman," he explained.)

On the stage, it occurred to Reed that while he had two championships he wouldn't trade for anything, the ringless Malone had two Olympic gold medals, having played for the '92 and '96 USA teams—and that was something Reed did not have. And there was a lesson in there somewhere, he was sure.

"I was up there thinking about how in the end, very few people can get everything from the game or from life," Reed said. "People talk about how many rings Jordan has, or Magic, and how that made them greater than this guy or that guy, but then you could look out in the audience and see West and Oscar sitting there, guys who were only fortunate enough to win one, but who were two of the greatest players in the history of the game. So you're thinking, 'Be grateful for what you've got, for the memories you have.'"

Be content, he was thinking, with the belief that if the effort was made, if the game and your team—especially your team—were not cheated, neither were you. This was what Reed would have told Karl Malone if Malone didn't already seem to know it—in no small part because that is what he had learned from watching Reed, 40 years earlier on a small black-and-white television screen, in a selfless act that would come to be the industry standard for courage and commitment.

An emotional man, overcome by the occasion, Malone wore his tears with a blue-collar pride, an unabashed joy. After acknowledging Reed, among others, he looked into the audience and the cable television camera and said: "I hope I did it in the way my peers did it before me."

The gray-haired Reed, class of '82, Captain of the Old Knicks, clenched his lips and gently nodded his approval.

ACKNOWLEDGMENTS

The endearing subject of the Old Knicks invokes memories of a carefree youth. Whether arguing profanely with badly outnumbered Celtics or Bullets fans in the high school cafeteria, or dribbling—back to the basket, like Walt Frazier—on outdoor cement courts or indoors at the Staten Island JCC, my childhood has always seemed bound with the Knicks.

From the occasional live game at the Garden, to the hundreds watched on television or brought to life by the mesmeric radio voice of Marv Abert, I suppose it's no surprise that the Knicks forged many lasting connections for me: the late Isaac Allen, Bob Baer, Emmett Berg, Ira Bistreich, Robert Busan, Tony Carter, the Edlebaum brothers, Mark and Ira, Chet Heald, Dennis Flanagan, Billy Fried, Mitch Gordon, Stephen Jackel,

Andy Rothstein, Dave Seidenberg, Lenny Stanley, and my forever friend, Lloyd Stone. To those who might have cared about the Old Knicks on a more casual basis—Sharon Pearlmutter Grossman and Robbie Hollender Levinson among them—sorry for tuning you out when the game was on the line. I was an addict; it couldn't be helped.

In my earliest newspapering days at the *Staten Island Advance*, Larry Ambrosino, Lou Bergonzi, Danny Colvin, Garry Ferraris, Jimmy Forbes, Terry Golway, Debbie Hartnett, Andy Lagomarsino, Bob Leggiadro, Julie Summers Lord, Joe LoVerde, Jim Meraglia, Jack Minogue, Larry Miraldi, Robert Miraldi, Joe Nugent, Jay Price, Chuck Schmidt, and Dan Siani knew great basketball when they saw it—even if our earthbound version of the game on the *Advance 5* didn't do it justice. Bless Tom Valledolmo for assigning me to my first Knicks games on those Saturday nights when the *Star-Ledger* copy couldn't come fast enough. And, speaking of indebted gratitude, I owe so much of my adult basketball life to an old friend, the one and only Phil Mushnick, whose fateful phone call landed me at the *Post*, which was great for me (if not, unfortunately, for Willis).

Setting out on this journey, no one helped me push through my initial apprehensions more than Zelda

Spoelstra, who connected me with many former players, who knew better not to return the call after Zelda told them they should. Selena Roberts was a special friend through challenging times, as were John Parlapiano, Michelle Musler, and Filip Bondy. Budd Mishkin gave me a great head start, as did many family members, friends, and colleagues, with their own splendid works and words and by just being there: David Albert, Hilary Albert, Dana Albert, the late Maury Allen, Barry Baum, Howard Beck, Marty Beiser, Ira Berkow, Howard Blatt, Bud Collins, Bob Cumins, Dave D'Alessandro, Bob Drury, Mitch Greene, Gene Goldberg, John Gruber, Arthur Hatzopoulos, Susan Hatzopoulos, Johnette Howard, Frank Isola, Dave Kaplan, Naomi Kaplan, Anita Klaussen, Gwen Knapp, Mark Kriegel, Fred Langbein, Peter McKenna, Michelle Musler, Paul Needell, Naomi Rand, Bill Rhoden, Ian O'Connor, Steve Politi, Shaun Powell, Richard Sandomir, Jay Schreiber, Barry Stanton, Alan Swyer, Susan Tepper, Fern Turkowitz, George Vecsey, Adrian Wojnarowski, Ailene Voisin, and the late Vic Ziegel.

Thank you to the Madison Square Garden and Knicks staff, including Barry Watkins, Jonathan Supranowitz, Dan Schoenberg, and Gregg Schwartz, as well as Brian McInytre and Tim Frank of the NBA.

Roughly 150 people were interviewed for this book, lending their time and patience when callbacks were necessary. A special shout-out to two Old Knicks who went above and beyond: Willis Reed and Senator Bill Bradley, whose support was unwavering and more than a onetime muckraker could hope for.

The very existence of this book is owed largely to the stubborn resolve of my agent, Andrew Blauner, who wouldn't take no for an answer. That led us to HarperCollins's David Hirshey, who had a strong vision for the project and, with Barry Harbaugh, distilled it into a crisper, richer tale. Will Palmer expertly copyedited the manuscript.

Finally, my wonderful family indulged me all the hours I needed, and never complained when I drifted off in the middle of a conversation, contemplating what the next chapter should be. Beth, Alex, and Charly, you are my everlasting inspiration for trying to move forward.

APPENDIX: BOX SCORES

EXIT THE COOZ: NEW YORK WINS 18 STRAIGHT
November 28, 1969

FINAL NATIONAL BASKETBALL ASSOCIATION
OFFICIAL SCORER'S REPORT

HOME: Cincinnati		MIN	FGM	FGA	FTM	FTA	REB	AST	PF	PTS
21	ANDERZUNAS	—	—	— DID NOT PLAY —			—	—	—	—
19	COUSY	2	0	0	2	2	0	0	0	2
24	DIERKING (C)	41	8	14	3	6	14	3	3	19
15	FOSTER	12	0	3	0	0	0	0	2	0
30	GILLIAM	—	—	— DID NOT PLAY —			—	—	—	—
20	GREEN (F)	41	8	11	3	3	20	1	0	19
22	RACKLEY	7	0	1	0	0	1	0	1	0
14	ROBERTSON (G)	43	15	23	3	4	6	10	6	33
10	SMITH	6	1	2	0	0	0	0	0	2
13	TURNER	7	3	4	3	5	3	0	2	9
5	VAN ARSDALE (F)	36	6	14	2	2	3	1	5	14
23	VAN LIER (G)	45	3	14	1	2	2	2	5	7
TOTAL:		240	44	86	17	24	49	17	24	105

FG%: 51.2   FT%: 70.8   TEAM REBOUNDS: 3   TURNOVERS: 18 conv. 6

VISITORS: New York		MIN	FGM	FGA	FTM	FTA	REB	AST	PF	PTS
12	BARNETT (G)	33	2	8	1	2	4	1	3	5
17	BOWMAN	4	1	2	1	1	1	1	1	3
24	BRADLEY (F)	32	6	12	1	2	2	1	4	13
22	DeBUSSCHERE (F)	33	2	8	2	2	9	1	4	6
10	FRAZIER (G)	44	10	19	7	9	7	5	3	27
20	HOSKET	—	—	— DID NOT PLAY —			—	—	—	—
5	MAY	—	—	— DID NOT PLAY —			—	—	—	—
19	REED (C)	44	8	22	3	4	13	1	3	19
6	RIORDAN	19	5	7	0	2	2	1	1	
33	RUSSELL	16	8	10	2	2	7	0	1	18
9	STALLWORTH	15	2	3	1	1	3	0	1	
16	WARREN	—	—	— DID NOT PLAY —			—	—	—	—
TOTAL:		240	44	91	18	25	48	11	21	106

FG%: 48.4   FT%: 72.0   TEAM REBOUNDS: 3   TURNOVERS: 16 conv. 4

PLACE: Cleveland Arena   ATTENDANCE: 10,438

REFS:	SCORE BY PERIODS	1	2	3	4	OT	OT	TOT
Bob Rakel								
Richie Powers	Cincinnati	30	22	26	17	—	—	105
	New York	23	32	22	29	—	—	106

REMARKS: Knicks set all-time NBA winning streak, at 18 in a row.

THE FALL . . . (GAME 5)

May 4, 1970

FINAL NATIONAL BASKETBALL ASSOCIATION
OFFICIAL SCORER'S REPORT

HOME: New York	MIN	FGM	FGA	FTM	FTA	REB	AST	PF	PTS
BARNETT (G)	44	6	17	4	5	0	3	3	16
BOWMAN	7	0	2	1	1	4	0	2	1
BRADLEY (F)	38	7	15	2	3	7	2	4	16
DeBUSSCHERE (F)	36	6	21	0	0	6	2	5	12
FRAZIER (G)	46	9	14	3	3	7	12	3	21
HOSKET	4	0	2	0	0	0	0	0	0
MAY	—	—	— DID NOT PLAY —				—	—	—
REED (C)	8	2	5	3	3	0	1	0	7
RIORDAN	5	1	1	0	0	0	0	0	2
RUSSELL	32	8	14	4	4	8	5	4	20
STALWORTH	19	6	12	0	0	6	3	3	12
WARREN	1	0	0	0	0	0	0	1	0
TOTAL:	240	45	103	17	19	38	28	25	107

FG%: 43.7   FT%: 89.5   TEAM REBOUNDS: 8   TURNOVERS: 10

VISITORS: Los Angeles	MIN	FGM	FGA	FTM	FTA	REB	AST	PF	PTS
BAYLOR (F)	43	8	15	5	6	11	5	2	21
CHAMBERLAIN (C)	45	9	12	4	9	19	3	2	22
COUNTS	12	0	4	1	1	4	0	2	1
EGAN	13	2	2	2	2	0	3	3	6
ERICKSON (F)	40	3	6	1	2	4	6	4	7
GARRETT (G)	33	7	12	4	4	5	0	4	18
HAIRSTON	—	—	— DID NOT PLAY —				—	—	—
LYNN	—	—	— DID NOT PLAY —				—	—	—
McCARTER	—	—	— DID NOT PLAY —				—	—	—
ROBERTSON	—	—	— DID NOT PLAY —				—	—	—
TRESVANT	8	0	1	5	7	0	0	2	5
WEST (G)	46	6	14	8	9	2	4	2	20
TOTAL:	240	35	66	30	40	45	21	21	100

FG%: 62.5   FT%: 75.0   TEAM REBOUNDS: 10   TURNOVERS: 20

PLACE: Madison Square Garden   ATTENDANCE: 19, 500

REFS:	SCORE BY PERIODS	1	2	3	4	OT	OT	TOT
Menoy Rudolph								
Richie Powers	New York	20	20	35	32	—	—	107
	Los Angeles	30	23	29	18	—	—	100

REMARKS: Technical foul on Erickson at 2:07 of 3rd quarter.

. . . AND RISE OF WILLIS REED (GAME 7)
MAY 8, 1970
FINAL NATIONAL BASKETBALL ASSOCIATION
OFFICIAL SCORER'S REPORT

HOME: New York	MIN	FGM	FGA	FTM	FTA	REB	AST	PF	PTS
BARNETT (G)	42	9	20	3	3	0	2	4	21
BOWMAN	21	3	5	0	1	5	0	5	6
BRADLEY (F)	42	8	18	1	1	4	5	3	17
DeBUSSCHERE (F)	37	8	15	2	2	17	1	1	18
FRAZIER (G)	44	12	17	12	12	7	19	3	36
HOSKET	—	—	— DID NOT PLAY —				—	—	—
MAY	—	—	— DID NOT PLAY —				—	—	—
REED (C)	27	2	5	0	0	3	1	4	4
RIORDAN	10	2	3	1	2	2	1	2	5
RUSSELL	6	1	4	0	0	3	0	0	2
STALWORTH	11	1	5	2	2	2	1	3	4
WARREN	—	—	— DID NOT PLAY —				—	—	—
TOTAL:	240	46	92	21	23	43	30	25	113

FT%: 91.3   TEAM REBOUNDS: 4

VISITORS: Los Angeles	MIN	FGM	FGA	FTM	FTA	REB	AST	PF	PTS
BAYLOR (F)	36	9	17	1	2	5	1	2	19
CHAMBERLAIN (C)	48	10	16	1	11	24	4	1	21
COUNTS	—	—	— DID NOT PLAY —				—	—	—
EGAN	11	0	2	0	0	0	0	2	0
ERICKSON (F)	36	5	10	4	6	6	6	3	14
GARRETT (G)	34	3	10	2	2	4	1	4	8
HAIRSTON	15	2	5	2	2	2	0	1	6
LYNN	—	—	— DID NOT PLAY —				—	—	—
McCARTER	—	—	— DID NOT PLAY —				—	—	—
ROBERTSON	—	—	— DID NOT PLAY —				—	—	—
TRESVANT	12	0	4	3	3	2	0	2	3
WEST (G)	48	9	19	10	12	6	5	4	28
TOTAL:	240	38	83	23	38	49	17	19	99

FG%: 45.8   FT%: 60.5   TEAM REBOUNDS: 12

PLACE: Madison Square Garden   ATTENDANCE: 19, 500

REFS:	SCORE BY PERIODS	1	2	3	4	OT	OT	TOT
Menoy Rudolph								
Richie Powers	New York	38	31	25	19	—	—	113
	Los Angeles	24	18	27	30	—	—	99

TWICE IN A LIFETIME: THE KNICKS WIN THEIR SECOND CHAMPIONSHIP
May 10, 1973

FINAL NATIONAL BASKETBALL ASSOCIATION
OFFICIAL SCORER'S REPORT

VISITORS: New York Knicks	MIN	FGM	FGA	FTM	FTA	REB	AST	PF	PTS
12 BARNETT	—	—	— DID NOT PLAY —			—	—	—
17 BIBBY	—	—	— DID NOT PLAY —			—	—	—
24 BRADLEY (F)	43	10	22	0	0	7	5	5	20
22 DeBUSSCHERE (F)	32	1	9	0	0	8	4	3	2
10 FRAZIER (G)	48	8	16	2	6	9	5	2	18
40 GIANELLI	—	—	— DID NOT PLAY —	—		—	—	—
18 JACKSON	18	2	7	2	2	7	2	4	6
32 LUCAS	19	5	9	0	2	2	1	3	10
7 MEMINGER	15	2	2	1	1	1	2	2	5
15 MONROE (G)	34	8	15	7	11	2	4	4	23
19 REED (C)	31	9	16	0	0	12	7	5	18
43 WINGO	—	—	— DID NOT PLAY —	—		—	—	—
TOTAL:	240	45	96	12	20	48	38	28	102

FG%: 46.9   FT%: 60.0   TEAM REBOUNDS: 8   TURNOVERS: 18

HOME: Los Angeles Lakers	MIN	FGM	FGA	FTM	FTA	REB	AST	PF	PTS
32 BRIDGES (F)	40	2	7	5	7	12	0	6	9
13 CHAMBERLAIN (C)	48	9	16	5	14	21	3	3	23
31 COUNTS	4	0	1	0	0	3	0	1	0
24 ERICKSON	25	1	4	0	0	5	0	6	2
25 GOODRICH (G)	40	11	23	6	6	5	1	4	28
33 GRANT	—	—	— DID NOT PLAY —	—		—	—	—
52 HAIRSTON	8	0	3	0	0	2	0	2	0
5 McMILLIAN (F)	41	8	17	3	5	6	3	3	19
15 PRICE	—	—	— DID NOT PLAY —	—		—	—	—
12 RILEY	1	0	0	0	0	0	0	1	0

HOME: Los Angeles Lakers	MIN	FGM	FGA	FTM	FTA	REB	AST	PF	PTS
30 TURNER	—	—	— DID NOT PLAY—			—	—	—
44 WEST (G)	33	5	17	2	3	5	4	1	12
TOTAL:	240	36	88	21	35	59	11	27	93

FG%: 40.9   FT%: 60.0   TEAM REBOUNDS: 10   TURNOVERS: 26

DATE: May 10, 1973   PLACE: The Forum   ATTENDANCE: 17, 555

REFS:	SCORE BY PERIODS	1	2	3	4	OT	OT	TOT
Don Murphy								
Darell Garretson	New York Knicks	23	16	32	31	—	—	102
Alt. Jake O'Donnell	Los Angeles Lakers	16	25	18	34	—	—	93

REMARKS: Technical foul on C. Holzman with 9:24 remaining in the 3rd quarter.

BIBLIOGRAPHY

The works listed below, as well as some others, were in most cases used for reference and were updated and expanded with fresh interviews where possible. Efforts were made to cite and credit within the text articles that were believed to be material exclusive to that publication. Other articles from the Associated Press, the *New York Times*, the *Boston Globe*, the New York *Daily News*, the *New York Post*, and the *Staten Island Advance* were helpful sources of reference. Other works of Old Knicks history were tremendously helpful, especially Budd Mishkin's wonderful reconstruction of the championship years for NBC radio and Dennis D'Agostino's "Oral History of the New York Knicks." In addition, the NBA's Brian McIntyre graciously provided videos of classic games—one of the countless times he has assisted me during my long career of covering the league. My wife, Beth Albert, saved Knicks programs from the glory days—bless her hoarder's soul. The *New York Times* archives online were a researcher's dream, as were the NBA Encyclopedia and those official NBA Guides that I never did get around to cleaning out of the closets.

BOOKS

Axthelm, Pete. *The City Game.* New York: Harper's Magazine Press, 1970.

Bradley, Bill. *Life on the Run.* New York: Quadrangle, 1976.

D'Agostino, Dennis. *An Oral History of the New York Knicks.* Chicago: Triumph, 2003.

DeBusschere, Dave. *The Open Man.* New York: Random House, 1970.

Frazier, Walt, and Ira Berkow. *Rockin' Steady.* Englewood Cliffs, N.J.: Prentice-Hall, 1974.

Holzman, Red, and Harvey Frommer. *Red on Red.* New York: Bantam, 1987.

Kalinsky, George. *The New York Knicks.* New York: Macmillan, 1996.

Keteyian, Armen, Harvey Araton, and Martin F. Dardis. *Money Players.* New York: Pocket, 1997.

Pepe, Phil. *The Incredible Knicks*. New York: Popular Library, 1970.

Shatzkin, Mike. *The View from Section 111*. Englewood Cliffs, N.J.: Prentice-Hall, 1970.

MAGAZINE ARTICLES

Deford, Frank. "Two Once and Future Champs." *Sports Illustrated*, January 11, 1965.

———. "A New Man for New York." *Sports Illustrated*, December 18, 1967.

———. "The Doctor Works His Magic." *Sports Illustrated*, November 4, 1968.

———. "In for Two Plus the Title." *Sports Illustrated*, May 18, 1970.

Kirshenbaum, Jerry. "Eeginnprst Ejrry Aclsu." *Sports Illustrated*, October 8, 1973.

Leggett, William. "A New Knick with a Knack." *Sports Illustrated*, January 17, 1966.

Papanek, John. "Clyde, Laughing Cavalier." *Sports Illustrated*, November 7, 1977.

NEWSPAPER ARTICLES

Bigart, Homer. "War Foes Here Attacked by Construction Workers." *New York Times*, May 9, 1970.

Cady, Steve. "Earl Monroe: A Spectacular Shooter and a Master Showman. *New York Times*, November 14, 1971.

Daley, Arthur. "Long Vigil Ends for Jerry West." *New York Times*, May 9, 1972.

———. "Exploding into Double Overtime." *New York Times*, April 24, 1973.

Frankel, Max. "Nixon Defends Cambodia Drive as Aiding Students' Peace Aim; Says Pullout Will Begin Soon." *New York Times*, May 9, 1970.

Goldaper, Sam. "20 Pro Basketball Stars Play in Benefit Game Here Tonight." *New York Times*, August 15, 1968.

———. "Elvin Hayes Bows Here as Pro." *New York Times*, August 16, 1968.

———. "Gianelli's Finest Hour Comes in Crucial Time." *New York Times*, April 13, 1974.

———. "End Comes Uneasily for DeBusschere." *New York Times*, April 25, 1974.

Keese, Parton. "Knicks Beat Bullets at Garden, 125–114." *New York Times*, November 23, 1971.

Koppett, Leonard. "Michigan Tops Princeton, 80 to 78, and Joins St. John's in Festival Final." *New York Times*, December 31, 1964.

———. "Knicks Set Back Lakers, 111–108." *New York Times*, April 30, 1970.

————. "Lakers Overcome Knicks, 121–115, in Overtime and Tie Final Series at 2–2." *New York Times*, May 2, 1970.

————. "Star Hurts Thigh in First Quarter." *New York Times*, May 5, 1970.

————. "Knicks Take First Title, Beating Lakers 113–99." *New York Times*, May 9, 1970.

————. "Knick Championship Culminates 24 Frustrating Years." *New York Times*, May 10, 1970.

————. "Knicks Down Bullets, 120–117, in 2 Overtime Periods." *New York Times*, May 27, 1970.

————. "Reed Set to Play Against Bullets." *New York Times*, April 16, 1971.

————. "Bullets Eliminate Knicks, 93–91." *New York Times*, April 20, 1971.

————. "Knicks. The Difference a Year Makes." *New York Times*, April 21, 1971.

————. "Knicks and Lakers . . . Then and Now: Astonishing Difference in 2 Years." *New York Times*, April 26, 1972.

————. "Wilt's Crowning Touches for Lakers." *New York Times*, May 9, 1972.

————. "Knicks Win in Two Overtimes." *New York Times*, April 23, 1973.

————. "Knicks Vanquish Celtics, 94–78, and Gain N.B.A. Title Playoff." *New York Times*, April 30, 1973.

———. "Knicks Win Title; Top Lakers, 102–93." *New York Times*, May 11, 1973.

Kornheiser, Tony. "Abe, Wes and Earl: A Family Circle That Will Never Be Broken." *Washington Post*, November 14, 1996.

Mallozzi, Vincent M. "Ex-Knick Trying to Stay Drug Free." *New York Times*, January 13, 1991.

Rogers, Thomas. "Celtics Halt Knick Rally to Win, 106–105, and Take Eastern Conference Playoff Final." *New York Times*, April 19, 1969.

———. "Knicks Down Royals, 106–105, in Last Two Seconds for Record 18th in Row." *New York Times*, November 29, 1969.

———. "Gambling Defense Marks Uphill Climb to Triumph." *New York Times*, May 5, 1970.

———. "Knicks, Scoring Final 19 Points, Top Bucks, 87–86." *New York Times*, November 19, 1972.

———. "Frazier Goes on Spree After Chaney Fouls Out." *New York Times*, April 23, 1973.

Seidman, Carrie. "Clyde Steals Show in Return to Garden." *New York Times*, December 16, 1979.

Vecsey, George. "An Ex-Knick Is Still Winning." *New York Times*, May 9, 1982.

Wise, Mike. "How Dean Meminger Turned His Life Around." *New York Times*, December 25, 2003.

HARVEY ARATON is a sports reporter and columnist for the *New York Times*, and the author and co-author of four other books. He lives in Montclair, New Jersey.